Rich AF

The Winning Money Mindset That Will Change Your Life

Vivian Tu

PORTFOLIO | PENGUIN

PORTFOLIO / PENGUIN
An imprint of Penguin Random House LLC
penguinrandomhouse.com

Most Portfolio books are available at a discount when purchased in quantity for sales promotions or corporate use. Special editions, which include personalized covers, excerpts, and corporate imprints, can be created when purchased in large quantities. For more information, please call (212) 572-2232 or e-mail specialmarkets@penguinrandomhouse.com. Your local bookstore can also assist with discounted bulk purchases using the Penguin Random House corporate Business-to-Business program. For assistance in locating a participating retailer, e-mail B2B@penguinrandomhouse.com.

LIBRARY OF CONGRESS CATALOGING-IN-PUBLICATION DATA
Names: Tu, Vivian, author.
Title: Rich AF : the winning money mindset that will change your life / Vivian Tu.
Other titles: Rich as fuck
Description: [New York, NY] : Portfolio/Penguin, [2023] |
Includes bibliographical references and index.
Identifiers: LCCN 2023026568 (print) | LCCN 2023026569 (ebook) |
ISBN 9780593714911 (hardcover) | ISBN 9780593714928 (ebook) |
Subjects: LCSH: Finance, Personal. | Saving and investment.
Classification: LCC HG179 .T8 2023 (print) | LCC HG179 (ebook) |
DDC 332.024—dc23/eng/20230901
LC record available at https://lccn.loc.gov/2023026568
LC ebook record available at https://lccn.loc.gov/2023026569

ISBN 9780593717172 (international edition)

Printed in the United States of America
1st Printing

Book design by Nicole LaRoche

TO MY BESTIES

This book is my love letter to you and anyone who has ever felt left behind, forgotten, or taken for granted. You deserve a life of richness, and I hope this road map can get you closer to whatever your dreams may be. I love you. I love you. I love you.

TO JEAN MAH, MY RICH BFF

Thank you for being the big sister I never had. Meeting you was the first time I ever saw an endless world of possibility for someone who looked like me. Your advice throughout the years has helped me navigate the best of times and the worst of times.

TO THE MAN WHO TOLD ME I WAS TOO GIRLY TO EVER SUCCEED IN FINANCE

Fuck. You.

Contents

PART II

Making Your Money Work Hard for YOU

Introduction

I hate to be the one to have to tell you this, but the American dream is dead. The rich get richer and the poor get poorer not because of some fluke, but because the system was designed this way—and guess what? Rich people designed it.

For generations, conversations about investments, money, and wealth were held in hushed tones on the sprawling greens of golf courses and over cocktails at members-only clubs. The secrets to financial success were traded among friends and passed down from "Rich Dads" to their "Rich Sons."

Meanwhile, if you weren't an old, rich, white dude, the financial services industry left you out to dry. While these rich dudes were busy creating and maintaining generational wealth, the rest of us were being sold the myth of the American dream—that if we studied hard, worked overtime, and gave up life's little luxuries, we'd be able to get rich just like the millionaires we saw in the pages of *Forbes* and *Vanity Fair*.

For most people, it's no longer possible to work or save your way to rich. And to make matters worse, if you don't know the rules around money, you simply never will, because we've been told that talking about money is rude, tacky, and off-limits. So how are we supposed to win life's game of chess when we only know how to play checkers?

By breaking those taboos.

By talking about money.

By thinking like a rich person.

And that's what I do.

Hi, I'm Vivian, and I'm Your Rich BFF.

I'm an ex–Wall Street trader, a former BuzzFeed sales partner, a current financial literacy creator, and a future bestselling author (okay, I'm manifesting—sue me).

I'm the founder and CEO of my own company. I own my own home.

And I made my first million dollars by age twenty-seven.

As Your Rich BFF, I'm here to cheer you on in your financial life. I'm here to teach you the rules rich people play by so we can beat them at their own game. My mission is to make money conversations normal, understandable, and—gasp—enjoyable for the next generation of Rich BFFs. Finance has been male, pale, and stale for entirely too long, but with this book, I'm turning finance into FUN-ance. I want everyone to recognize that they can become financially independent if they're armed with the right information and tools.

Because here's the thing: I am not special or unique.

I haven't always been good with money. I had to learn how to be.

I grew up in an immigrant Chinese home with two very loving but very frugal parents—where clipping coupons and reusing ziplock bags was the norm. I was taught that becoming rich meant swapping out my name-brand purchases for the store brand and packing a brown-bag lunch every day. I was told that if I could just stop buying Starbucks I'd be a millionaire in no time . . . right?!

Wrong.

It wasn't until I began my career on Wall Street that I realized real rich people were less concerned with scrimping and saving and more focused on investing and growing their wealth.

When I started on the J.P. Morgan equities desk in New York City, there were about thirty to forty traders and salespeople on the team. If you asked most of them why they joined the industry in the first place, I'd bet money that most of them would tell you they had a genuine interest . . . in making a shitload of money. Anyone who says otherwise is a liar.

I was no different. I wish I could tell you I had a burning passion for financial markets, but in reality, I just wanted a job where I'd never have to ask my parents for money ever again. Sure, I wanted to work in a fast-paced environment and get to do something new every day, but the idea of a penthouse apartment and a seven-figure paycheck definitely didn't hurt. Ultimately, the job helped me get rich, just not in the way that I originally thought it would—and a lot of it is thanks to *my* Rich BFF.

Because one thing I *didn't* have in common with those traders and salespeople?

All but one of them was a white man.

As fate would have it, the only other outlier, another Asian woman, ended up becoming my manager and mentor. She was everything I wanted to be—smart, sharp, successful, and sporting a new designer bag to work every day.

My Wall Street job had put me on the fast track to earning, but it was meeting my mentor that was the real game changer. For the first time in my life, someone was looking out for me. She would pull me aside and ask if I was contributing to my 401(k) (I wasn't), ask if I knew how to use the company's corporate travel catalog to save on hotels (I didn't), and even buy me lunch every day for nearly two years (I couldn't afford it— even on my fancy salary. I was paying New York City rent, people!). From her, I learned invaluable lessons about money, finance, and life that I never would have on the trading floor.

My mentor became the model for what I do and who I am now. She was the blueprint. The OG baddie. And the person behind the massive shift in my relationship with money. She was pulling back the curtain on wealth and teaching me the stuff that I never learned within the four walls of a classroom. Not only did she help me build a foundation to create financial wellness for myself, but even more importantly, she became an inspiration: a daily reminder that someone who looked just like me—a young Asian woman, from a modest family, with few connections—could make it big.

By the time I left Wall Street two and a half years later for the greener pastures of tech and media, I began to notice that my friends were constantly peppering me with the same questions I had once asked my mentor. Things like: *Can you help rebalance my 401(k)? Which health insurance did you pick? What are you investing in?*

I got so many of the same questions over and over again that at the end of 2020, I made a New Year's resolution to start a little passion project and share my knowledge publicly. I posted my first TikTok on January 1, 2021, and eight hours later my video had gone viral. By the end of the week, I had over 100K followers, tons of engagement, and an "oh no" moment of my very own.

How was I going to keep creating enough content to satisfy my community? How could I possibly do right by my fellow millennials and Gen Zers who were yearning for more financial information? Could I really do this—me, lil ol' Vivian?

But then I gave myself a reality check.

I had worked in high finance.

I had gotten my own personal finances in shape.

I was *more* than equipped to answer those questions.

Besides, what would my mentor do?

And then it dawned on me. The student had become the teacher.

I had become the Rich BFF.

So I decided to stay true to who I was and keep posting, and I haven't looked back since. Every day, I create the kind of content my friends would want to watch by blending topics like investing, student debt, and home buying, with pop culture anecdotes and funny personal stories.

Over the past three years, the Your Rich BFF community has grown to over six million followers and counting across eight social platforms. These lovely humans are young people, women, LGBTQ+ folks, people of color, first-generation Americans, hard workers from low-income backgrounds. I know rule number one for staying sane as a creator is supposed to be "don't read the comments," but IDGAF. Because take a look at these:

Thank you! Just got laid off and need this!

That was so easy thank god

This was such an amazing thing to know! I waited more than 70 minutes to get someone on the phone, but it was worth the refund!

Omg I have had so many jobs and didn't know about this! I hope my money can get found years later.

Ain't nothing wrong with knowing your worth!

Thank you for clarifying this info. You are absolutely correct.

Good to know because you're right, I've seen a lot of that nonsense on my fyp . . . ! 🫣

such a great explanation thank you

This is so important! It might feel awkward now, but someone having to drop out due to cost is way more awkward.

Thanks for the reminder, went straight to set it up. All done!

I just did this! Thanks Rich BFF!!

Those are comments from my videos.

Those are people who happened to watch sixty seconds of me explaining a concept, walking them through a process, or demystifying an acronym.

And then they did something to change their life.

Maybe it was a small change (like nabbing 2 percent cash back on their holiday shopping) or maybe it was a major change (like snagging thousands of dollars in tax credits). But it was a positive change, no matter the size. And it's one they never might have made if they hadn't heard from me. They are learning, earning, and growing, and they are *my* Rich BFFs—and with this book, now *you* are too.

This isn't me tryna brag, though. Because, again: I'm not that special. I'm no supergenius.

In fact, what I do on social media—and what I'll do in this book—is what I want *all* of us to do.

Talk about money.

Because when we talk about money, everyone benefits.

More people can get the raises they deserve.

More people learn what credits, refunds, and discount programs they're eligible for.

More people walk away from bad deals, money sucks, and rip-offs.

More people get more money.

More people live Rich AF.

So let's do it.

I'm going to reveal the secrets the rich have been passing down within their family lines and social circles for generations: the secrets that I only learned when I came to Wall Street myself. Because women, people of color, LGBTQ+ folks, and marginalized communities deserve a seat at the table, and if they're not going to get it the traditional way . . . well, we're just going to build our own damn table.

In fact, we built our own club. This isn't the exclusive club where the bouncer keeps you out unless you're some kind of VIP, or the country club where you need to pay out fifty grand to join. This club is for everybody. Throughout this book, you'll see invitations to come on in to our inclusive club: this is where you'll find resources like budgeting templates, spreadsheet calculators, brainstorming worksheets, and other helpful stuff to get you putting your new knowledge to work. So keep a lookout for those handy-dandy tools throughout the chapters, or pop on over right now: the URL is richAF.club.

We're smarter than we think, we're better together—and we all deserve the opportunity to be RICH AF.

Your Rich BFF's Money Map: How to Navigate This Book

Here's the deal with this book. I'm not your father's financial advisor. I'm never going to tell you to skip the avocado toast or Starbucks—there's no shame or judgment here—but I can help you improve your overall financial position.

I will start off by ripping back the curtain and showing you how rich people *really* do: how they think, how they act, how they spend, and how they're not just born rich, but stay rich and get richer. I'll also lay out all the reasons that the most recent generations of young people have had it exceptionally harder, money-wise (hint: it's not your fault).

From there, I'll cover Personal Finance 101: that crucial financial foundation you *wish* you got in school (but never did). I'll start by teaching you why you need to be taking *in* as much money as you can—and *how* to make that happen. From there, I'll guide you through assessing your spending, making a budget, and fine-tuning your plan so that you don't live on just beans and rice.

The rest of the book will be dedicated to the fundamentals of getting rich, the Your Rich BFF way: banking, saving, investing, using credit and paying down debt, and taking on the whole damn world.

I've also put together a glossary that you can flip to anytime you need a refresher on certain terms or concepts—so if you don't know an IRA from an HSA, no prob. I gotchu.

Finally, each chapter will end with a money management guide. I'll give you a handy to-do checklist to complete before moving on to the next chapter.

And yes, I deadass expect you to do *all* of them before you move on. Those checkboxes aren't just decorative, people. They are action steps you *need* to take. I want to hold you accountable because *doing* these things—not just reading about them—is the only way you're going to meaningfully improve your financial life.

So get out a pen, boss up your life, and X that sucker out. (And then tag me with your completed list—you deserve to brag!)

PART I

You Work Hard for the Money

1

EDUCATION FOR THIS ERA

Why This Book Is For You

A while back, I was spending a long weekend in the Hamptons with some friends—a cute little couples getaway, one of those day-drinking, sunbathing, very chill kind of mini vacations. One afternoon, before heading to the beach, we swung by the local CVS to pick up some snacks, and on the way out my girlfriend stopped dead in her tracks.

"Oh my God," she said. "I *have* to have that."

It was a Monopoly game. Not just any Monopoly game, but a Hamptons-themed Monopoly game.

Not gonna lie, I definitely rolled my eyes as I took our M&M's and gummy bears to the self-checkout. But Lauren was *so* excited, and inevitably her enthusiasm rubbed off on me. If my bestie was so excited about this novelty tourist trap of a board game, then who was I to rain on her parade?

By the time we got back to the car, Lauren had sold me on game night and we were fully stoked. We were *ready* to play this game. We slid back into our seats, handing out the goods, and when Adam, Lauren's boyfriend, asked what we were so amped about, I told him, "Oh, Lauren just bought this cheesy Hamptons Monopoly game for us to play tonight."

No response. It was like the summer air had gone chilly all of a sudden. And then, from the front seat, Adam turned around. Not smiling. Super intense.

And he said, "You guys do *not* want to play Monopoly with me."

Naturally, we were like, "Uh . . . why not?"

Another pause.

"Because," he said. "There's a secret. Most people have never actually read the full instruction brochure for Monopoly. But I have. And when I play the way I know how to play, there's no way I lose."

"So what's the big secret?!" I asked.

But he just shook his head. Wouldn't tell us. Lauren and I brushed off the conversation and headed out to the beach.

Later that night, we broke out Hamptons Monopoly. It was corny, with little lighthouses and windmills all over, but the wine was flowing and we were fully invested. After we each picked our little pieces and divvied up our fake money, we rolled the dice.

Adam proceeded to *dominate*.

Personally, I think I'm *okay* at Monopoly, like above average to actually decent, but I never stood a chance. This was a bloodbath. Tensions ran really high, really fast. Voices were raised, words were exchanged, arguments broke out over the exorbitant rent for the hotel on Shelter Island (the Hamptons version of Boardwalk).

Now, if you've ever played Monopoly with a competitive friend group, none of this comes as a surprise. It is probably the quickest and most devastating way to push friendships (and any relationship, really) to the brink. But this particular session was different, and not just because we were playing Hamptons Monopoly instead of the regular version.

It was because of Adam's *secret strategy*.

The secret was basically a weird loophole in the rules that allows you to use money *you don't have* to buy property. It turns out that if you do read the rule book the whole way through, and understand how the lending system works, the rules actually allow you to get leverage with the Monopoly bank (pretty much the same way you get rich in real life, TBH), which makes piling up those pink and orange bills go *so* much faster.

Lauren and I did not know that, of course. We'd laughed about this "big secret" earlier, but now that we'd been absolutely beaten down, we were mad about it.

"That's not fair," we said. "You didn't *tell* us that we could do that!"

Adam shrugged. "You guys had the same rule book as I did. You just chose not to read it."

Aside from guilt over almost starting World War III on our fun little couples trip (pour one out for our other friends who were innocent bystanders in this mess over tiny fake money), what I take away from this story is that the way Adam was able to win (and the rest of us . . . didn't) is basically the same way our financial system works in real life.

In theory, we all have access to the same information about money. We all have some version of the rule book. Everyone has a smartphone. Or a laptop. Or a library. It isn't *Downton Abbey* times anymore, when nothing was publicly accessible and only people rich enough to afford daily telegram delivery knew what was up. You can pull up any number of books, articles, websites, Wikis, whatever, right at your fingertips, all for the low, low cost of zero dollars, and learn everything there is to know about getting rich for real.

In theory, anyway.

Because no one really does that, right?

No one reads the rule book all the way through. Not when playing Monopoly, and not when managing our actual, authentic, cold, hard US dollars.

I'm willing to bet you probably learned to play Monopoly the same way I learned to play Monopoly: you sat down for your first game with someone else who had already played, and they talked you through it. It's quicker, it's less boring than squinting at all that tiny type, and it just gets you in the game faster and makes it more fun.

But then there are some people like Adam. He'd read the rule book all the way through. He found the loopholes and technicalities that could make him a winner *without* cheating and *without* a ton of effort.

Was there anything stopping me and Lauren from reading the entire little pamphlet front to back too?

Nope.

But did we?

Also nope.

We all had the same information available to us. But only one person really dug in and learned how to take advantage of it.

The reality is, just because we can all read up on the *rules*, that doesn't mean that we all have the same access to good *strategy*. Some people go through life leveraging the bank, and some of us play Monopoly the traditional way that we learned from our dad or our aunt or our big brother or our babysitter.

In other words, just having access to the rules alone is not enough. If you'd never played Monopoly before, you'd probably be confused just opening up the box: *There's a thimble and a Scottie dog in here? Why are all these streets named after states? What is this game even about?* You'd have to spend at least fifteen minutes reading the pamphlet, and you'd probably forget half of what you read once you start playing and have to go back and check all the time. The game would generally be slow, annoying, and not that fun, let alone easy to win.

Whereas if you play with someone who's played before, who has a strategy, they can teach you not only the rules, but which rules *matter*— and how to use them to your advantage. They can walk you through buying the deeds and how you have to build four houses before you can build a hotel, but also advise you on which color properties to snap up first, when to offer other players a trade, and whether or not it's actually worth buying utilities and railroads.

Finance theory is *most* useful when it's actually articulated as actionable advice. Instead of reading about things that *could* happen to you at some point, you're getting step-by-step info and instructions for what to do *right now*, given your circumstances. You have insights into which information is crucial and which you can kind of disregard.

That's the difference between knowing the rules and having a strategy.

And financial *strategy* is what we actually need to be teaching.

Because guess who learns financial strategy early on? Rich people.

And the rest of us? Well . . .

We Don't Learn About This Stuff in School

When was the last time you busted out the Pythagorean theorem?

Or wrote a five-paragraph essay?

Or played dodgeball?

It's probably been a loooong time.

And you're probably not going to do any of those things more than a handful of times for the rest of your life.

But when was the last time you bought something?

When was the last time you paid rent, or budgeted for groceries, or looked at your student loan balance and thought, *WTF do all these words mean and why are there still so many zeroes?*

We are not taught how to balance a checkbook . . . or even what "balance a checkbook" means. We are not taught how to file our taxes. We are not taught how to budget, how to save, how to invest wisely, or even what most of these words and terms *mean*. Personal finance for far too long has been this big gatekept secret—if you know, you know, and if you don't, you never will.

Every single person reading this book can likely tell me that the mitochondria is the powerhouse of the cell, but very few of you can confidently define what the stock market is or does.

And in my mind, that's a failure of our educational system.

Good News: It's Never Too Late to Learn

First off, it really *isn't* too late to learn. The best day to get financially literate was yesterday, but the second best day is today. Hopefully you get that by now, since you're already here and into chapter 1. (Stick with me, besties.) You still have plenty of time to harness the power of time to make you money (we'll get to that). Even if you're in debt and worth negative half a million bucks. Even if you're constantly getting slapped with overdraft fees. Even if you grew up broke and bullied and ashamed and deep down still feel like that dorky kid in secondhand clothes.

Better News: It's Not Your Fault

Second off, there's a very real reason you *don't* know this stuff, and it is basically beyond your control: you were not taught this in school. (I'm gonna say that until it sinks in.) But why *not*, exactly? If this information is so important to succeeding in life and eventually getting Rich AF, and the information is very much out there and not some big gold-plated secret, then why doesn't our education system make it a priority?

Because a lack of basic financial literacy keeps our working class working.

Look, I'm not trying to sound like a conspiracy theorist, but I do think a big part of why some of these basics of good financial strategy haven't "trickled down" (lol) to the middle class and beyond is because rich people want the rest of us to stay working. There is always a need for people to do the "dirty jobs," to pump gas and drive trucks and earn subminimum wages bartending and waitressing. Most people aren't stupid: if they know how to make more money, to establish a nest egg and a financial cushion, they *will*. And do you think they'll want to keep their shitty $7.25-an-hour job once they're no longer living hand to mouth? You think they'll sign up to work the third shift and never see their kids for the eighteen years it takes for them to grow up?

Of course not. People always want the best life their money can buy.

Back in the day, people actually aspired to be blue-collar professionals—because, once upon a time, a steady middle-class paycheck *was* enough to build wealth over time. That's no longer the case (and we'll get to why later in this chapter). For now, the point is just that our current system depends on blue-collar workers *not* having that upward mobility, not having the luxury to leave sucky jobs, to keep a consistent labor force hungry for whatever work they can get. You can look no further than the COVID-19 pandemic for proof: while white-collar corporate desk employees were sent to work from home, "essential workers" in construction, food service, and sanitation were still forced to show up day in and day out. By making financial literacy feel inaccessible and confusing, we've been able to keep our working class working— and carrying all of us on their backs.

But let's take off the tinfoil hats and get to the third and final, most important point here, which is . . .

Best News: You're Not a Bad Person If You *Don't* Know This Stuff

I mean it: *not* knowing the rules, *not* having a strategy, does *not* make you a bad person.

Which, like, okay, sounds fine on the face of it. We love ourselves, we respect our worthiness, all that good stuff.

But at the same time . . . how many times have you thought something like:

I'm so bad with money.

I'm just irresponsible.

I don't have the kind of discipline to save.

I'm a chronic overspender.

I'm a shopaholic.

I have a serious Amazon Prime problem.

I'm just resigned to being in debt until I die lol fml.

You see what all these thoughts have in common? They're making *you* the problem. Not even your choices or your mistakes. *You.* Your character. Your self.

And I'm sorry, but that's fucked up.

For one thing, we've already established that *you didn't learn this shit in school.* So you're probably unfamiliar with the rules. If you weren't lucky enough to get financial strategy advice from your rich parents and uncles and grandparents, you don't know how to *do* stuff even if you vaguely know you "should" save or "should" budget.

For another, the media and our culture in general *love* to lean into this character-assassination kind of money narrative. I strongly suspect that before you had any of those negative thoughts for yourself, you heard them somewhere else—on a TV show, in a movie, online.

Unfortunately, this blame game is particularly bad when it comes to anyone who isn't a straight white dude. Everything from dumb "women be shoppin'" memes to sitcom-level jokes about those gay guys and their wacky extravagances to harmful and false stereotypes about "welfare queens" and "job-stealing immigrants" hammers home the same message: you, and people like you, are inherently unable to handle money well. Your personal shortcomings are why you're broke. And there's nothing you can do to fix it, it's an essential part of who you are, so go cry about it, poors.

Nope. Not today. You're here and you're going to learn to think the way rich people do. You're going to get the lowdown on the rules and the inside scoop on how to make those rules work for you. You're going to learn how to make more money without working any harder, without giving up all the stuff you love, without being miserable and stingy and eating ramen for the rest of your life.

No, you didn't learn this stuff in school. No, you didn't have a rich great-aunt teaching you the ins and outs of the market or giving you savings bonds on your birthday or whatever.

None of that matters. Because it's never too late, so you're going to learn now.

And it's going to work.

And you are going to be Rich AF.

Take it from me. Yes, I got my ass handed to me in Hamptons Monopoly that one time. But after that? After I figured out the strategy?

I haven't lost since.

How Rich People Think

Short answer? Not like regular people. Because rich people are out here breaking all the rules that we're all "supposed" to follow.

Case in point: When I was just starting on Wall Street as a baby trader, I remember seeing this one sales guy come in on a Friday in the same outfit that he had worn on Thursday. Why? Because after work on Thursday, he'd taken a client to Atlantic City, New Jersey, to go gambling. They played poker and blackjack all night, did not sleep, and then chartered *a private helicopter* to bring them back on Friday. So this dude rolled in wearing yesterday's fit with a duffel bag of—no joke—*thirty-five grand in cash*, which he opened, and then he took out a hundred-dollar bill, gave it to his junior associate, and begged him to get everyone breakfast sandwiches because he was so hungover.

Now, my first reaction was to be psyched, because hey, free food. But as I ate my goodwill breakfast sandwich, I started running the numbers in my head. This guy probably spent $5K in a night—and that was just for the experience, not even the actual gambling part, which would have been God knows how much. And I knew the corporate expense policy was about $175 a person. So all I could conclude was . . . *Damn, did he just foot the bill?!*

None of it made *any* sense to my regular-person brain. I'd for *sure* think that, on paper, a stunt like this would get you fired. But no. This guy—a guy who literally *fell asleep* on his desk later that afternoon—ended up getting a *massive* trade order from his client that same day, plus every day for the following two weeks. He ended up being one of the top-paid people that year. This man broke literally every rule I had ever been told about being a good employee, and it *worked*: I watched him spend big, win big, and get rewarded.

This is *not* to say that we should all go empty our checking accounts and put it all on black in Atlantic City. It's simply to say that I have seen firsthand just how much rich people do *not* act, think, or behave the way the rest of us are told to. Rich people do it *their* way.

So if you're wondering, *Where are the rich learning all this secret money info if not at school?* the answer might surprise you: *talking among themselves.*

While *we* have been told that discussing money is tacky, taboo, and rude, *rich people* have been discussing their salaries, their tax strategies, and what they're paying for stuff for generations. It's been their little secret, the "rule for thee but not for me" that they're happy to break. Take it from someone who's been part of this world for a while now: money talk is *more* than welcome in this environment. When you're out in Martha's Vineyard, you can hear people talking about cash flow and return rates all the time. When you go to a golf course, and guys are having a few beers, smoking a cigar, and teeing off, they're talking about their portfolios and real estate investments like the rest of us talk about football scores.

The same way walk-of-shaming your way into work with a sack full of gambling cash doesn't make you a bad employee if you end up landing the Big Deal, talking about money isn't rude when *rich people* do it.

So what makes it tacky for two young women who *don't* have money to talk about *not* having money?

Nothing, actually. Nothing except our rich-person-dominant culture saying that it's rude.

But if we want to get rich, then we have to do as the rich people do, not as they say. (As far as money talk is concerned, anyway. If you wanna go gamble in New Jersey, you're on your own.)

Let's take a look at eight key characteristics of how rich people live that are probably *not* what you think.

1. Rich people are lazy.

You heard me right. Rich people do *not* want to work hard.

(I mean, do any of us?)

Sure, they *say* hard work matters. But in reality, they just want *you* to work hard, especially if you're dropping off their DoorDash order or babysitting their kids.

As for themselves? They want to take it easy—very easy.

The whole "just work hard and you'll get rich" mentality drives me insane for this exact reason: the rich aren't making money the way that regular people are making it.

Rich people know that everybody *else* is making money through labor (though, granted, sometimes they labor themselves, they fully intend— and have a plan—to scale back on active work hours ASAP). Often rich people are themselves just . . . lazy. But lazy in a brilliant way.

Because it's not just that they don't want to labor. They simply know that they *can't* work around the clock.

But you know what can work 24/7? Their money.

Since they know that they can have their money working for them literally all the time, and that they as a human being cannot, they simply understand the pretty logical conclusion that their money is a much better moneymaking tool than their bodies or their minds.

2. Rich people don't just have higher-paying jobs.

This brings me to my next point. Most people assume that rich people just have better-paying jobs than they do. But that's not true. It's not the whole picture, at least.

A person who is, for example, a billionaire does not just get a paycheck every two weeks for $85 million and stick it in a bank account. Yes, if this billionaire is still actively working, then they'll have a salary or some other kind of take-home cash pay, and it's probably quite high, at least compared to most working adults. (Though Mark Zuckerberg, CEO of Meta, notoriously only collects a one-dollar annual salary, that's more for tax purposes than anything else.) But most of their "money" is actually tied up in assets (company stock, bonds, mutual funds, real estate, fine art, whatever).

The way rich people make *and have* money is fundamentally different. And one way that it's fundamentally different is that their wealth is basically invisible.

3. Rich people don't care about impressing you.

You don't *see* a lot of what actually makes rich people rich.

They don't have some big pool of gold coins or anything. Their "riches" are *not* shown in things like Lambos and Louboutins. Their wealth is in fact something dead boring, like money in a bank somewhere earning interest.

Because rich people do not need to impress you.

In the Instagramification of society, when keeping up with the Joneses has become *Keeping Up with the Kardashians*, it's really easy for us to see just enormous amounts of wealth on our feeds and think, *Oh, I guess that's normal rich-people stuff.* It's not. Even at the lower end of the scale, I'm willing to bet that a *lot* of your friends, even the ones showing off their beach vacations and shiny gel manicures online, are broke just like you.

When rich people buy stuff, they don't buy it just because it's a luxury they want to enjoy. They buy it because it will make them more money. In other words, they put the vast majority of their spending power into buying assets (stuff that makes them money over time) instead of liabilities (stuff that costs them money over time).

Here's what this looks like in practice. Instead of buying, for example, that flashy Lamborghini that literally loses a third of its value as soon as you pull it off the lot, a rich person will take that same chunk of change and buy . . . a two-family duplex. Not exciting, not glamorous, maybe even a little run-down and in need of a face-lift.

But, like, YOU'RE RICH, you might be mentally screaming at them. Why did you buy a shitty, run-down duplex in a sketchy part of town? You already have a house.

Well, they can make that shitty duplex less shitty by investing in some repairs. They can take out a mortgage on it because they have collateral (their primary residence) and a high credit score. Then they can rent it out and use the rent payments to pay the mortgage. Eventually, they'll have paid off the mortgage and own the duplex outright without ever having paid out of their own pocket.

Oh, but it doesn't end there. This rich person probably also realized that they were able to take the money that *would* have gone to mortgage payments (but doesn't need to, thanks to cash coming in from rent) and invest it in the market instead. They see that the market is making them eight to ten percent a year, while their mortgage debt is going up by only two or three percent per year—and the amount is shrinking with every payment. The delta between that—the difference they get to pocket—is that 8- to 10-percent growth in the market minus the 2 to 3 percent in debt, which equals a nice 6 to 7 percent. Which, again, is money they are straight-up keeping.

Meanwhile, the Lambo they could have bought is now worth maybe, what, 30 percent, 40 percent of the purchase price? It still looks flashy, but it has *cost* the buyer a real amount of money. The duplex, though, is earning money through rent, through appreciation of the property itself, and through freeing up cash to be invested. Our rich person now owns a physical piece of the earth with a structure that you can touch and feel, which will provide value almost indefinitely, and they did it without you "seeing" any of it happen.

They don't care what you think of them or whether they impress you. They're happy to just cash your rent checks and let *you* pay their mortgage.

4. Rich people have an abundance mindset.

Us regular people have a terrible scarcity mindset—a constant feeling that we're never going to have enough money, that we're one slipup away from disaster, that we have to hoard every scrap of money we can because we'll never get a second chance to earn it back. Sometimes, this mindset is for sure valid—if you only have ten bucks in your bank account, visualizing abundance or whatever is not going to magically create more dollars. The problem here is that this scarcity mindset makes regular people very, very, *hyper* competitive with other people in similar financial situations.

So you have people at the bottom of the pyramid fighting with each other tooth and nail instead of trying to overthrow the people at the top of the pyramid.

No surprise, but this is *great* for the rich people.

The broke normies aren't coming for them, because they're too busy fighting each other. But the other rich people aren't coming for them, either.

Rich people are apex predators. They are the biggest dogs. They are chill AF about their place in life.

This is because rich people have an abundance mindset. Since they know they're gonna be able to take care of their bills tomorrow, they're not worried about them. They don't cling to every last cent because they know that money can always make more money, that "there's always more where that came from." They're able to decide what they *want* to do with their time rather than figure out what they *need* to do to survive. They don't have to see life as a zero-sum game where they're duking it out with other people at their level and fighting over the last scrap. The abundance mindset means that they are not as competitive with other people in their socioeconomic class—and they enjoy *so* much less stress as a result.

5. Rich people share, swap, and scratch each other's backs.

Rich people *love* helping each other out.

I was pretty shocked when I saw this kind of thing in action when I was starting out on Wall Street. See, there's a restriction that says if you're a trader in equities, you are legally not allowed to trade the things you trade at work—so if you're the tech trader, you can't trade tech stocks in your own personal portfolio, or if you're an industrials trader, you can't trade industrials in your personal portfolio. But what I found to be so interesting is that constantly, whenever there was ever a lull, or when we were all having our fifteen-dollar lunch salads, people would just be sharing their stock picks or their investment ideas. For free! With other people! Not only that, but these were ideas that they legally could not take advantage of themselves. But they didn't care. They were *happy* to dish out tips for PA (personal account) trades to anyone else.

It's not only stuff like stock tips, either. Rich people love being known in their friend group as the smartest person, the one with the best taste, the one on top of the trends. The phrase I hear all the time from other rich people is "I have this—you should get one too."

I have this great tax person—you should work with them.

I found the best cocktail bar—you have to try the martini.

I joined the best country club—and I'll sponsor you to join too.

The thing is, they *also* recognize that because they're sharing that knowledge, other people will open up and share what *they* know. They're indebted to them for the advice. It's the same reason rich people also love nothing more than putting their besties in positions of power. The thought process is something like: *Okay, I'm not qualified for this job, but my friend is, and once she gets it, she'll owe me a solid. Then, as soon as she's in a position of power, I'm automatically tapped into that whole network, which will definitely come in handy someday.* Yes, it's partially because they like to see their friends succeed. But it's also because they're thinking strategically— and thinking toward the future. They're thinking of collaboration, not competition.

6. Rich people think long-term.

Speaking of which, rich people are in it for the *long haul.*

Rich people know that sometimes stuff takes time, and they are happy to wait. They are kings and queens of delayed gratification. They know that it's better to weather out a minor deprivation in the short term to cash in majorly in the long term.

Again, in *theory* this makes total sense. But we've all painted our nails, immediately realized we had to pee, and said "fuck it" and scuffed up our manicure because we just can*not* wait. So yeah, in theory we know it's better to be patient. But in practice, it's incredibly easy to sabotage a long-term goal (gorgeous at-home mani) to solve a short-term problem (literally about to wet my pants).

But not for rich people. They can hold it *forever.*

A rich person has no problem, for example, socking away money in a retirement account. Yes, that money they invested in their IRA account this year is off-limits until they're 59.5. But they know that just because they can't spend that money *now*, it's not like it went *poof* and disappeared entirely. In fact, it's the opposite: because it's in an investment account, it's likely going to earn them a decent percentage back every year. So the *longer* they're locked in to wait, the more money they get when time's up. They almost enjoy making themselves wait, because they know that the more time they give their money to grow, the more their money will reward them for their patience.

7. Rich people love giving away their money— and watching it come back.

The boys that I sat around on that trading desk, talking about PA trades and swapping stock tips? They were not sweating over the fifteen bucks they'd just spent on their lunch salad. They were worried about how they were gonna take the six, maybe seven figures they had stashed, and *give it away.* They could not *wait* to hear about opportunities to get that money out of their savings accounts and into someone else's business.

Inevitably, somebody would mention, "Oh, my cousin is launching this startup," or "My wife and I are interviewing hard-money lenders for a twelve-unit complex," and everybody's first questions were "Do you need money? Are they looking for investments? What's the buy-in here?"

This was so confusing to me at first (since I was panicking over the cost of my quinoa bowl). Why are these rich people trying to give their money away? Dude, you seem like you just want to light this on fire.

Now I get it. The mindset rich people have isn't *How do I scrimp and save and keep every last penny locked up in my account?* It's *How can I get this money flowing and growing—and waste no time doing it?*

8. Rich people (especially the generation above us) have had it easy.

I've mentioned *time* in a general sense as something rich people harness to get rich. But there's one key aspect of time I haven't really mentioned: *when* you're making your money.

In the past, it was a *lot* easier to get rich.

Not for everyone (and don't worry, we will break all that down in a sec) and not across the board, but trust me. There's a reason a lot of rich people right now are from the generation *above* ours. You've probably seen new stories to the effect that "millennials are the first generation to be worse off than their parents, blah blah blah," but it's actually true. If life is a game of Guitar Hero, those people played in tutorial mode, and we're playing advanced on an old broken TV.

This is where the "rich person" mentality doesn't always map to the reality of where we—the millennials and Gen Zers—actually are.

We're all been sold this American dream, right? Back in the day, in our parents' generation (so boomers, roughly), the attitude was that if you worked your tail off, you went to a good college, and you got a four-year degree, then for the most part, you'd be financially successful.

Whatever debt that they took on to get that degree was minuscule, small enough to be paid off with a few shifts at the campus pizza place. They'd have a nice job. If they worked hard and they were a good employee, they'd get raises. They would make enough money to put food on the table, to start a family, and to save, and then they would take that saved-up money and buy a house.

And since the housing market has really only gone one way—up— since our parents entered the market, the money they put into that house made money back in equity. Their job kept promoting them up the ladder until finally they retired with a gold watch and a nice pension.

Then they start giving us advice.

The first big problem here is survivorship bias. We're only hearing advice from people who had opportunities to succeed in the first place. But there were massive swaths of the population that were left out of this "normal" American dream trajectory. Black people who were redlined out of property ownership, women who couldn't open lines of credit without their husbands' permission, queer people who were (and sometimes, sadly, still are) discriminated against in hiring for jobs.

The other thing is that while these older rich people aren't *wrong* about what worked for them—obviously, it did—they fail to recognize that what worked for them *worked* for them. As in, past tense. They're not entering the job market *now*. They're not starting from scratch in Today's Economy™. And that makes a *huge* difference in what's possible for those of us who *are* actively building wealth, now, at this time in history.

The current state of things in this country is, financially speaking, a hot mess. Massive systems like the housing market, the student-loan-industrial complex, and the international supply chain have been going absolutely buck wild in a way that is truly unprecedented in modern history.

So if you've ever felt like the deck is stacked against you, allow me to validate that: It is. Majorly.

That's what the next section of this book is all about: why things right now are *way* different (and way worse) than they used to be, and why so much "conventional wisdom" sucks. Once you understand where we are and how the hell we got here, you'll finally understand why typical "money wisdom" just Does Not Apply—and how you can start making intelligent, informed, rich-person decisions instead.

The Money Advice Out There Sucks (and Here's Why)

If reading about the way rich people think about money is a wake-up call for you, then these little tidbits of advice here might be a tad more familiar. These are the money pro tips you've seen online, read in old books, vaguely absorbed from ~somewhere~, and heard from "financial gurus" (or from your parents).

They're also the pro tips that need to *die*—because they are keeping us broke.

Just switch careers to make more money!

Yeah, that's infinitely easier said than done.

If a person grew up in a blue-collar family in Appalachia and moved to a midsize city after school to work at Dunder Mifflin, what exactly is their path to, say, working at Google? Seriously, think it through. They don't know anybody who does computer programming. They don't live near a company where they can do an internship for experience and they probably can't afford to work for free anyway. Even if they got the degree or got the boot camp certification, how are they going to get their résumé in the door? How are they going to take time off work for an interview? And would they even *want* to uproot their whole life and move across the country just for a bigger paycheck even if they *did* get the job?

No. Google is going to hire one of the zillion people in their current referral chain from other people who know each other from Silicon Valley or New York City. This paper salesman is going to be reluctant to up and leave their family and friends and that cute receptionist at work just to get a "better job," even if they could stand to earn more money.

Jobs aren't just about paychecks. They're cultural, they're local, and they shape our identity. So suggesting that a "better job" or a "new career" is all it takes to end brokeness forever is hardcore out of touch with reality.

Just find a cheaper place to live! Or get roommates!

First of all: *What* cheaper place? Take it from me and my fellow millennial Zillow obsessives: they're just not out there.

In the *real* world, housing prices have jumped a ton since the middle of the last century—specifically, 118 percent since 1965—and that's accounting for inflation *and* despite all the news about the pandemic home-buying boom. Even if you're renting, you're not shielded: higher overall prices for landlords mean higher rent payments for you . . . and *that's* assuming you're in good enough shape to pass the credit check, have a job with a paystub, and aren't given the runaround by shady brokers.

But most important of all here is that housing isn't just a boring line item you can reduce like a gym membership or an app subscription. For one thing, homeownership has long been the bedrock of middle-class wealth-building, the most expensive investment a person makes and the one they count on to fund stability up until (and well into) retirement. Not being able to get in on that? Sucks. Telling us to "find a cheaper place" not only isn't a feasible short-term solution, it's steering us *away* from a fundamental vehicle for amassing wealth.

For another thing, a house (or apartment) is a necessary physical structure that you can chuck your family in and protect yourself from the rain. Changing where and with whom we live comes with an emotional and physical trade-off that sometimes we're just not willing to make—nor should we be. (And that's before we even get into the pain in the ass process of finding a new apartment, negotiating with a landlord, moving all your shit, and hoping your roommates aren't annoying.) In fact, sometimes it's actually worth spending *more* on housing.

Case in point: When I was working trading hours on Wall Street, I had to be in my seat at 5:30 in the morning. I'd work until 6:30 or so at night, and then I'd leave for client events in the evening. Get home at 10 or 11, rinse, repeat.

I was lucky that my commute was manageable enough that I didn't have too miserable of a subway ride there and back. But as soon as I was financially able, and my lease was up, I sprung for a new place that was closer to work and *more* expensive.

Why? Because I was fucking tired. And I knew I couldn't run on fumes forever.

If I'd stayed in that cheaper apartment, eventually, the commute and the long hours would've ground me down. I'd have gotten physically and mentally exhausted faster than I should have for someone my age, and eventually I'd maybe even burn out so hard I simply couldn't do the job anymore. Sure, I'd be "saving" on rent, but it'd come at a real cost.

Meanwhile, I was watching the analysts who lived closer to the office than I did. With a shorter commute, they were able to get more sleep, show up earlier, and generally just look like they were more dedicated to the job. Essentially, they were seen as better employees. And for what? Because they had more money to spend on rent.

Compare that with someone who's coming from generational poverty, maybe someone who needed to send money home to their family. They know that they cannot spend all their money on rent because that support is non-negotiable. So they either decide they're going to sacrifice an additional forty-five minutes of sleep (which you're not getting much of anyway, working those hours) or they're going to show up slightly later and be seen as a less good employee.

(Finally, who's to say I don't already *have* roommates? Literally only about one in ten young people lives completely solo. The rest are bunking with roomies, partners, spouses, or—yes—parents: one in three adults aged eighteen to thirty-four still lives at home.)

Just spend less on lattes and avocado toast!

Avocado toast: $18

Avocado toast x 2 times weekly x 52 weeks/year: $1,872

Daily latte: $5

Latte x 365 days a year: $1,825

Median price of a home in the United States in 2023: $363,000

Average amount of student loan debt per capita in 2023: $28,950

Average price of a used vehicle in 2023: $26,510

Short answer: IT AIN'T THE AVO TOAST, BABE!

Long answer: Short-term small expenses aren't making or breaking our financial lives and keeping us from achieving our goals the way most financial gurus want you to *think* they are. For one thing, you might look at these numbers and be like, "F it, I'm never going to afford all that stuff anyway, so I'm at least going to get myself a nice brunch once in a while," which is a pretty valid response. (Although, as we'll see, you *can* actually work toward those bigger buys without feeling totally hopeless . . . but more on that later.)

But for another thing, the reason so many expenses these days—small, big, and everything in between—feel so much more out of reach than we've been taught they should be is because, well . . . they are, thanks to *inflation*.

You've probably heard about inflation ~generally~, but if you can't explain it in a nutshell, don't sweat. This conniving force of darkness is pretty simple at a basic level. Inflation refers to the gradual increase in prices over time. In practice, this generally means you'll be paying more than you previously did for the same item or service.

You've probably seen this happen in your lifetime. Think of the movies you've seen over the years: the ticket you bought to see Robert Pattinson as a sparkly vampire in *Twilight* (no judgment) probably cost less than the one you bought to see Robert Pattinson kick ass in *The Batman* fourteen years later, right?

Inflation in general can be tracked at a macro level (averaging out all the price increases across different sectors of the economy—so, movie tickets, but also gas, groceries, industrial goods, that kind of thing). When the general price level rises, each unit of money buys fewer goods and services, and thus there is a reduction in the purchasing power of money. Pretty simple.

The problem comes when inflation gets out of hand—when average prices go up faster than average wages are going up, in other words. Economists generally consider a rate of around 2 percent per year to be "healthy" and indicative of an economy that's growing steadily. (Negative inflation, or *deflation*, is actually its own kind of bad news.) More than that, though, can be bad news—and lately, that's just what's been happening. The still-ongoing aftermath of the COVID-19 pandemic that caught tons of companies, banks, and manufacturers by surprise; the sporadic supply chain issues that keep cropping up; the labor market wildin' out as people are laid off, retire early, and come *out* of retirement; and the general *instability* of it all have contributed to the inflation we see now, making stuff more expensive than it used to be.

Just relax! Money can't buy happiness anyway!

Um, false. So false. Falser than you even think.

Back in 2010, there was a pretty famous study you might have heard about regarding money and happiness. Basically, it concluded that people's happiness increased in lockstep with their income—but only up to a certain point, around $75,000 per year (which is about $90,000 in today's dollars). After that, it leveled off.

People love to throw this factoid around because it kind of had its cake and ate it too: it essentially meant money *could* buy happiness because it provided basic necessities and stability, but also that billionaires weren't much happier than the rest of us.

Well, I hate to break to you, but: new study just dropped.

A 2021 study titled "Experienced Well-Being Rises with Income, Even Above $75,000 per Year" found that the $75,000 figure is absolute bologna (yeah—even adjusted for inflation). Turns out happiness continues to increase well past that threshold—and I quote: "There was . . . no evidence of an income threshold at which experienced and evaluative well-being diverged, suggesting that higher incomes are associated with both feeling better day-to-day and being more satisfied with life overall."

Preach. But let's go deeper. Because "just relax" isn't simply empirically shitty advice; it's advice that ignores our lived reality. The years in which we've come of age have seen crazy amounts of cataclysmic, once-in-a-lifetime events that destabilize markets. Even before most of us had jobs and were earning our own cash, we existed in a world that was constantly getting turned upside down. You didn't *need* to be an adult with a stock portfolio to see that 9/11, the Iraq War, the 2008 housing crisis, Brexit, COVID-19, the January 6 insurrection, the FTX fiasco, and the 2023 collapse of major regional and national banks had massive, unavoidable effects on the way we live. In fact, *because* we were young when many of these things happened, they taught our impressionable kid and teenage and twentysomething brains some truths about the world: *It's volatile. It's scary. It could all be ripped away in a split second.*

Sure, "just relax" was good advice—once. Boomers (and some older Gen Xers) got to live their prime earning years through a bull market (aka when the line goes up and to the right and the economy is doing well). Back then, as long as you participated in the stock market and bought a diversified portfolio, you won. But anyone born from the nineties onward lived through collective trauma—economic and otherwise. The ideas we've been taught about "how the market works" do not match with our lived reality of *how the market actually works.* Call us coddled, or sensitive snowflakes, or whatever, but this shit was *real* for us.

Bottom line: it's okay to feel a little spooked and unsure, *and* it's okay to want to have money.

Just stop choosing to be poor!

UGHHHHHH. I hate this one.

Maybe it's just my FYP, but I feel like I've scrolled past *so* many celebrities and influencers talking about how "being broke is a choice."

Which is a fucking idiotic thing to say.

For one thing, medical bankruptcy, which was unheard of a generation ago, is now the leading cause of bankruptcy in the United States.

I don't have to tell you this is super fucked up, but I will. It's fucked up. Who would *ever* "make the choice" to run up a sky-high hospital bill? No one *chooses* to have a kidney stone or a seizure the way people *choose* to run up credit card debt at Sephora. Those folks end up broke, still probably sick, *and* judged by internet randos on their "choices."

For another thing, it's actually *more* expensive to be poor. Covering ongoing costs with stopgap cheaper options can actually cost you more in the long run—and you don't have a choice.

For example, when I worked at J.P. Morgan, I had to wear pantyhose to meet the dress code. After food, rent, and other necessities, the best I could afford were the cheapies that come in little cardboard boxes at Walgreens for $6.99. These pantyhose *sucked*, y'all. I'd wear each pair two, maybe three times before a hangnail snagged one of the legs, or a hole appeared in the crotch, or they just got one of those mysterious out-of-nowhere runs. So I'd have to buy more. Over about six months, I went through thirteen pairs of those suckers, aka just about ninety-one dollars' worth of pantyhose.

Meanwhile, a pair of Wolford sheer nude hose from Saks Fifth Avenue—which would last me a solid six months or more, if I was careful—cost sixty dollars. Except I never had sixty dollars, not all at once. That was my whole-ass clothes budget for the month, and I needed other stuff like "skirts that fit" and "shoes not worn down to the heel peg." So I was stuck buying L'eggs at $6.99 a pop, because I *did* have $6.99. I was overpaying in the long term—not because I was "making bad choices" but because I was too cash-strapped to have an alternative. (If you've ever read Terry Pratchett's Discworld series, you might be familiar with Captain Samuel Vimes's observations about cheap boots versus expensive boots. I was basically living out my own version, but with pantyhose.)

When people are actually in a cycle of paycheck-to-paycheck brokeness, it's not that they don't want out of that situation. They *do*. They want to make the right choices. The problem is that there are factors working against them: exhaustion, illness, a lack of time, a lack of resources, and a lack of role models. Urgency, timing, convenience, and limited options can squeeze us into paying more over the long term (and that's before we even get into things like predatory payday loans, credit card interest, or the fact that high-ticket items from phones to laptops are now basically designed to stop working every five years).

So no, being broke is not a choice. And overcoming brokeness is not easy (but you've got me, Your Rich BFF, to help you do it!).

Why Race, Gender, and Diversity Are Important to Acknowledge

I can't just wrap up this chapter on a note of "Yeah, it's harder *now* than it used to be."

For some people, it's always been hard. For some people, the money traumas are systemic and generational. So many groups—like women,

POC, and the LGBTQ+ community—have simply not had the equal opportunities to build wealth.

Because, real talk, when most people think of "a rich person," they probably picture a white guy, whether it's Warren Buffett or Elon Musk.

But this is *not* because white guys are better at stuff. In fact, they are the ultimate tutorial-mode players. They've just had it easier.

That's not being "politically correct" or whatever: it is facts.

Here's a quick history lesson.

The abolition of slavery in the United States was supposed to usher in freedom and equality under the law, but the (white) (male) people in power just innovated new ways to discriminate. Eight generations after the first Juneteenth, the typical Black American family has only thirteen cents for every dollar held by the typical white American family. Black veterans were denied benefits of the GI Bill, such as free college tuition. And Black families would face redlining and racist lending policies when attempting to buy homes, effectively locking them out of the postwar economic boom.

These disadvantages were negative interest compounding generation after generation, denying Black people the ability to move upward economically. Today, Black women in the United States are still paid 36 percent less than white men and 12 percent less than white women. They're also 10 percent less likely than white men to be an active part of the workforce. Black people who are homeowners get less resale value for their homes—just because Black people lived there! (Seriously: a Black family in California swapped out their family photos with photos of a white friend's family, and their home appraisal went up by HALF A MILLION DOLLARS. For the *same. Exact. House.*)

But Black Americans aren't alone in struggling to get a foothold in generational wealth. As much as I loved seeing *Crazy Rich Asians* representation on the big screen, please don't let the glitz and glamour blind you from the challenges the Asian American community faces as a whole. (Not to mention the fear of being attacked in the street.)

While Asians overall rank as the highest-earning racial group in the United States, that is not a status shared by *all* Asians. We aren't a unified, singular, monolithic group, but rather a melting pot of many different countries, languages, and cultures—and income brackets. In fact, Asian Americans are now the most economically divided racial group in the country: in 2016, Asians in the top tenth percentile earned over ten times as much as those in the bottom tenth percentile. This is at least partially due to American immigration laws, specifically the H-1B visa that allowed US employers to employ foreign workers in high-earning specialty occupations—think doctors, computer scientists, engineers—which led to many highly educated, high-earning Asian people immigrating to the United States post–World War II.

The Latino community in America also grew in the twentieth century—but their bank accounts haven't always, thanks to a racist grab bag of fearmongering, union busting, and oppressive immigration policies. In the early twentieth century, Latino farmworkers were crucial to the organized labor movement, striking for fair working conditions and pay . . . only to be attacked by militias. The 1942 Bracero Program granted millions of Mexican citizens the right to work temporarily in the United States . . . but also took a mandatory 10 percent "savings" from their pay that was rarely restored *and* actively blocked them from contacting their families back home.

Today, Latino Americans earn on average just seventy-three cents to the dollar compared to white Americans and are collectively underpaid by an estimated $288 *billion* (with a b). Still, for the past twenty years, Latino wealth has been growing at an average rate of 7 percent per year, more than twice as fast as white wealth . . . yet despite absolutely crushing it, growth-wise, the median wealth held by Latino households was just one-*fifth* that of white households ($36,000 versus $188,200) as of 2019. Not only that, but Latinos start more businesses than any other racial group in the United States (and at twice the rate of white folks) . . . yet are less likely to be approved for start-up loans despite having, on average, the same credit scores as white entrepreneurs.

It's not just race-based, either: queer folks have also been subject to historical disadvantages. Before same-sex marriage was legalized nationwide, lifelong partners had no legal recourse for inheriting wealth if one of them passed away, enjoying the tax benefits of marriage, or sharing spousal health insurance coverage. Today, it's still perfectly legal in many instances to just plain fire (or not hire) someone because they're gay or trans (thanks to sneaky things like religious exceptions), and it's only been illegal to reject an LGBTQ+ person for a mortgage since *2020*.

And, lest we forget, good old-fashioned sexism is still alive and well. For one thing, it's just expensive to be a woman. The "pink tax" on stuff like razors and soap, the cultural expectation for all of us to wear a full face of makeup every single day (and the fact that we're seen as less competent if we don't), the lack of a social safety net that makes childbearing a huge burden on a woman's lifelong earning potential—it's exhausting.

But for another, it's sadly quite easy for us gals to get really, really stuck in a bad situation because of money. Trust me, I have received *way* too many DMs from women telling me that they caught their husband cheating and now he's locked her out of their joint accounts, or that their partner who "took care of all the bills" just passed away and now they have no idea what to do with their money, or that they are trapped in a relationship they know is toxic but they simply can't afford to move to their own place.

All these reasons, for all these kinds of people, are why we *all* need to be Rich AF.

And it's why we all need a Rich BFF.

2

I KNOW MY WORTH

The Earnings and Career Section

Right about now is when most money books would jump into budgeting.

They'd run down how to calculate your expenses, track your spending, and make savings goals. Maybe you'd get some sweet spreadsheets going, or draw an adorable chart in your bullet journal full of little motivational stickers.

And that's all well and good—eventually.

Because most money books have it backward. They're just not seeing money the way rich people see money. They're focusing on downsizing and minimizing and scrimping before even considering the other, much more powerful side of the equation: how much you earn.

Now, don't get me wrong—rich people *do* budget (and we'll get to that). But they also live by one core truth above all, a truth that absolutely should be first in your mind before you even *think* about making a spreadsheet.

This truth is the best, craziest, most solid-gold piece of financial advice I've literally ever gotten in my life, and now I'm going to share it with you.

Ready? Here it is:

You can only save as much as you earn.

It's kind of obvious, I know. But think about it: you can only save so much before you're cutting into basics like the roof over your head and nothing but rice and beans for sustenance. Even if you somehow spent zero dollars, got rid of all your expenses somehow, and bought absolutely n-o-t-h-i-n-g, not even essentials, you *still* couldn't save more than you get in your paycheck. It's just not possible, right? There's no way to sock away 110 percent of what you earn unless your job is up to some seriously shady accounting practices.

Now, here's the second part of this mind-blowing advice:

You can only save as much as you earn . . . but you can always earn more.

Rich people take this to heart. They're out there asking for raises, trading up to better-paying jobs, buying rental properties, and investing like crazy. And they're not trying to fix shortfalls with scrimping and cutting back. Why? They know that earning more at their job is step one . . . because money can *make more money.* Earning more leads to investing, and investing gets you harnessing the power of time to make your money grow, and *that* is exponentially more impactful than just never going to Starbucks again or living with six roommates until you're fifty. (Also, rich people know it's just plain easier to make more money and have the lifestyle they actually want than to slash their expenses to the bone in the name of saving.)

Essentially, rich people know that you can't just budget your way out of a spending hole. And you definitely can't budget your way out of poverty.

So that's why we're starting here: with your career, with your *earning power.* Because before we go any further, we're gonna find a way to get you some more cash.

I'm not going to explain how to get your boss to like you, or how to polish your résumé, or how to ace an interview. But I will tell you how to get *paid.*

Because we don't do this shit for free.

The Your Rich BFF Career Saga (Or: How I Learned to Go Where I'm Valued and How You Can Too)

I didn't start my career as a TikToker. Or as a digital marketing salesperson. Or as a Wall Street hotshot.

Actually, my first paid job was as an intern at a "marketing company" in Chicago, the summer after freshman year of college.

I put it in quotes because it was not a marketing company. It was, in fact, a club-promoting company. It was a club-promoting company that had no problem hiring me, a nineteen-year-old child, for the job of getting people to go to bars that I myself could not legally enter.

Now, you might think an outfit this shady would pay, like, nothing. I was pretty much expecting to make nothing. And that's what the pay scale was on the face of it: one body in the door = five dollars for Vivian.

But this was summer break. Most of my college pals were hanging out in Chicago, on campus taking extra classes or interning somewhere. When the weekends rolled around, they were bored, they were broke, and a decent number of them were twenty-one . . . or had identification stating that they were twenty-one. And since I knew basically everyone who was on campus for the summer, I had a captive audience. I just had to mention to my fellow UChicago students that such-and-such bar was offering a drink deal, and they were *in*.

As the summer went on, I put together a crew. Every Friday and Saturday night, they would go to whatever bar I told them was giving away free shots or half-price beer buckets or whatever. Then my underage ass would collect five dollars for each of them walking in that bar and stand outside for the rest of the night putting wristbands on.

I recognized pretty quickly that being a club promoter was not in the cards for me. However, I did really like the overall setup of the job, that I ate what I killed. The idea of commission-based pay didn't scare me like it did a lot of people, and it worked out pretty damn well: I would make $250 or so on a Friday and another $250 on a Saturday.

Now, $500 a week is a *lot* for a college kid. But I also had no problem spending it. And as I did, I started to realize something else: I liked working for more money a lot more than I liked giving things up. Because I was commission-based, I could literally calculate exactly how much work I'd need to do to earn five, ten, fifteen more bucks for the week—like, a few minutes of texting and I could drum up two or three more people to tag along that weekend. That felt so much easier and so much *better* than comparison shopping for the cheapest brand of yogurt to keep my grocery bill down.

The moral of this work story is exactly what I said up top (and something I will say over and over again until I'm literally on my deathbed): you can only save as much as you earn, but you can *always* earn more money.

However, not all jobs are as straightforward (or unsupervised) as "underage club promoter." Sometimes working harder *doesn't* get you paid more. For one thing, some of the hardest jobs out there (looking at you, essential workers) are laughably underpaid considering they involve feeding people, teaching people, or literally keeping people alive. Meanwhile, corporate attorneys are billing $350 for a ten-minute phone call where they mostly talked about golf scores.

For another thing, when it comes to moving up in your career, your workplace environment matters just as much—if not more than—your hard work. Because as much as we would like to think that your pay, your role, and your nonmonetary compensation are directly tied to your performance, they're not. They're always tied to the politics at your company. To stick it out in your career and to ensure your financial success, you need to be able to network both inside and outside of your current company—*especially* if you're a woman, a person of color, an LGBTQ+ person, or in any way marginalized.

Rich people get this. They know their worth, but they don't *just* know their worth. They know when that worth is being overlooked and when it's appreciated. They can tell when they're in an environment where they're not going to succeed and they can tell when they're somewhere they're going to flourish, grow, and make bank. So for my first "real job," I knew I had to go somewhere I would be valued: Wall Street, baby.

When I started at J.P. Morgan, I, like all junior traders, sat between two senior traders, who were my managers. To my right was the woman who became my mentor: an Asian woman like me, someone who understood the cultural things I was dealing with but could explain point-blank, "This is how Wall Street works." She traded industrial and material stocks and she was hardcore.

To my left was my second manager, a white guy in his forties who traded energy stocks. We did *not* have as much in common as my mentor and I did. But he also treated me quite well. And while I don't know for sure that this had anything to do with the way he treated me, this guy did happen to be the father of two little girls.

At the same time, both he and my mentor? They were hard as shit on me.

If I made a mistake, I knew I was going to hear about it. If I missed something, it was pretty much a given that I would get yelled at. But it was always about the quality of my work. It was always "Vivian, you missed XYZ, and you need to do better." It was never personal.

It wasn't *fun*, but at the same time, I could handle it. I could handle being not perfect at my job on day, like, thirty-seven. The feedback was fair, and people knew that was normal—even the smartest guy on the desk would joke about when he got *sent home* because he fucked up so bad in his twenties.

And that was the thing: these were the kinds of people who made me want to join J.P. Morgan in the first place. These more senior people were hard on me, but they were hard on *everyone*, and these people were truly invested in my work. Even this brilliant, revered guy on the floor was at one point *also* making mistakes, but people had his back and he ascended. So even when my managers truly let me have it, I knew deep down, *This person is going to advocate for me. This person is going to be in the back room pounding the table to make sure I get paid, I get promoted, I get a raise.*

Then the head of my desk got let go, and they brought in a new guy. And this new guy fired a *lot* of those people who helped me get the job in the first place.

In the aftermath, the new big boss pulled me aside one day. "You had an internship in banking before you came to the trading side, right? I've heard you're good at Excel."

Now, as a junior trader, you're trying to curry favor with everyone on the desk, so I told him yep, totally, and asked what I could help with, and then next thing I knew I was fielding requests from a bunch of people, writing my little Excel sheets to fix their problems and getting thanked *profusely* for something that (ngl) was pretty easy for me.

Eventually, word got around that if you needed an Excel thing, you should go to Viv. And the big boss noticed, because soon after that he came back with another question for me: basically, *Do you want to leave your two managers and come work for my BFF?*

Except the way it was posed to me was not a question. This BFF was the guy the big boss had handpicked, who was going to be his right-hand man. So all I could think was *Well, I'm not trying to get fucking fired, and I'm not trying to blow up all the success I've had thus far, so sure, I'll come work for your guy.* I figured it might not be ideal, but hey, if I was valuable there, then maybe it'd be a good trade up.

The change was immediate. I went from being the star child whiz kid (who, to be sure, still got yelled at when it was merited) to *trash*. When I got to this new boss, it felt like I couldn't do anything right. Even when I thought I had done great work, he would be like, "It's fine," or just . . . not say anything. I started getting used more and more for my Excel skills, and then this man would take my work and present it as his. I'd have to watch him talk about his spreadsheet setup in a meeting as if he knew how to use Excel, knowing that he'd spent hours literally leering over my shoulder as *I* did the work.

Oh, but it got worse. Because this guy? He would say horrible things to me—just *horrible*. "You're too girly to be in this seat. I can't believe you work here." But it was one day in particular that pushed me over the edge. I came into work with a long cardigan on, and this guy—I am not kidding—fucking *bowed* at me, and asked if I was wearing some kind of kimono.

That was the moment I knew it wasn't for me anymore.

But it wasn't just because he was treating me badly. Yeah, he was clearly a racist, sexist bigot. Yeah, he was shitty at his job and leaned on me to cover for him. But beyond all of that, I knew this guy was never going to advocate for me. He was never going to be in the back room with his boss, pounding the table, saying, "This girl's got to get paid. We can't lose her. She's a great talent. She's amazing." And I realized that it didn't matter how hard I worked, how talented I was, how high I performed. If my manager wasn't going to push for me, then my career at that company was at a dead end. It didn't matter that there *were* people who would advocate for me, like my mentor and my former manager, because they no longer had the power or influence. In fact, both of them ended up leaving the company. And so did I.

I left because I wasn't going to waste my time, talent, and energy in an environment where the inner circle was very clearly not going to open for me, no matter what. I left because I wasn't valued the way I should have been, and I wanted to—*deserved* to—be somewhere my hard work and talent rewarded *me* too.

Fortunately, I quickly found that kind of environment—the opposite of where I'd been on Wall Street.

Working in sales at BuzzFeed, there was a very clear inner circle: the top sellers. People across the company would bend over backward for these salespeople because everyone knew they could bring in monster deals if they got what they needed—things like quick legal approvals, niche research stats, and beautifully designed pitch decks. That, to me, did not feel like an inaccessible group. I could get there with my work: not just by closing massive deals but also by taking fifteen minutes out of my day, every day, to go meet with research, to go meet with accounting, to go meet with *all* the teams, and just give them a quick "Hey, how's it going? I'm Vivian—just wanted to introduce myself and to put a face to a name."

It worked. Over my almost four years at BuzzFeed, I politicked my way into that group. By the end, people were bending over backward to help *me* close deals. And it worked because the environment at BuzzFeed was one where politicking, meeting people, and having advocates beside *and* above me really made a difference. If I kicked ass, I was more valuable—and treated (and paid!) as such. I got to earn a commission just like my nightclub-promo days, and I had the respect, trust, and confidence of my managers *and* peers.

But there's one last twist to this career story (though it's . . . probably not a surprise at this point). Real talk: I did not have dreams of becoming a Big-Deal Influencer. When I started making TikToks, it was *for fun*, period. Making money was not even remotely on my radar—I put my first video out because my coworkers were bothering me with questions, and I was like, "Ha *ha*! Sure, I'll answer you, but I'll put the answer on the internet so *everyone* from work can get the information!"

It wasn't until my first brand partner reached out to me that I was like, "Oh, shit . . . I can get money from this?"

From there, it genuinely took me a long time (a year and three months to be exact) to realize that my hobby-turned-hustle had become lucrative enough to go full-time. But since I had the sales experience, I could negotiate for what I knew I was worth. Since I was my own boss, I knew that I'd be getting paid what I deserved—because I was in charge! And since I genuinely love love love making the content I make, I knew I could put my full authentic self into it instead of trying to please someone else.

The moral of the story is basically this: We work to earn money. But when it comes to getting what you're worth, it's just not as straightforward as *harder work in = more rewards to you*. Like, my nightclub gig was sweet, but there was a definite limit to what I could earn no matter how much harder I worked (not least because eventually, I'd have run out of friends). My job at J.P. Morgan was challenging, but I gave it my absolute all *and* got results—which were ultimately taken for granted at best.

In reality, to reap the most out of your job (money-wise and otherwise), you need to find your sweet spot, where harder and better work from you equals more value to the company—and where that value is recognized, supported, and *paid for.* Sometimes, this means staying in your current role, working hard, *and* working your way up: build your network internally, forge connections with advocates, hopefully have a manager who will stand up for you, and always negotiate for more pay.

Other times, it means getting a whole-ass new job. Because if an environment is toxic or stagnant or otherwise just not going to honor your skills and your talent, you will *never* earn what you're worth there. Leaving sucks, but you know what? Their loss.

Both staying *and* leaving can be viable paths to more money, and neither is impossible once you start thinking like a rich person. Why? Rich people are especially good at three things: selling their skills, networking, and knowing when to get the fuck outta Dodge.

So if you're looking at your current job (or current paycheck) and thinking, *This is absolutely not it*, then you owe it to yourself (and your net worth) to get good at all three.

1. Sell your skills.

I see too many people, *especially* young people, treat their skills as locked into whatever their work history has been so far. They get stuck in this idea that their career trajectory is just going to be "this same thing, but more," and if they don't like that same thing, or it's not earning them enough money, they're in for a bad time.

In reality, if you want to work somewhere different, you're not limited to just working for your company's competitor. As long as that next job has some shared quality or responsibility with your previous job (or jobs), you are a solid candidate for it—regardless of the industry. For example, when I left the equities desk at J.P. Morgan for a sales position at BuzzFeed, I wasn't just going to a new company, or even a new industry: I was going to a new *role*. New lingo, new objectives, new ~vibes~. The only true transferable skills I had were the ability to sell and to communicate well. But with those in my back pocket, and a convincing case that they would smoothly transfer over, I went from slinging stocks and trade ideas to hedge funds to selling ad products to corporate partners.

In other words, think less climbing a career ladder from rung to rung and more scrambling up a climbing wall where the next foothold could be above, below, or to the side of where you are now. For example, if you start your career out in the accounting department of a pharmaceutical company, your second job could be in the accounting department at a *tech* company. Then your third job could be a junior software engineering role at a tech company. Your next role could be a project management role at a competing tech brand. Then—who knows? Maybe you become COO at that tech company, maybe you quit and found your own pharmatech startup, maybe you're recruited by the CIA to build spy robots.

Or maybe you start in accounting at that pharma corp and then move into a marketing role there. Then you become a senior communications officer. Then you're headhunted by a celebrity PR firm. Then you meet some A-lister on a red carpet, fall in love, and become an influencer couple with your own wellness brand.

It might sound over the top, but this is literally how successful careers work: listen to a rich person tell you their career history and many, many of them will have these kinds of zigs and zags or straight-up twist endings. Rich people don't see their career trajectory as copy-paste, copy-paste. They're playing a game of word association, strung together with the skills they've acquired and the knowledge they bring.

So step one in maximizing your opportunities is to **know your skills**. And if you're like, "*What* skills, Vivian?" listen to me: We young people are children of the internet. We know how to use Word. We know how to use PowerPoint. We know how to use Excel. We know how to turn a

.docx into a PDF and back to a .docx. There are *so* many jobs now that can be done with that baseline set of skills (slash the ability to google solutions), and you should not take for granted just how useful you can be across the board.

Beyond those LinkedIn-friendly, résumé-ready bullet points, think of what you're just *good at*, naturally, and the kind of work you tend to crush. Are you an HBIC* who can run a full meeting with five minutes to spare? Huge skill for project management roles. Are you the friend everyone can count on for a good pep talk when they need it? Major plus for any job where you train direct reports. Are you a good writer? PR, copywriting, technical writing, writing corporate speeches for CEOs to deliver to shareholders—you've got choices.

And if you want to load up on some new skills, there are ways to make that happen, whether that be a part-time MBA, a programming bootcamp, or just some DIY self-study on online learning platforms.

Step two is to **compile your knowledge**. If you're working that accounting job at a pharmaceutical company, yes, you're mostly crunching numbers—but you're also going to be picking up some insight into how the pharma industry works. That's something *you* have that a run-of-the-mill CPA might not, and that could be a huge selling point in your favor. Maybe a nonprofit that helps people afford their prescriptions is looking for a CFO. Maybe a real estate developer needs a sales rep to get drug companies leasing their office parks. You could be their dream candidate and not even realize it.

So don't discount the institutional knowledge and industry info you're picking up. As the saying goes, at your job, you should be either earning or learning (ideally both).

---

*HBIC = Head B in Charge (a very technical professional term)

> **Takeaway:** Write yourself a new pitch line that focuses on those skills and your knowledge instead of your plain old job title. Don't box yourself in. A good self-pitch is like offering prospective employers (slash anyone you network with) a charcuterie board they can pick and choose from instead of a premade sandwich.
>
> For example, instead of introducing myself with "I'm Vivian and I'm an influencer," I might say, "I'm Vivian, and I'm a top-performing salesperson with a background in finance and digital entertainment media. I'm a creator, I've built companies that earn seven figures annually from scratch, and I am open to opportunities that allow me to help businesses reach their next generation of users."

2. Work your network.

This is the other thing that sets rich people apart from the average person: they're never, ever satisfied, and they are *always* looking to trade up.

Seriously, they could be happier than a clam at their current job, ten out of ten, love their boss, love their work, love their team . . . and they are *still* eager to have a conversation with somebody at another firm, just cuz. They know that opportunities are had when you're in the right place at the right time, so to get the most opportunities, you want to be in the most places, as often as possible. Networking allows you to be in two rooms at once.

But it's not *just* a way to get yourself in the door, either. We know that rich people love them some quid pro quo, some positive karmic payback, some I'll-scratch-your-back-if-you'll-scratch-mine. Successful networking means that someone's not just mentioning your name, but actually *vouching* for you. Because when they say, "Yeah, she's good, hire her," they're putting their reputation on the line too. That's what makes it so valuable. A recommendation like that lends you credibility in a way that no piece of paper with your name on it, no CV, no interview will ever be able to do. And by the same token, they'll expect something from you down the line—because, again, they gave you something with serious value.

Having a network is especially important if you're looking to switch industries or otherwise make a drastic career change. It's *hard* to get buy-in as a candidate if you've never done X or Y role before or never worked in Z industry. But if someone internally can speak to how awesome you are, that can sand over that rough edge. How do you think I went from finance to media? My OG mentor vouched for me, and her best friend ended up becoming my very first manager at BuzzFeed.

There's this idea that networking has to be this weird, corny, cringey thing, or that it's something that only tryhards do, or that you only need to do it when you're actively looking for a new job.

False—at least for the way rich people do it. They see networking as expected at every position in every stage of a career. It's a mutual activity, with something in it for everyone, and it's really only weird if you make it weird.

The easiest way to start is just to get to know people you already work with. Make the rounds in other departments, introduce yourself, understand who's who around the office beyond who you interact with as part of your role. Learn about what they're working on, maybe even see if you can help. Then, when a sweet internal position opens up in, say, sales, and you already know Lindsay in sales *and* happen to know that she's trying to expand the company's reach into a new territory, you not only have a personal rapport but a specific Thing you can share ideas on if you apply for the job.

More generally, you just want to be open—especially to recruiters. These are people whose *entire job* is just finding candidates for open positions at companies. They are literally professional networkers.

If you're a ways into your career, you might get emails from headhunters already. But if not, you can still get them in your orbit. Are there industry networking events near you? That's a breeding ground for eager recruiters, so hit one up and bring business cards. Did your current job just hire someone new on a recruiter's recommendation? Subtly stalk that recruiting firm and maybe send them a note on LinkedIn (speaking of which, LinkedIn has a feature that lets you basically raise a little invisible flag that says "Hey, I could be interested in a new job, whatcha got?" so do that too while you're at it).

Then, when recruiters *do* reach out, *talk to them.* You don't have to take the job or even apply for it. You can just gather info on what skills are in demand and what the going rate for certain jobs is. Plus, one recruiter can work for multiple companies, and once they get to know you, they're much more likely to hit you up for an opening down the road.

Personally, I have done this my whole career. I consider it part of my job to network like this. While I was at J.P. Morgan and while I was at BuzzFeed, anytime a recruiter would hit me up, I would set up a call. And let me be clear: my second-to-last year at BuzzFeed, I made $625,000. I was one of their top sellers and I got paid like it. I felt that I was being compensated incredibly fairly, I loved every single person I worked with, and because I was bringing in monster deals, the company would bend over backward to make shit work for me.

And *still*, I would have a call with a recruiter around once a week. I was talking to Facebook. I was talking to Twitter. I was talking to TikTok. I was talking to everybody. Anybody who would talk to me, I would talk to them.

The final aspect of networking is pure mindset: always have one foot out the door at your job. That's not to say you shouldn't be giving 100 percent, or that you can't love your boss, love your team, love everything about your work, but—as rich people know—loyalty doesn't pay these days. (Literally: according to *Forbes*, people who stayed with a company for more than two years on average ended up making 50 percent less over the course of their working life.) Rich people know corporations are selfish, that they'll fire you in an instant if it's good for business, and figure, *Fine, I'm gonna be selfish too. I'm gonna look out for number one.*

Is it more work to do this kind of networking? Yes, absolutely. But, again, rich people embrace it because they are all about that delayed gratification and bigger payoff. If a little legwork now can double or triple their income in five to ten years, they say, *Bring it on, cuz I know I'm worth it.*

> **Takeaway:** Who don't you know in your company? Go talk to them. Play it cool—just a quick hi and "want to put a name to a face" kind of chat (or email). Then go to your LinkedIn, right now, and turn on that little "open to recruiters" beacon. (Also, make sure all your skills and job history are up-to-date.)

3. Know when someplace sucks for you.

Rich people may love to schmooze, but they're also not going to waste their time if they're schmoozing at a brick wall. If their job is giving major nepo baby energy and they know the promotions are always gonna go to the CEO's great-nephew or secret mistress or whatever, they're gonna bounce and find a job where they *can* cozy up to the people in power.

As I learned from my time at both J.P. Morgan and BuzzFeed, there are basically two kinds of workplaces: ones where you can break in, work laterally, and fraternize your way into the inner circle, and ones where, no matter how hard you pat yourself on the back, no matter how good you are, you're not going to be able to politick your way into the boys' club.

To make those rich-person moves, you need to be able to understand the difference. Are you working somewhere you can, with a little effort, improve your workplace social status and become not just a top performer but a name-brand, known performer? Or are you working somewhere you're stuck in a box with no ability to change how people perceive you?

Fortunately, there's a lot you can pick up about a company just on vibes alone, and if the vibes are off, it can take you from corporate baddie to corporate saddie *real quick*. Here are some key green flags and red flags to look out for at your job.

> **GREEN FLAG:** The criticism you get is about your work product and your performance.
> **RED FLAG:** The criticism you get is about you: your personality, your entity, your *self*.

> **GREEN FLAG:** You're given resources to solve a problem when you ask for them.
> **RED FLAG:** You're told to "just figure it out" and left to fend for yourself.

> **GREEN FLAG:** Expectations are clearly outlined. Whether or not they're ridiculous, at least having a benchmark in writing of what makes a good employee gives you a place to start.

RED FLAG: Expectations are ??? What makes a good employee? What's the standard protocol for XYZ task? How are raises determined? No one knows.

GREEN FLAG: You can look at upper management and think, *Yup, I'd love (or be fine with) that person's lifestyle and career.*

RED FLAG: You look up the ladder and see that people with the "good jobs" (high paying, fancy titles, whatever) are miserable.

GREEN FLAG: Generally some camaraderie around the team— people are willing to help each other even when it's not in their job description.

RED FLAG: "We're a family here." NOPE.

GREEN FLAG: You don't have to "look busy." There are clear expectations about your work, but no expectation that you stick around late or keep your status active 24/7 just for optics.

RED FLAG: You're role-playing a worksona five days a week. Whether or not you have work to be doing, the expectation is that you're in your seat, active on Slack, or somehow "on call."

GREEN FLAG: People are—for the most part—welcoming. Your colleagues invite you to lunch with them, make pleasant water cooler chat, seem to care about knowing you as a person.

RED FLAG: Nobody seems to care who you are. There are no opportunities for you to chime in or mingle—or, for an even redder flag, things are downright cliquey.

GREEN FLAG: When people get promoted, you think, *Oh, that makes sense! They're so good at what they do and they've done X and Y things for the company.*

RED FLAG: When people get promoted, you think, *Oh*, that *dude is now a vice president? For real?* (Again, nepo baby energy = bad news.)

GREEN FLAG: Senior members of the team are invested in junior talent. They take the time to spend time with more junior people generally, and always have time for their direct reports.
RED FLAG: It's so hierarchical that junior employees shouldn't even look in the *direction* of the C-suite.

GREEN FLAG: Everybody on the team generally likes the person in charge.
RED FLAG: Everybody on the team thinks the person in charge is an idiot.

These are just some jumping-off points—and, honestly, you probably have a sense of where you are already simply by virtue of having worked there for a while. If you're in an environment where you recognize that you have no ability to politick your way upward, where your manager does not give a flying fuck about you . . . well, I hate to be the one to say this, but you want to look at other jobs. Maybe internally, maybe externally, but you can't stay where you are and advance.

On the other hand, as long as you're feeling positive about your chances if you work hard, don't just be that top performer—make sure your manager knows, and go out of your way to make *their* work easier. Having a manager who actually values you and understands how hard and smart you're working is literally a cheat code for your career, but this person can be your advocate only if (1) they truly see how much you deserve it and (2) they know what you need. So do everything you can to kick ass at your role (hint: ask what *you* can do to make *them* look better to *their* boss) and then talk to your manager about your goals, your needs, your concerns. Ask them to help you get to know managers in other departments and become more connected across the wider net of the company. And definitely use your manager as a resource to make sure that you have an inroad with the LGBTQ+ employee resource group or the AAPI Resource Group or the Women's Network or whatever affinity groups your company might offer (your manager may not even be aware that you identify in that way, and they can't legally discriminate against you for disclosing that you're a member of a protected class. That said, I don't know your exact situation, so use discretion, especially if your boss is giving weird discriminatory vibes. But then you should definitely be looking for a new job).

> **Takeaway:** Run your current job through the green flag/red flag checklist and proceed accordingly. Finally realize the place isn't for you and you need out? Good thing you've got those skills listed out and that network, right? Start looking for a new gig pronto. Feel pretty happy with your potential? Schedule a sit-down with your manager to talk long-term goals . . . and maybe a pay raise.

How to Ask for More Money

Imagine if I told you that you could get $5,000 for just two hours of work.

Yes, seriously (and no, this is *not* a sales pitch to get you to join my skinny tea or essential oils pyramid scheme—this is legit).

It's 100 percent possible. Because that work is called *negotiation*.

Negotiation can be *sooooooo* cringey and uncomfortable—I get it. Plenty of us (basically anyone who's not a straight white dude) have been socially conditioned to think that standing up for ourselves, driving a hard bargain, sticking to our guns, and so forth is unacceptable, rude, too much, extra, etc. Asking for more can make you feel like your skin is melting off your body, so it's no wonder most people don't do it.

That's why I like to frame it in terms of that hourly rate. Negotiating for a raise—including all the prep work, the conversation itself, and the follow-up—can take as little as two hours. If you get, let's say, a $5,000 salary bump out of it, that's like making $2,500 an hour.

And would you *ever* turn down the chance to make $2,500 an hour?

I wouldn't. Neither would most rich people.

So, given that the hourly rate here is wildly good, and given that most people are working hard, providing value, *and* earning less than they're worth, I believe everyone should ask for a raise.

And that's where we're gonna start you taking action.

Asking for a raise is not only a true-up for what you're actually doing in your work but also the quickest way to increase your disposable income—remember, you can only save as much as you earn, but you can always earn more money. It's hard to build up a surplus by cutting out everything that brings you joy in your life, but it's relatively easy to ask for more money at work. (And yes, you *do* have to ask; even if you're good at your job, reliable, and put in the hours to exceed expectations, you can't just wait around for the Salary Fairy to hit you with her magic wand and grant you more money.)

That said, I also get that asking for more is probably the number-one most terrifying experience for the vast majority of employees out there. Anecdotally, I've noticed that most people can't even think of the last time they negotiated for a raise. They're not sure, or they just never have, or they've crystallized the memory of ~*That One Time I Asked*~, but it was either years in the past, unsuccessful, or both.

Rich people *don't* have to think about it: *My last raise? Brought that up in Q1 / two weeks ago / right after my last major client deal.*

It turns out that for every fear your average broke-ish person has about asking for a raise, rich people have an equal and opposite mindset. So before we get into the nitty-gritty of your approach, it's time to learn the rich way of thinking about this convo—and unlearn the blocks that are holding you back.

> **BROKE PERSON:** I don't want to, like, offend my manager! I *like* them, so why would I want to hurt them like this?! It just feels too weird.
>
> **RICH PERSON:** Companies are selfish. The only way I'm getting paid fairly is if I'm selfish too.

The most important piece of professional career advice I was ever told was this: "Your company or corporation *doesn't* care about you."

Your coworkers may care about you. Your boss (if you have a good relationship) may care about you. But your corporation does not care about you.

Rich people get this. A rich person knows that raise money is not coming out of their manager's pocket. It's coming out of a corporate bank account that is literally allocated to pay labor staff. It's okay to ask for more money because that's literally what the company is prepared for you to do (and, again, as rich people know, if things get tough, the company won't hesitate to cut your pay or even lay you off—even if everyone likes you. It's not personal, it's business).

As for "making it weird," you're not. I think of this as the pedicure principle: like, yes, you might feel kind of self-conscious because you think you have Hobbit feet and you haven't shaved your legs in five days and you still have chips of nail polish from when you painted your nails three months ago. But in all likelihood, you don't have the grossest feet the pedicurist has ever seen. They're a pro. They've seen some shit. And they literally look at feet like it's their job. (Because it is.)

So in most cases—especially if you're working at a large corporation—this is not your manager's first raise-request rodeo. You are not the first person to ask for money. You are not the first person for them to say yes to and you're not the first person for them to say no to. You're not asking for the biggest or smallest number they've ever seen. You're not "making it weird" because it's not weird for them at all. It's how work *works*.

> **BROKE PERSON:** If I ask for more money, then they're going to get mad and fire me on the spot.
> **RICH PERSON:** Worst case, they say no. But the answer is *always* no until I ask.

Realistically, the worst-case scenario here is you get a no. Maybe your manager tells you no and also tells you your performance has not been good enough for you to get this raise at this time, in which case, okay, that's great feedback for you to know for next year. But being straight-up fired for asking? That's just . . . not what happens.

Fun fact: Did you know it can cost a company as much as three to four times an employee's salary to replace them? Firing and replacing takes up a *lot* of valuable time: your manager would lose weeks, if not months, out of their schedule searching for a replacement, interviewing candidates, onboarding them, getting them up to speed . . . and that's still a gamble, because that new person might totally suck. So it just doesn't make business sense to fire an otherwise capable employee just because they asked for more money.

But more than that, rich people's abundance mindset is helping them out here. Even if being fired were likely—which it isn't—they just aren't as worried about losing any one job. They've developed all these connections among their rich-person network and they know that if they end up losing this job, well, there's more where that came from. I know, when I see headlines about big tech or household-name-brand companies doing layoffs, that even though many of those employees were making over six figures, they're going to have a soft landing somewhere. People who stayed at the company will vouch for their former colleagues. They'll gather up alumni databases to share around. Rich people take care of each other.

> **BROKE PERSON:** I get a yearly cost-of-living raise, so I don't
> wanna look like a greedy dick or like all I care about is
> the money by asking for *even more.*
> **RICH PERSON:** I get a yearly cost-of-living raise, which is a
> joke compared to inflation. I *have* to negotiate for more or
> else I'm letting myself lose money.

Sorry to say, but this "not wanting to be greedy" self-sabotage plagues women even worse than men. We've been told our entire lives that if you care about money you're a shallow, materialistic, a gold digger. (No, like . . . I just like to afford rent and eat food at the same time? It's this weird lil hobby of mine???) And so we become complacent. We think that the "inflation" raise of two or *maybe* three percent we get every year is good enough.

In reality, these "raises" are not keeping pace with inflation (especially in an environment like this, where inflation is spiking anywhere from five to nine percent, as has happened in recent memory), and we're losing money year after year. Rich people know this, but it doesn't dawn on *most* people that they should be asking for more until someone literally comes out and says it.

So here I am, saying it: you—and I can't emphasize this enough—should negotiate everything.

> **BROKE PERSON:** Okay, okay, FINE, I'll ask for a raise . . . in five months at my annual review. Are you happy now?!
>
> **RICH PERSON:** Hey boss, it's been two months since we last sat down—can we set up a meeting next week to talk about my performance?

Most people get *so* nervous to say anything about a raise that they just wait and wait and wait and wait, until finally it's time for end-of-year reviews. They screw up all their courage, blurt out, "I want more money!" and their boss is like, "??? Where is this coming from?"

Rich people, though, are *On. Top. Of. It.* They will ask, ask, ask, once every two to three months, they will set up those meetings and remind their boss that X raise is what they're looking for and Y accomplishments are why they deserve it. And then, by the time the end-of-year reviews roll around, they are at the top of the boss's list when it comes to handing out those raises.

This works so much better for two reasons. For one, asking for a raise is like planning a vacation. If you want to go to the Bahamas in December, when *everyone else* is dying to go to a white-sand beach, you are not going to get a good deal if you wait until November 31 to book your tickets. No, you need to be buying your flights and snapping up a hotel room in June, when no one else is thinking about December travel, because that's when it's easier, that's when it's cheaper, and that's when the deals are to be had. In other words, if you ask for money when every single person on your team is asking for money, you can easily get lost on that long, long list. What you *want* is for your boss to always be thinking about *you* when it comes to raises, promotions, or really any opportunity. And the easiest way to do that is to ask for them in that "offseason."

No, you don't have to hit your boss up every week. Don't be *annoying*, but ask to meet in thoughtful intervals, genuinely bring something to discuss in terms of your performance, and they will be more likely to remember you when it actually counts.

The other thing is that, as I mentioned earlier, there's a budget for raises. And the budget decisions are not made in that annual review meeting you have with your boss. They are made months in advance. By the time those conversations are happening, your boss already has an idea of what they're going to grant you—if anything. So if they have already seen throughout the year that you've been . . . not *annoying* about that raise, but let's say *persistent*, by the time you get to the end of your review and you bring up money, they're that much more likely to say, "Cool, I'm going to cut you off right there. I already got it for you, so it's all good."

That's what you want . . . and honestly, that's probably also what your manager wants. *They* don't want to disappoint *you*, either. Plenty of managers are people pleasers by nature, and if you are bringing the goods and delivering that performance, they genuinely want to give you your due.

> **BROKE PERSON:** I'm just grateful to have a job at all. This
> place is doing me a favor just by employing me.
> **RICH PEOPLE:** To quote the philosopher Drake, know
> yourself, know your worth. And baby, I do.

To be clear: sometimes people take less than they deserve because they have to. There is no other option, rent is due, and ends have to be met. And there can be times when you've just gotta grind like that.

But not all jobs are created equal, right? Shitty jobs are *shitty*, and given the opportunity, almost everyone will jump ship if something better comes up.

This is perfectly represented by the mass exodus of fast-food and other low-paid hourly workers right after everyone got their stimulus checks. As it turns out, slinging food for ten straight hours to people who gripe about how slow you are? It fucking *blows*, especially when you're not being paid enough to do it. But when you actually have $2,000 sitting in your bank account, you don't feel the need to do that. You're willing to take an extra week or an extra month to find a job where you know you'll actually get paid fairly.

So I don't believe that deep down, we should all just be grateful for having a job at all. Because it simply is *not* sustainable to take less than you're worth over the long haul. And unless you are truly hand-to-mouth, if your job is shitty and taking advantage of you, then they are not doing you any kind of favor. You are worth more.

Rich people know their worth—not least because they've been told their entire lives that they are amazing and special and smart from their parents, teachers, au pairs, whatever. But they also know their worth because they're competitive as fuck, and they want to be at the top of that leaderboard. They know that when they're asking for a raise, they are there to try and convince their boss that they are deserving . . . but also that they deserve it more than the guy sitting next to them. There's only so much budget in the pool, and if that raise money goes to him, it ain't going to you.

So when I say you've gotta know your worth, I don't just mean you need to be confident and have self-esteem and not settle for shitty pay that *no one* deserves. I mean you have to know, in every aspect, the worth you are creating in your role.

This means you might have to have a real hard talk with yourself: *Am I truly performing at a high level? Am I at least in the top quartile? Am I really doing my best?* Because if you're coming in late, leaving early, only getting half your work done, and unreachable during the middle of the day because you're taking an hour-long nap . . . you should not be asking for a raise—yet. You've got to improve and then *prove* that you've improved.

But when you know your worth and you can prove it, you are ready. You are competitive. You are justifiably confident and ready to kick ass.

And if you do all you can to ask and deliver and that job is *still* blowing you off? Then maybe it's time to trade up and find a new gig.

THE BEST-KEPT SECRET FOR YOUR CAREER: A BRAG BOOK

Yeah, it's good to *know* your worth, but it's even better to have *receipts*. If you want to get paid more, if you want a promotion, if you want to be the person who gets nominated for awards at the end of the year—you need to have a Brag Book.

A Brag Book is just a collection of cold, hard proof of what you've accomplished, and it's super easy to set one up.

1. Create a folder in your email called Brag Book, Promo Pitch, Raise Receipts—whatever you want—and add the year.

2. From now on, every time a client tells you they "couldn't have done it without you," every time an internal team

praises you for streamlining a process, every time you get thanked in an email chain—drop it in that folder.

3. Get tangible numbers for as much as you can. Did you bring in more revenue than other sellers? Did you grow the social media channel by X number of followers? Did you ideate more concepts than any other creative director? The more you can quantify, the better—it's hard to argue with numbers.

Because this Brag Book? It's not just for stroking your ego. (Although it's a great pick-me-up if you have a crappy day at work.) This folder will be your secret weapon come review season. You're not going to need to scour your past year's worth of emails to fish out a few things you did and show them to your boss. You will have a folder bursting with every success you had this past year, and you can then point to these accomplishments to justify whatever you're asking for. Personally, I used this strategy both on Wall Street and in tech—and it works.

Your Brag Book can also come in super handy to prep yourself for interview questions like "What's your greatest strength?" or "Tell me about a time you rose to the occasion." Oh, and don't forget to pay it forward—if your colleague absolutely crushes it on a project, send them an email to let them know how helpful they were. Karma is real!

How to Ask for More Money: The Script

STEP 1: Prepare your tool kit.

If you want the conversation to be a W, make sure you have all 5 W's on this checklist:

1. Know **what** you are asking for. More pay? Higher title? To move to a different role?

2. Know your **worth**. If it's more $$$ that you want, make sure you know what your peers are making. You can ask candidly if you have colleagues you trust, or use resources like Glassdoor or Fishbowl online. If you're looking to advance, don't be afraid to ask HR for a job description sheet for that next-level position so you can tick off all the skills, accomplishments, and qualifications you already have.

3. **Wins**—organize them. Grab your Brag Book receipts, use numbers and quantitative facts to point to your success, and keep it objective and relevant ("I deserve it" is not a qualification, my friends).

4. Get someone **who** you can practice with. Ask a friend to role-play the convo as your boss so you can get a hang of saying the words out loud.

5. If you need to keep yourself calm the day of negotiation, **write** up a script (or adapt the one that follows 😊).

STEP 2: Set up a meeting.

Slack, GChat, email, or just go by your boss's office—don't overthink it. Whatever your usual method of contact is will work.

> "Hey, [boss], do you mind if I put thirty minutes on your calendar for sometime this week? I'd love to discuss my growth at the company."

STEP 3: Start strong.

Don't leave your boss wondering what you're here to talk about. Remember, they're a boss, and they have been asked for raises before. You're not dropping some huge bombshell on them.

"Hi, boss—thanks for sitting down with me. Excited to share some of my recent accomplishments, and I'd also like to discuss my salary for next year."

STEP 4: Make your case.

Lay out some of your wins from your Brag Book. You don't have to list every single accomplishment—feel free to stick to two or three of the greatest hits for now.

"I've learned so much over the last two years. Not only has my work grown the e-commerce business by twenty-five percent and garnered over ten pieces of positive PR, but I've also grown the Instagram account to fifty thousand followers. Additionally, I've trained two new coordinators and I'm ecstatic to be growing out the team."

STEP 5: Make your ask.

Again, no need to draw this out. Make a quick pivot to talking money, and lead by reminding them that you're basing this on what you've done *and* what's competitive in the market (because you did your homework, ofc!).

"With all that in mind, I'd love to discuss my compensation. I've done some research, and based on my experience, skill set, and accomplishments here, a raise of X dollars would be appropriate."

STEP 6: Stop and wait.

Odds are there will be *some* kind of pause here, and even though it's human nature to keep talking and fill the silence, resist the urge!

One of three things will happen here. If your boss *basically* agrees on the idea of a raise but pushes back, or if they don't *quite* say no, or if they're basically anywhere on the fence, go to step 7.

If they say yes, then HELL YEAH!!! Skip to step 8.

And if they give you a flat-out no, don't freak out. You're no worse off than you previously were, and you can use this moment as an opportunity to lay the groundwork for the future. Say something like:

> "I understand, and I appreciate you being candid with me. I'd love to make this an ongoing discussion since I'm always looking to grow. What skills or accomplishments would you like to see from me before increasing my pay?"

Listen to what they say, take notes, and use that list to set your goals for the next three to six months. At that point, *knock knock knock*, boss! Guess who's back?

STEP 7: Go deeper.

So maybe your boss seems warm to this idea, but there's some sticking point. Let's walk through that together. Your boss maybe agrees that you've contributed greatly to the company but that the raise amount of X dollars isn't possible. What you want to do is find out more about their reasoning.

> "From my research, an X-dollar increase is reasonably in line with what I've contributed. Can you tell me more about why that increase isn't possible today? I'd love to hear your thoughts, and I'm happy to provide more quantitative examples of how I provide value to the team."

The answer they give will vary, of course, depending on what's actually going on with your company and your boss. The best-case scenario is that they do agree to a raise, just a smaller one than you've asked for, or on a different timeline—in that case, you can jump to step 8 and proceed.

But there are *plenty* of other reasons they could be hesitating: Maybe that amount isn't in the budget right now but they feel they could make the case for it in the future. Maybe there's a temporary salary freeze and they need you to ask again in a few months. Or maybe they need to see more results and/or accomplishments from you and just weren't comfortable giving you a hard no up front.

Whatever they say, *listen*—this is a golden opportunity to get inside your boss's head and see what they're trying to get done, what restrictions they're under, and how you could potentially make some of that easier.

No matter what, try to end on a note of establishing specific benchmarks and a timeline:

"Understood. Thank you for explaining. How can I help you make that case in the near future? And what timing feels feasible to you?"

Depending on what you discuss, and how concrete of a plan you end up with, you can follow this up with an email (in step 9) to confirm how you'll move forward.

STEP 8: Stick the landing.

YOU DID IT!!! Thank your boss (of course) and ask them for a timeline for when the raise will kick in (if it's not already predetermined, like in an end-of-year review).

Also, you'll want to have some kind of follow-up in writing. Usually, your boss will be responsible for sending an official notice (to both you and HR), but it's a good idea for you to follow up with your boss, too, just to confirm that the conversation took place—you don't want this slipping through the cracks, after all.

> "Thank you! I appreciate that, and it means a lot to know my work is valued. When will that increase take effect, and is there anything else you need from me right now? I'll be sure to send you an email by the end of today to follow up too."

STEP 9: Get it in writing.

Then, obvi, send the email: remind them what you discussed (including the agreed-upon number), and offer to help with any logistics to get the paperwork moving, with a timeline if appropriate—again, even well-meaning bosses are busy, and you don't want this getting lost in the shuffle!

> Dear [boss],
>
> Thank you again for taking the time to meet today and discuss my compensation. To recap our conversation, we discussed my proposal of an increase to my salary of $X, which you agreed would be effective as of Y date.
> I appreciate having the chance to share some of my accomplishments and discuss my future with [company]. I value my role here and I look forward to future successes as part of the team.

From there, your boss should follow up and get the ball rolling with HR to make it happen, but don't hesitate to follow up if things slip off the agreed-upon timeline.

OTHER THINGS YOU CAN NEGOTIATE FOR (ASIDE FROM JUST MONEY)

Compensation doesn't start and end with you trading your time and work for X number of dollars per year. Actually, you can get pretty creative with what you get in return for your hard work—and rich people *love* being creative this way. In fact, by suggesting alternatives that let you defer that money (so that your employer doesn't feel it as acutely right now, but you still get the benefit) or gets you some "free" (i.e., nonmonetary) benefits, you're doing the company a favor by protecting their bottom line. How's *that* for out-of-the-box thinking, boss?

So if you've hit a ceiling in terms of cold, hard cash, try asking for these perks as a serious way to grow your wealth.

- **Restricted stock units (RSUs) and incentive stock options (ISOs):** Restricted stock units and incentive stock options are both a kind of equity compensation, where instead of just giving you cash for your work, your company also throws in some equity in the company. RSUs are actual *units* of stock (i.e., shares) and they're *restricted* because you only get a portion of your total RSU grant every so often, over what's called a *vesting schedule.* ISOs are not stock shares themselves, but the *option* to buy shares at a *strike price* (usually the price of stock when your option is issued) any time after the *vesting date.* So RSUs are kind of like free stuff paid out over time, while ISOs are like exclusive access to a major discount. In both cases, time is your friend—the more valuable the stock gets over time, the more your shares will be worth, or the more of a "discount" you'll get by buying at your strike price.
- **Paid time off (PTO):** Can't get more money? Ask for . . . well, not less work, precisely, but more *time not at work.* These

are days where you're on vacation, or decompressing, or just *not answering email*, but still getting *paid*. It doesn't cost your employer more, but it definitely gives you something good. (Best part, in certain states, like California, your PTO is also paid out in cash if you leave and haven't used all of it!)

- **Flexible working arrangements:** Forget the 9 to 5. What if you want to work 10 to 6, or noon to 8, or do half-time in the office or full-time WFH? Fab news: you can negotiate for it. And because employees have started voting with their feet (i.e., up and quitting if management insists on full-time office work) post-pandemic, lots of companies are *fiiiiiinally* including some kind of baseline flex work options, making it that much easier to ask for. That said, there might be some restrictions: if you work in one state but live in another, for example, going full-time WFH might have tax implications your company isn't willing to put up with—but it never hurts to ask.

- **Signing bonuses:** Unlike a regular bonus, a signing bonus comes only once—when you sign your employment contract. But surprisingly, even though it's just an extra chunk of change for you, these can still be attractive to employers: they have to accommodate a signing bonus only once per employee, and if the amount is reasonable, then they might just say, "What the hell, let's just get this person working," and grant it to you. These one-time bonuses are also great to ask for if you're moving somewhere new for a job—for example, when I signed my contract to work for J.P. Morgan, my new-hire colleagues and I all got $10,000 signing/relocation bonuses (and although the "OMFG, I'm rich" feeling faded once the taxes were taken out, it was still a nice jumpstart for my life in $pendy NYC).

- **Job titles:** No, this isn't some "assistant *to* the regional manager" pettiness. For one thing, titles are 100 percent free, and unless you're in a highly regulated industry, they aren't fixed and can be earned just by asking. For another, an impressive title in *this* job makes you more likely to be paid more at your *next* one.

Side Hustles

You thought rich people don't have side hustles? Let me tell you about Jerry.

When I was at J.P. Morgan, I sat near, as you might imagine, a bunch of kinda dorky numbers guys. One of them was Jerry.

Now, Jerry was a run of the mill vest-wearing, mild-mannered guy—*not* what you would consider a fashion connoisseur, in other words. But Jerry had a secret double life. He happened to be a sneakerhead in a *major* way. Seriously, this guy probably spent $100,000 on Nike and Adidas in the time I knew him.

And not *just* for himself, either. No, Jerry had a side hustle: buying and flipping sneakers.

This was not raking in crazy bucks for Jerry. He'd make maybe a couple hundred per pair—maybe one to two thousand over market price if they were insanely rare (and he didn't end up keeping them). But he kept it up.

Eventually, after watching him post what seemed like his ten thousandth StockX listing, I had to ask: "Jerry, I'm curious. You make high six figures. You literally work on Wall Street. Why are you doing this?"

And Jerry was like, "I don't know. There's just something about that rush of getting that sneaker and being able to sell it for more, I guess."

"But you're *busy*," I said.

Jerry the Sneakerhead just shrugged. "Yeah, but . . . I like doing it. So I'm still gonna do it. It's just free money."

At that point, another one of the guys nearby perked up. "Did someone say free money?"

"Yeah," Jerry said. "You guys wanna learn?"

And that's how Jerry ended up teaching me and two of my colleagues how to flip sneakers. And you know what? In my short time trading in Jordans and Yeezys, it did feel like free money.

Obviously, I wasn't cut out for the secondary sneaker market long-term (it's hard to compete with bots that can scoop up a dozen pairs in three seconds, after all), but my point is, basically, that if there's a hustle to be had, rich people want in—and the rest of us could learn a thing or two from them.

To be clear, though: Let the record show that I, Your Rich BFF, am *not* pro hustle culture. I am not #nodaysoff. I am 100 percent #daysoff. I do not think we need to spend every waking hour working. I also recognize that if you are living paycheck to paycheck on a sixty-hour workweek, or already juggling multiple jobs, the advice to "Just get a side hustle!!!" can feel a little tone-deaf.

But at the same time, side hustles can be a serious boost to your path to a rich lifestyle. They let you live out that core truth of "you can only save as much as you earn, but you can always earn more money." They can be a meaningful way to increase your income and set yourself up for a financial situation where you are not making decisions out of a place of desperation. They give you the chance to have choices instead of being forced into the only option you can afford.

Yes, it might take more work and discomfort and *hustle* in the short term. But long-term? *That* is freedom: choices, options, stability.

So if you've maxed out your earning capacity at your day job for the time being, a little part-time side gig can be a *great* way to put extra cash in your pocket. Plus, with the rise of work from home and the digital economy, there's never been a better time to earn a little extra $$$ *without* your side hustle taking over your life.

Here's everything you need to know about doing side hustles the Rich AF way.

Side Hustles Don't Have to Be Passion Projects (and Vice Versa)

People use the phrase *side hustle* to describe a lot of things, from gig work to creative projects, but I want to make a distinction here. Personally, I distinguish a *side hustle*, which is something you do for money quickly, from a *passion project*, which is something creative you do because you like to do it.

Passion projects *can* make you a little money, and that's totally fine, but I do not think every passion project, hobby, or casual pursuit needs to be monetized—and I say this as someone who literally turned a hobby into a job. I found that as my TikTok following ramped up and things got harder and more complex than when I was just goofing for my friends, the pressure could suck just a *little* bit of the joy out of making my content—even with a passion project where I was my own boss. Once money got involved, I had to slow my roll a bit to make sure I was still actually having fun (and I am!).

The other thing is that, while creative projects *can* make you tons of money if you hit it big, the time you'll pour in is not likely to pay off, at least in the short term (like, only 4 percent of content creators make enough money to do it full-time—sorry to all the kids out there whose dream job is "YouTuber," I guess?).

This isn't to say that you *can't* do things that you enjoy as a side hustle (I give you exhibit A: Jerry the Sneakerhead). It just means you don't *have* to turn whatever you love doing into a second job. Turning that thing you enjoy into a money-making venture *seems* like an obvious side hustle, but not every hobby has to be monetized, and that's totally cool. It's okay just to cross-stitch because it's relaxing, not because you want to start an Etsy shop.

Side Hustles Should Be Low Risk

When you're brainstorming up a side hustle, think in terms of a temporary gig that's low risk and low barrier to entry. For example, signing up for a Wag account and walking someone's dog? Low risk—doesn't cost you much in terms of initial startup costs and easy to cut your losses and quit if it doesn't work out. Mowing lawns and pulling weeds? You've gotta have that lawn mower, and maybe some work gloves, but still pretty low-ish startup costs (especially if you already own a mower). Babysitting? Doesn't cost you anything—you just show up to that person's house.

Low startup costs are also important because you're going to want to test this side hustle out to see if you actually like doing it, right? For example, if you lease a car and start to drive for Uber, and then find out that you don't have time to do it for forty hours a week, and if you don't do it for forty hours a week, you're not going to make what you thought you were going to make . . . well, you're still trapped in that car lease, and that sucks.

Side Hustles Should Actually Make You Money

Getting that first "free money" payment is an amazing moment . . . until you realize what you had to spend to earn it.

Fact is, side hustles can come with a lot of *hidden* costs—and you'll definitely want to account for those too. If you're driving for DoorDash or Uber, for example, you'll want to factor in the expenses and the wear and tear on your car, the gas, the insurance . . . all of which can add up. If you're painting custom pet portraits, you'll have to account for the cost of the paint, the canvas, and all the time you spend not just painting but communicating with the pet parents over how exactly they want little Fluffy to look in the final product.

So keep a close eye on how much time *and* money your side hustle is asking of you, and make sure you're netting back enough to make it worthwhile.

Oh, and don't forget that you're going to have to pay taxes on your side hustle money, because unlike a paystub, the government is not going to take them out for you. Your individual tax rates will vary depending on where you live, but as a *very* broad rule of thumb, assume that anywhere from 30 percent to 40 percent of your income after expenses will have to go to the IRS and your state treasury.

HEY HUN! WANNA JOIN MY TEAM OF #BOSSBABES?

If you've ever gotten an out-of-nowhere DM from the girl who bullied you in high school asking if you want to join in her "business opportunity" selling weight-loss shakes or cheap floral print leggings or mascara that gives you creepy spider eyelashes, you've had a brush with an MLM, or multi-level marketing company.

MLMs sell products not in stores or online, but through individuals selling products to the people in their network—often by word of mouth (or Facebook). They're often peddled to people (usually women, and especially stay-at-home moms) as a super-easy, "work in your sweatpants" side hustle opportunity, but they're also . . . controversial, to say the least.

So what makes them controversial? Well, while the individuals peddling these products do get paid to sell products (like mystery hair oil, dodgy supplements, and low-quality skincare), that's not where the real money comes in. MLM sellers actually get paid *more* to recruit others into the sales force. This means the incentive isn't really on sales to consumers . . . it's on bringing in new "reps" or "consultants."

Think of it this way: the founder of the MLM recruits people to sell the product. We'll call those first recruits the A squad. A squad gets paid to sell product, but they *really* get paid to recruit others, which they do—we'll call those friends and family they rope in B squad.

Now, A squad is thrilled, because they're not only getting paid kickbacks for every person they recruit to B squad, but they *also* get a commission from all the products B squad sells. Of course, the trade-off is that B squad makes less commission . . . even though it's *on their own sales*. But no worries—they can offset that loss by recruiting their *own* team, aka C Squad. B Squad gets a chunk of what C Squad earns in commission . . . and so it goes, forever and ever until the earth literally runs out of people.

This model makes it exponentially easier for the folks at the top of the MLM to make money, and all but impossible for the C Squad and below folks. According to a report by the Federal Trade Commission that studied the business models of 350 MLMs in the United States, at least 99 percent of people who join MLMs don't just not make money—they *lose* money. Because on top of barely making any commissions at the bottom of the, ahem, pyramid-shaped business model, those sellers have to buy the products themselves, with their own money, often piling up on low-quality inventory that doesn't sell and they can't return.

This means that your odds of making money in an MLM are *very* low, but your odds of *losing* money are great. As side hustles go, it's a no from me, dawg. Because net net: if something seems too good to be true, it likely is. And if a company's business model is based more on recruiting new members than actually selling the product, proceed with caution.

Side Hustles Should Fit into Your Life

But beyond those basics, the real side hustle sweet spot is finding the right work for you to do at a time that's convenient to your schedule.

For the work, look for a task that's straightforward and not *too* taxing, but different enough from your day-to-day so that it doesn't drain you or bore you to tears.

So, if you're an office employee and you side hustle by mowing lawns or walking dogs or helping people assemble IKEA furniture, you might enjoy doing something more physical and less brainpower-intense (like, you need the exercise anyway, right?). Whereas, say you're an electrician or a personal trainer or an art teacher and you pick up a side hustle as a data entry specialist. Copying numbers into an Excel sheet can be *d-u-l-l*, but since it's very different from what you typically do, it lets you flex a different part of your brain that allows you not to get so bored so easily.

As for the time, consider when you have those pockets of a few hours during the week and what's feasible to do then. If your only spare time is between 9:00 p.m. when you've tucked in your kids to 1:00 a.m. when you finally go to sleep, you can't exactly mow lawns for some extra cash in the dead of night . . . but you could turn those hours into a shift driving for Uber in the family minivan (and there are plenty of suburban parents who do). If you're a teacher and have summers off, you could work doing test prep or college essay coaching during those months. If you work 9 to 5 and have an hour-long train ride each way, find some online freelance work like transcription or bookkeeping that you can do during your commute.

**MONEY MANAGEMENT
TO-DOS FOR CHAPTER 2**

☐ Schedule a time to talk with your manager about your role, your performance, and your future. This is a necessary first step whether you're actively angling for a raise or just want to start creating that rapport that will help them help you in your advancement.

☐ Privately, take some time to reflect on your current workplace, office politics, and manager. What does it take to get to the top here? How far could you see yourself going, realistically? Think about whether you want to keep pushing up this ladder or if it might be time to look elsewhere.

☐ Either way: get networking. Commit to spending at least fifteen minutes per week doing outreach either internally or externally.

☐ Research your job duties (both the ones officially in your job description and the ones you're doing anyway) and compensation. How much do people make elsewhere to do what you do?

☐ Compile your Brag Book.

☐ Schedule another meeting to connect with your manager. Make it a regular thing.

☐ Review your company's benefits packet and make sure you're taking full advantage of everything you can use.

☐ Explore some side hustles that fit your schedule. Pick one to try for a week or two and commit to giving it a shot.

☐ Schedule *another* meeting with your manager. Ask for a raise and/or more perks and benefits. You can do it, bb!

☐ Find even more career tools, negotiation resources, info on work-specific finances, and side hustle ideas at **richAF.club.**

3

I AM IN CHARGE OF MY MONEY

The Budgeting Section

I remember my first big purchase after I'd started working full time on Wall Street: a beautiful black leather Prada bag.

It was the most money I'd ever spent on something. I'd had my eye on it for weeks—months—and I was literally sweating at the boutique when it was time to actually buy it. I had worked my ass off for it—not just *at* that Wall Street job, but to get that job in the first place, and now I was reaping the luxurious fruits of my labor in the form of this gorgeous designer piece. By the time I swiped my card at the register, I knew I had earned every stitch on that bag. I was trading blood, sweat, and tears for Saffiano leather. And I swear, in that moment, I really felt like I had made it. I was legit thinking, *Yes, I am the American dream.* When I carried it around in public, when I got a compliment on it, I felt a sense of pride precisely because I *knew* how hard I had worked to afford that bag.

But I wasn't able get that bag *just* because I worked so, so hard.

I was able to buy it because I had a budget.

Yes, I was making good money, but I wasn't, like, fuck-you rich. I wasn't so ungodly wealthy that money was no object for me, and I wasn't surrendering to the void of consumer debt because YOLO and we're all going to die anyway. I still had to plan ahead for that purchase. And really, that's how I've always seen budgeting—and still do: planning ahead so that I can indulge my dream of owning buttery Italian leather without screwing myself out of rent.

Now, if you hate the idea of a budget, I toooooootally get it. When people think about a budget, it instantly makes them imagine this incredibly restrictive thing, like a diet, or a punishment. Financial talking heads like Dave Ramsey are out there giving us straight-up shame and judgment about our budgets (or lack thereof) and calling it "tough love." And it ends up feeling like a monster list of "STUFF YOU'RE NOT ALLOWED TO HAVE, YOU POOR."

So, yeah, given all that? No wonder you hate budgets.

But what if I told you about this amazing system that'd make it possible for you to march into that Prada store and pick your fave bag off the shelf and pay for it outright, no prob? You'd probably be into that, right?

Well, that's a budget.

The real talk is this: budgets don't suck, and if you think they do, it's because you haven't been taught about them correctly.

Budgets aren't about slapping your hand out of the cookie jar. They're more like the recipe that allows you to have the biggest, fullest, most delicious jar of cookies that you can enjoy for the rest of your life.

Sadly, too many folks feel that "ew, budgets" feeling and never get past it. They end up deciding it's better to just wing it. But when has winging it ever been a good idea? We've just established that money is important. So why leave something so important up to ~whatever~ and just hope for the best? Fact is, when it comes to money, if you fail to plan, you're planning to fail. Yeah, maybe I sound like your middle-school gym teacher, but it's true.

Because you know who doesn't like failing? You know who *hates* to fail?

Rich people. Rich people hate failing.

But they do love planning. Especially when it comes to money.

In other words, rich people budget. They budget like hell.

I do. All my rich besties do. My rich mentors sure do.

Rich people who were born rich budget, because that's how they're going to keep the family home on Martha's Vineyard and send their kids to Harvard and retire at forty-five. Rich people who used to be broke budget, because that's how they got to where they are and that's what's going to keep them there. The only rich people who *don't* budget are the ones who aren't gonna be rich much longer, you know what I mean?

The thing is, unless you are making a truly astronomical amount of money—and I am talking Bezos bucks, like you-literally-have-your-own-private-fleet-of-spacecraft rich—you're gonna have to budget to ensure financial well-being for future you.

"But Vivian," you're probably yelling at this book, "I thought the whole *point* of being rich is not having to worry about money anymore!"

To which I say, "When did I ever say anything about *worrying?*"

That's the thing about rich people and their money management. The *way* they budget is what makes all the difference. For them, budgeting is not a stressor—it's an opportunity. It's what fuels those moneymaking machines that create rich lifestyles. It's maybe even a little . . . fun?!

That's what it means to budget the Rich AF way. And I'm gonna teach you how.

What *Is* a Budget?

Let's get back to basics here.

A budget is just a plan for what you're going to do with your money. It's strategizing about how to make the most of the resources you have to get the results you want on the timeline you're working with.

Which I guarantee you already know how to do—even if you've never had a budget in your life. Budgeting uses the same brain skills that you use when—for example—scheduling your workouts around when you want to wash your hair. The same way you go, "Okay, Thursday is date night, so I'll push my Tuesday night workout to Wednesday morning and have forty-eight hour hair by happy hour—perfect," you can come up with a strategy to deploy your dollars effectively.

So trust me here: you've got this, bb.

With that definition in mind, allow me to bust down some myths or preconceptions you might be holding around budgeting.

Budgeting doesn't mean deprivation.

I mean—I budget, and I'm not deprived at all. But seriously: regardless of how much money you make, I 100 percent believe that every budget should have room for the things that make you happy, whether they're "essentials" or not (and we'll get to nonnegotiables later on). More than that, if your budget makes you miserable, you're not going to follow it, and then it's as good as no budget. So there's zero point in depriving yourself in the name of budgeting . . . especially when budgeting is the very thing that will let you be a fancy bitch with all the money you've stashed away.

Budgeting doesn't mean not being spontaneous.

By the same token, budgeting lets you plan to be spontaneous.

I know, it sounds like an oxymoron, but think about it: rather than make a last-minute decision to meet up with your friends only to panic over whether your account is overdrawn when you slap down your card, you can ring up another round of cocktails no prob because you know you have the $$$ for it. Thanks, budgeting!

A budget doesn't keep you from being spontaneous because a budget doesn't dictate exactly *when* you'll spend that fun money. It just means you've planned ahead to have some fun—and spend money doing it—at some point in the future. It's an outline, not a word-for-word script.

Your budget plan can and should adapt as life changes (for worse *and* for better). If anything, knowing you're prepped for whatever *might* happen frees up a lot of mental energy to be *more* spontaneous in the day-to-day, because you know you've already got your basics covered.

Budgeting is about self-acceptance, not punishment.

I think most, if not all, people who "suck at budgeting" are really just dealing with shame and embarrassment.

Those feelings are real. As we'll see in a bit, the first step in budgeting is basically just taking a deep, hard look at yourself and your spending habits. And unsurprisingly, seeing your credit card statement and saying, "Damn, I spent seven hundred dollars on delivery last month?!" is just . . . not a good feeling.

So when you take that deep, hard look, and you feel that not-niceness, that sense of dread, that overwhelming embarrassment about how you've been spending your money . . . most people just stick their head in the sand. Instead of changing the habit, most people choose not to acknowledge that the habit is going on at all, with a kind of "Well, if I don't know, I don't know!" kind of attitude. If they budget at all, it's a weird punitive "I've got to get back on track and atone for my past sins" kind of overboard approach that's impossible to stick with. That just triggers *more* shame at being a "failure" and then lands them right back in "ignorance is bliss" land.

Well, ignorance is *not* bliss, trust. But I'd be lying if I said budgeting was always super fun and easy-breezy. It's definitely going to feel worse before it feels better—but it *will* feel better.

Budgeting is basically pregaming for your life.

If you take three shots at your friend's place before heading out for the night, you're not going to have to spend as much at the bar to keep having a crazy-wild, drunk-ass night. This is a scientific fact.

That's really all that budgeting is. Same principle. Having a budget—and specifically, having enough money in your budget to *invest*—is what will allow the rest of your life to be as crazy and wild (or calm and stress-free) as possible.

I'm going to go deep into investing and why it's important in chapter 5. But as a quick teaser, you need to invest if you plan on retiring. Period. Seriously, if you have any desire to lie down for an extended period of time at any point in your life, *you need to invest.*

Budgeting is what makes investing possible. It's what kickstarts and sustains that buzz. And this, more than anything else, is the fundamental truth of budgeting that rich people just *get.* For rich people, budgeting is just a plan that lets them maximize the value of their wealth (aka invest their money so it *makes* them money) and keep up the lifestyle they want for the entirety of their lives.

And speaking of which . . .

What Rich People (Really) Know About Budgeting

Remember that abundance mindset we talked about in the first chapter? Rich people bring that to everything, but especially budgeting—aka financial planning, money management, cash flow oversight. Whatever you want to call it, it's the same thing: budgeting.

But it's more than just a mindset: rich people actually *need* to budget— sometimes more than broke folks do—for a couple of reasons.

Rich people have unusual opportunities they want to take advantage of.

Whether it's the chance to quickly close on a property at auction and make it an income-generating rental or the option to cut a big fat check to their favorite charity (and get a sweet tax-write off) before the end of the year, rich people get a lot of opportunities knocking that the rest of us might not. In fact, they tend to find opportunities where the rest of us see obstacles (stock market's down? Buy, buy, buy so you can profit when it rises later).

But all those opportunities require *money*.

Rich people can be just as cash poor as the rest of us.

When rich people say something like "My net worth is ten million dollars," they don't mean that they literally have ten million dollars in their checking account right this instant.

What they *do* mean is something more like "I own a portfolio of assets, and the value of those assets, minus all of my liabilities like debts, loans, mortgages, and so on, is ten million dollars."

Cash is only one kind of asset—and almost every rich person is going to have more than just cash making up their portfolio. In fact, odds are good that the majority of their wealth will be in held in *illiquid* (non-cash) holdings like their personal homes, any other real estate they own, investment and retirement accounts, ownership stakes in businesses, and a whole bunch of other assets that can't be "spent" freely like cash.

Budgeting is what makes it possible for them to access their money in a timely way—and not overdraw their cash accounts in their everyday spending. A solid budget is what allows them to plan for when and where they should rebalance their portfolio so that any cash they need will be available for them to spend when they need it.

Rich people want their money to make them more money.

Rich people also just don't like keeping money in their checking accounts. Why? Because they want the money they have to make them *more* money, remember? They want their money to be working *hard*. And if it's just hanging around in a checking account, it's not working. Most checking accounts don't earn interest at all—and if they do, it's usually something like .07 percent. Even traditional savings accounts pay out around 0.42 percent interest annually. Rich people take one look at those minuscule interest rates and go, "Yeah, no."

So, instead of just parking their millions in a bank account—aka having no plan—they figure out a setup for those millions that will maximize their returns. They strategize. They divide and conquer. They calculate how much risk they can tolerate, research (or hire people to research) different investment vehicles, and allocate their money accordingly.

In other words, they *budget*.

Remember, the rich person mindset is always "How can I take what I already have and use it to make me money?" And doing *that* takes a plan. Always.

Rich people who don't budget aren't going to get away with it for long.

Even people who make hundreds of thousands of dollars a year can be broke *if* they don't use a rich person's mentality.

Why? Two words, friends: *lifestyle creep*.

Lifestyle creep is just a fancy way of saying "spending more money as you earn more money." As people get more and more money coming in from their job or their investments, they can also—if they're not planning ahead—have just as much money going *out* the door. You get that promotion at work, so you move into a nicer apartment, you buy a new handbag, you get a new car, you overall just spend more and more, little by little, on whatever you're regularly buying.

Lifestyle creep can be *so* tempting and *super* insidious (hence the "creep" factor) but it's possible to avoid it with some advanced budgeting techniques, like value-based spending and factoring in nonnegotiables (which we'll discuss in a hot sec!).

What Is MY Budget?!

When you go in for a facial, does the esthetician just lay you down and start slapping random creams and oils on your face?

Hell no.

She takes a good, hard look at your face first. Maybe she even whips out a magnifying glass or one of those pore microscopes.

Which brings us to the first part of budgeting—the spending audit. Think of it like the money version of one of those little pore microscope things (except hopefully less gross). We're going to get up close and personal with every last detail of your spending—warts and all.

The Spending Audit

There are two basic steps to getting started on your spending audit:

1. Track down all your stuff.
2. Put it all in one place.

"All your stuff" means any records you have of your spending over the past month. If you slap everything on your credit or debit card, you can just pull up your last statement from your bank or credit card provider to comb through—the statement being the record of every dollar that exited your account that month.

Here's how to get the statements:

1. Log in to your bank or credit card's online portal.
2. Select the account (if you spend mostly on a debit card) or the card (if you spend mostly on a credit card) you use.

3. Look for a link/button to "Statements" (and if you haven't already, sign up for paperless delivery while you're there, so that they come right to your inbox every month).

4. You can usually get your statement as a PDF, although some banks will give you the option to export as a spreadsheet, which is handy if you're an Excel whiz (or want to become one with the Your Rich BFF templates!).

5. Repeat steps 1 to 4 for as many debit/credit cards as you regularly use each month.

> **Key Items:** I recommend exporting the statement for one to two months prior than the current month (so if it's June, export April or May). But whichever month you select, just make sure it's the same across all of your accounts. I also generally recommend avoiding November and December statements for your budgeting audit, because the winter holidays can mean abnormally high spending.

Alternatively, you can use a spending tracking app (many of which are totally free) that securely accesses your credit and bank statements, aggregates them, and categorizes your expenses. (You can grab the list of my favorite apps at richAF.club.)

That said, even if you use a credit card for all your spending, there will be a few major things that likely won't be on your credit card statement: your rent or mortgage, your car note, and any debt payments you're making. These are all likely some of your biggest expenses, but odds are you don't charge your student loans, for example, to your credit card, so just be sure to either cross-reference with your bank statement to get those amounts, or write them down from memory.

With all your stuff gathered, it's time to put it all in one place. You could literally just print the statements out if you have a printer, or you could input all your expenses in a spreadsheet, or you could hand write them into a bullet journal. Truly, just do whatever works for you—we all have different learning styles. Personally, I'm partial to the Your Rich BFF spreadsheets (naturally), but maybe you're my dad and are literally going to print everything out and whip out a yellow highlighter. No prob.

Okay, phew! That's a lot of info gathering. But you're doing amazing. Trust me, I know your spending might feel like a huge pile of chaos right now, but it's all part of the process. Think of figuring out your spending like the Marie Kondo Netflix cleaning show: you empty your closet, clear out your dresser drawers, and dump everything on your bed.

And now . . . you get to sort it!

> Grab a copy of the Your Rich BFF Budgeting Spread-sheets here: **richAF.club.**

Categorize, Calculate, Re-Calibrate: What Did You Get for Your Money?

There are two steps to sorting your spending.

1. First, you'll group all your expenses into categories.
2. And then you'll classify those categories based on how essential they are to, basically, keeping you alive.

So: categories! These will vary depending on what your life is like and what you're spending money on, but here's how I like to do mine. For a typical month, I categorize my spending into *about* six different areas:

1. Housing (rent or mortgage, utility bills)
2. Basic food (i.e., groceries)
3. Dining out (aka takeout, going to the bars, getting coffee)
4. Transportation (Ubers, Metrocard, etc.)
5. Entertainment (streaming services, concert tickets, etc.)
6. Self-care (haircuts and haircare, lash extensions, massages)

But I say *about* six different categories because it really varies. If you shop for clothes pretty much every month, you're gonna want to make clothing into its own category. If you own a house and are running to Home Depot twice a week, you could create a home maintenance category—or you could choose to lump your light bulbs and shower curtains under housing. You could put health insurance premiums in the same medical category as copays and cold medicine, or you could create an insurance category that also includes your car insurance and homeowner's or renter's insurance. (If you're using the Your Rich BFF spreadsheet, I've included a starter set of categories ready to go, but you can def get in there and change things up. Same goes for automatic programs like Mint—double-check that their categories are accurate and haven't gone rogue.)

Whatever categories you end up with, keep in mind that the main goal is just to see at a glance where your money is going. What's most important about any individual category isn't so much what kind of thing you're spending on, but how much of a necessity that set of expenses is as a group. I do also suggest avoiding having too big of a miscellaneous category, because that sort of defeats the purpose of categories at all. Beyond that, the only rule here is *you do you.*

> The three categories that most people don't remember? Saving, paying down debt, and investing. And if you're like, "Vivian, I didn't *forget* those categories, I just don't do those things!!!" well, that's why we're here. Your new and improved budget is going to make *sure* you have the cash freed up to sock something away, crush your debt, and make your money make *you* money. But right now, those categories might all be zero bucks per month, and that's okay. Just keep them in mind for later—because remember, the whole goal of your Rich AF budget is to get you investing ASAP.

With all your expenses grouped up and totaled (either manually or in a spreadsheet), it's time to ~evaluate~. Does this involve color-coding? Hell yes, it involves color-coding.

We're going to keep it super simple and do this stoplight style—red, yellow, green—so grab three highlighters or get those colors loaded up in your little Excel paint box.

Red is for expenses that are truly not flexible. All the stuff that you simply can't cut out or cut back on whatsoever without dying, losing your job, or, like, breaking the law? Those are your red categories.

Two categories that are almost certainly going to go in this "not flexible" red zone are housing and transpo. With housing, you already have a contract in place (either a lease or a mortgage) so that amount is not going to change until the contract is up, and you can't just *not* have a roof over your head.

Yellow is for expenses that are necessary, but may be flexible in amount or frequency. This is where you're gonna start using some self-awareness and make some judgment calls. Groceries, for example, are a necessity—a girl's gotta eat—but maybe meeting a friend for lunch at the Whole Foods hot bar is more of a "dining out" experience than a staple meal. Stuff like your phone and internet service that you need to live your life (and have a fixed monthly cost) will go here too, because these expenses are necessary, but the *amounts* can be negotiable (spoiler alert for later!).

Finally, green is for your straight-up discretionary expenses: you go to the movies. You grab drinks at a bar. You get your lashes and nails done. Hopefully pretty self-explanatory (and should technically be everything left that isn't red or yellow).

Once you've gotten your greens done, you can start making some assessments. (In other words, this is the part where you hold up a sweater and ask yourself if it sparks joy.) Start with the greens and just . . . look at the numbers to start. Seriously, just do a vibe check. If you feel a lurching "oh shit" when you see how much you've spent on DoorDash, or you're *still* grinning over the $$$ you spent on Taylor Swift tickets, take note of that feeling (and don't beat yourself up over it, whatever it is!).

After that initial vibe check, try looking at your green expenditures through the lens of *opportunity cost.* Opportunity cost is basically the idea that whenever you make any single choice, you are taking some *other* choices off the table. It's like dating: if two cuties from Bumble message you to go out on the same night, that "Who am I going to pick?" feeling is you anticipating opportunity cost. Because you know if you go out with Cutie #1 and they turn out to be boring or gross or secretly a terrible person, you're going to spend the whole night thinking *Ughhhh, what a waste of my life, I can't believe I shaved my legs for this.* You missed not only the opportunity for a better date with Cutie #2, but also the chance to just, like, stay home and save your energy.

Opportunity cost thinking helps you see where you can cut (or cut back on) your spending in a way that fits what *you* actually care about. It frees you from those stupid "never spend more than X dollars on Y thing" rules of thumb, and it reminds you that *you* are the one who gets to make the judgment calls, because you're the one who'll feel the after-effects of whatever your spending decisions are. That feeling of regret at the lost opportunity only really creeps in when you feel like you've wasted your time, wasted your money, or wasted your resources—so if you feel that about any of your spending here, make a note (mental or otherwise).

Once you're done vibe-checking and opportunity-costing those green categories, move on and repeat with the yellows and ask the same question, keeping in mind that these are probably categories that you can *shrink* if need be, but not eliminate entirely. (You can also take a look at your reds, too, but since they're your core expenses, they may be a little less flexible.)

Remember, you don't need to make any specific cuts or adjustments just yet. For now, you're just trying to see where you're at and forming a direct understanding of how and where your expenditures bring value to your life. You're cultivating the mindset that value is (a) based on your personal subjective feelings and (b) relative to the *other* things you might spend money on—aka thinking like a rich person.

Wait, How Much Money Do I Make Again?

Okay. You've just done an amazing, head-to-toe organizational make-over on your money *outflow*.

However, outflow isn't everything. Spending—and therefore your budget—is actually kind of relative, because it all depends on how much money is coming *in* the door.

So there's one last piece of your finances you're gonna want to take a look at before you try on some fresh budget styles: your income.

Now, I'm guessing you could probably tell me your salary or hourly rate off the top of your head. But we're interested in the money that's available to spend, aka your net income. *Net income* means just the dollars that actually hit your bank account. You might *earn* $100,000 a year, but some of that is going to be immediately forked over for income taxes (local, state, and federal), as well as pretax benefits like insurance premiums, commuter benefits, or flexible spending accounts if you get them.

If you have a straight-up salaried position with no other sources of money, then you can take a look at your "net pay" on your pay stub and multiply it out by however many pay periods you have per year (e.g., if you get paid twice a month, there are twenty-four pay periods in your fiscal year) to find your annual net income.

READING YOUR PAY STUB:

HOW MUCH DO YOU ACTUALLY MAKE?

Real talk: When was the last time you looked at your pay stub? If the answer is "never," don't sweat it. Pay stubs are basically receipts for your paycheck—and just like receipts, they're boring to read and easy to forget about . . . until you suddenly need to decipher them.

Never fear. Each company's pay stub is going to look a little different, but the basic breakdown is the same. At the top or on the left you'll usually see something labeled **gross pay**. That's what you "made" . . . but then come some things that are withheld.

TAXES WITHHELD:
- Federal income tax: to the US government
- State income tax wherever you live (though some states like Florida don't have state income tax so if you're lucky this may not be a line item for you)
- Local income tax: to your city, town, or municipality
- Social security and medicare tax: basically us paying for these public services for our more elderly citizens

OTHER DEDUCTIONS WITHHELD:
- Your health insurance premium
- Any commuter benefits contributions
- Childcare, if you get it through work
- FSA or HSA contributions*
- Contributions to a 401(k), 403(b), or any other type of employer-sponsored retirement plan*

Finally, at the end, you'll have some kind of *summary section*. This will show in a nutshell:

- Gross pay
- The total amount for all the stuff that was withheld
- Net pay, aka what you'll see hit your bank account, which is gross pay minus all those taxes and deductions

I'll explain all these abbreviations later, promise!

But honestly, very few of us have *just* one source of income these days, so if you get a chunk of your money through side hustles, freelance work, or anything that doesn't give you a pay stub, you can ballpark your annual income with last year's tax filings. Dig out form 1040 from your most recent tax return (if you didn't save a PDF, your tax software should let you log in and download a fresh copy) and find your *adjusted gross income* (AGI) on line 11 and your *total tax* on line 24. Subtract the total tax (line 24) from the AGI (line 11) and voilà: your *net income*, aka all the money you had at your fingertips to spend last calendar year. (Again, this is very much a "back of the envelope" calculation—if you know that something major has changed since you filed, then do your best to account for that new nannying gig or the $$$ you won in Vegas.)

> Wait—what if I have money going to a retirement account? Should I include that in my income calculation here?
>
> Excellent question! If you know you're automatically contributing to retirement accounts (such as a 401(k) through your employer), make a note of how much you contribute each year. (Even if you don't really understand how or why you're doing it—we'll get to that in a later chapter!) That money is money you earn—so it's part of your income—but it's already earmarked, because it's going right to those retirement investments. In other words, it's already budgeted, and you'll include it in the "saving/investing" category you'll set up in a bit when you lay out your actual budget plan.
>
> And if you're not contributing to retirement yet, do not panic. I'll show you how (and how much), all step-by-step.

Now that you've got your net income, let's do that gut check. Take your monthly spending and multiply by twelve, then compare that yearly spending total to your annual net income.

Which one's bigger?

[*Jeopardy!* music plays]

Time's up!

If your income is bigger, amazing! Jump right on to the "Build Your Budget" section.

If your spending is bigger, don't panic!!! Seriously, don't. Go back to your monthly spending, but this time, ignore all the green categories. Add up just your reds and yellows and multiply *that* total by twelve.

Now compare that red + yellow annual total to your annual income— is your income now the bigger number? Then yay! While you're techni-cally spending at a deficit right now, you won't be for long once you map out your budget. Read up on the budget strategies coming up, and *definitely* pay attention to the "Value-Based Spending" section—trust me when I tell you that it will be the *perfect* way to take those opportunity-cost-y, why-did-I-pay-money-for-this green categories and free them up into a magic source of cash.

UM, VIVIAN? MY SPENDING'S MORE THAN MY INCOME . . . 🤐

That you?

First off: take a deep breath. Yes, if you're spending more than you take in, then this conversation changes a lot. But it does not mean you're a failure, you're doomed, or you should give up. Not. At. All.

If your annual expenses are more than your annual income, even once you're down to just your red and yellow categories, then you're operating at a deficit. And that means even the very "best" budget (whatever that means) is not going to solve this for you because—as I will say forever and ever until I die—you cannot budget your way out of a deficit.

So here are a few things to try instead.

- **Negotiate at work.** Jump back to chapter 2 and give it a good reread. Did you ask for a raise? What about applying to new jobs? These aren't quick fixes by any means, but over time, even a 5 percent pay jump will add up. If you haven't tried either yet, now's the time.

- **Start a side hustle.** For a short-term infusion of cash, side hustles are where it's at. Even if you can only squeeze in two Rover walks per week, that's money you wouldn't have otherwise, and every bit helps—not least because you'll feel so much better knowing you're taking action.
- **Shrink your bills.** Hop on down to chapter 4 and read up on how to negotiate down some of your red-category bills (like cell phone or internet). Just like salary negotiations, a quick conversation could land you with a few hundred back in your pocket over the course of a year.
- **Get a handle on debt.** If debt payments are a major part of your spending, you can take steps to minimize the sting of high interest rates or even shrink the monthly obligation to your creditors. Jump to page 236 in chapter 6 to see how.

You did it! Ctrl+s that spreadsheet and cap up those highlighters, girl, because you're ready for the next step.

Hell *yes* it's time to build your budget!

Remember how budgeting is just the act of allocating dollars to savings, expenses, debt, and investing? Your individual budget is how you, personally, are going to do that—and baby, your budget is going to be *custom-made*.

Build Your Budget

Building a budget is like getting a manicure. You've got *options*.

Acrylic or natural? Powder, gel, or regular? Color? French tips? Cut down or just filed? Square, round, or almond shape? Nail art? Rhine-stones?

Personally, I like to get my nails done when I've got something big coming up and I want to look extra nice. That's all I need out of my manis. But I know some girls who are ride-or-die for their gels, or who get schmancy subscription boxes every month with new polishes to try.

Point is, when we do our nails, we're not all doing the exact same thing with them. Everyone gets to choose what works for them, fits their life/events they may have coming up, and really just makes them happy.

The following styles of cash flow management are my Your Rich BFF–approved, top-four favorite budgeting methods—BUT! They are just jumping-off points. They are that wall of polish colors in the nail salon, so just pick one that speaks to you—there are no wrong answers and nothing has to be permanent. If after a few weeks or months it's not working, just buff it off and pick out something new.

50/30/20 Budgeting

Not to play favorites, but this might be my favorite budgeting strategy because it is so easy. It's the slice-and-bake cookies of the budgeting world. HelloFresh for your bank account.

Here's how it breaks down:

- 50 percent of your posttax income goes to needs
- 30 percent goes to wants
- 20 percent goes to saving/debt/investing (we'll get to *how* to save and invest it in the next chapters, but for now, it's fine to just earmark that money)

That's it. Seriously.

I've found that 50/30/20 works best for folks who don't ~nEeD~ a budget, but do want to have guardrails to guide their spending. It's also great for people who are into the spectator sport of budgeting: the ones who love using tracking apps to see what their money is being spent on but don't necessarily want to have to set up a super-complex spending allocation system on their own.

Also, since you literally categorized and labeled your spending, it's easy to start: use those color-coded categories to figure out what goes where in your 50/30/20 breakdown. But because 20 percent needs to be available for saving/investing, this means that *all* of your spending—red, yellow, and green—should add up to about 80 percent of your income (aka 50 percent + 30 percent). If it's soaking up more than 80 percent, then it's time to start tweaking your spending plan, starting with that middle 30 percent—the "wants," aka green categories.

> If you find yourself struggling to figure out what should stay and what should go from that middle 30 percent, check out the "Value-Based Spending" section at the end of this chapter.

One final note: as you start to make more and more and more money, these particular percentages aren't going to make as much sense. Your saving, investing, and debt category will eventually be so much bigger than just 20 percent of your income—in fact, that's the goal. 50/30/20 is just the jump-off.

Zero-Based Budgeting

Don't let the name fool you: this is *not* going to leave you with zero dollars. With zero-based budgeting, you take the total amount of money you have to spend and start assigning it to your expenses (your needs, your wants, your fun money, as well as your savings and investing goals). Every dollar you take in gets a specific job, even if that job is "covering random expenses I forgot about." By the time you're done allocating, your income minus your expenses should equal zero—because you have a plan to spend exactly as much money as you're taking in that month, no more, no less.

MONTHLY INCOME (POST-TAX)		MONTHLY SPENDING	
Paychecks	$3,400	Rent	$1,600
Side Hustles	$420	Groceries	$375
		Utils	$200
		Transpo	$125
		Renter's Insurance	$75
		Drinks/Outings/Fun	$250
		Nonnegotiables	$150
		Debt Payments	$550
		Savings	$375
		Misc/Stuff I Forgot to Plan For	$120
TOTAL	$3,820	TOTAL	$3,820

$3,820 – $3,820 = 0

This prevents you from spending at a deficit because it makes spending at a deficit technically impossible—a dollar can't be in two places at once, after all. (In the olden days when everyone used cash for everything, people would literally divide up their dollar bills into separate envelopes—hence why you might see this called the envelope method.)

If you're thinking that zero-based budgeting sounds like more work than 50/30/20, well . . . it is, not gonna lie. But the extra effort is worth it, *especially* if you're someone with an irregular income.

What's an irregular income, you might ask? Allow me to explain using *Swamp People*.

For those of you unfamiliar with this masterpiece of modern reality TV, on *Swamp People*, the main guy is basically a farm-to-table alligator hunter. He goes out in the swamp and hunts down the gators so people can eat the meat and harvest the skins for leather. It's incredibly lucrative work—think of how much an alligator-skin bag goes for—but there's a sort of catch to it.

See, the thing about alligator hunting is that there's hunting *season*. The *Swamp People* guy works three months a year, and *only* three months a year. It's basically three months of nonstop gator-chasing. In other words, his entire livelihood for the year has to be made in that short hunting season. He only works three months a year, but that money has to sustain him for a full twelve.

Of course, *Swamp People* are not the only ones who earn money in irregular chunks throughout the year. Professional athletes competing for tournament money, teachers, freelancers, full-time Uber drivers, authors, artists, musicians . . . even folks with full-time jobs can have inconsistent cash flow if they're commission-based, seasonal, or rely heavily on tips. If that's you, zero-based budgeting can help you strategize your spending so that you don't run out of cash before your next payday. And no matter how your money comes in, it's also a great way to sneakily force yourself into making tradeoffs: you *can* buy anything, but you *can't* buy *everything*.

Reverse Budgeting

With reverse budgeting, you just commit to putting a chunk of cash in savings and investment accounts before making literally any other spending decisions. That's pretty much it. You don't figure out how much to save alongside figuring out how much to spend on wants and needs (like 50/30/20) and you don't zero down your paychecks in any old order (like zero-based budgeting). It's a "reverse" method because your very *first* move is putting money in savings and investments (instead of just saving however much is left after expenses).

This is an especially genius strategy if you struggle with overspending, or if you're one of those so-called savers who puts a few bucks in a savings account at the end of the month only to transfer it all back out a week later. Reverse budgeting gets your money out of sight and out of mind—especially if you're paying yourself first into a retirement account, where that money is effectively locked away until you're much older (and more on that in chapter 5!).

The set-it-and-forget approach of reverse budgeting isn't just great because it automates your willpower, though. It's also super flexible. There's no minimum percentage you're aiming for here—you're just trying to get the pay-yourself-first habit going. Getting in that groove makes it so much easier to sustain over the long run. And smallish contributions may not feel like much now, but they can definitely add up over time (hello, compound interest!) and make you richer almost effortlessly.

Half-Payment Budgeting

The half-payment method is a super simple way to budget, particularly if you get paid twice a month. Basically, you split the cost of your bills into two lump sums. Your first paycheck of the month covers one half of your expenses, and the second paycheck covers the other half.

Again, simple . . . but honestly, it's kind of a mindfuck how well it can work. It definitely was for me. I fell in love with half-payment budgeting pretty soon after I moved to New York and found myself getting really bummed out in the second half of every month, because even though I knew I was going to get a paycheck, it basically all had to go to rent. Yet for whatever reason, it felt *less* bad to set aside half of that *first* paycheck for rent, live off the other half of that first paycheck for two weeks, and then cover the rest of the rent with half of that second paycheck and still have another half paycheck to ride out the end of the month. Something about not having to rip the entire rent money out of one paycheck made me *feel* so much more competent and on top of things—and not feeling broke made it that much easier to live within my means with those two half paychecks for expenses.

Half-payment budgeting is great if you feel like you start every month with the best intentions only to get desperate and depressed and cranky by the end of the month. In other words, it's a dope method for procrastinators. You can even think of it like writing a paper in college: if you know that your teacher is giving you a week to write it, you *could* spend six days avoiding the assignment and then bang out a shitty essay that you submit at 11:58 p.m. on deadline day. Or you could write half the paper in the first three days of the week, and then the second half of the paper in the back three days—and still have one day off to go party.

> Still not sure which budgeting type makes sense for you? Take a quick quiz at **richAF.club** to help you decide!

Value-Based Spending

Remember that Prada bag I mentioned earlier?

A few days after I bought it, my work mentor happened to notice the bag and asked about it. I excitedly babbled out that yes, it was new, I'd just gotten it, and I loved it so so so so much.

She just smiled. "Nothing ever feels as good as your first bag."

I smiled back and laughed in a kind of "Oh, yeah, haha, whatever!" kind of way. She laughed too, and eventually we went back to work.

Since then, I've bought many a bag. And you know what? She was totally right. Nothing ever felt as good as that first bag. In fact, as I started to pick up a few more luxury items, I started to have feelings of buyer's remorse: *Did I really need this? Is this something that I'm actually going to use regularly?*

In some cases, I was wrong. I would end up wearing a new piece all the time. I loved it, it became a wardrobe staple, the whole deal.

But in other cases, I was totally right. I spent thousands on a bag and I never took it out of the dust cover. It ended up feeling like a big ol' waste of money. It was, undeniably, not worth it.

Now that I've explained how budgeting works, I want to pause and get down to the root of overspending: *value.*

Generally speaking, a purchase has value for us when we have more positive feelings about having it than we have negative feelings about *not* having the money anymore. It feels "worth it," in other words—"it" being the dollars we've given up to get the thing. The problem is, many of us don't understand the value of a dollar—not because we don't work hard, but because we aren't visualizing exactly what that dollar equates to.

In hindsight, I think I got so much value out of that first Prada bag because I *did* know what those dollars equated to. I'd worked and saved specifically in order to buy it—like, your girl was setting aside a couple of hundred bucks every paycheck and putting it into the Bag Fund. I literally promised myself out loud "I'm going to work my butt off this year because I'm buying this damn bag no matter what." I could have calculated the exact number of working hours that went into that bag and felt *great* about every single one of them.

I'm willing to bet most of us have had a moment like this early in our working lives. Doesn't have to be a bag, of course: it might be moving to your own apartment, or being able to pick up the tab when you go to dinner with your parents, or buying a car. The first time you realize that you have financial agency, the first time you know you don't have to rely on another person to get you what you want. In that moment, nothing is more valuable than whatever symbolizes that feeling of freedom and power.

Like my mentor said: nothing ever feels as good as your first bag.

Because things change. *You* change. And how you *value* things changes with you.

When I saved up for my big Prada adventure, I *wanted* what I bought to represent a big chunk of my earnings and sweat equity. But once I already had a few bags, I started reevaluating. I thought about all the work hours that would effectively be going into each new purchase. I imagined myself hustling at the trading desk, answering emails, doing research, even commuting, and thought, *Would I do that for two full weeks and be happy getting this bag in return?*

Eventually, the answer became no. I didn't want to buy more bags. I realized I was overspending—not because I was spending money I didn't have, but because I wasn't getting the value I wanted in *exchange* for that money anymore.

Those "Is this worth the effort?" calculations I was doing were essentially practicing *value-based spending.* Value-based spending means you weigh the price of a potential purchase against the work you've done to earn that amount of money, and then ask yourself, *Okay, so is it worth it?*

Value-based spending is easy, it's powerful, and it'll probably save you money. When we start to lose touch with how much work—how much of our blood, sweat, and tears—went into getting those dollars into our bank account, it gets a lot easier to just fritter them away and somehow still end up unsatisfied with what our money got us. Value-based spending changes the question from "Do I have the money for it?" to "Is it worth the work I put in to get that money?"

The secret Your Rich BFF value-based spending formula looks like this: **price of item / your effective hourly wage**.

You then ask yourself if you'd be willing to work those hours in exchange for, say, this dress or that vacation.

Value-based spending is also a quick check-yourself-before-you-wreck-yourself moment. For example, instead of automatically thinking, *Well, I was meh on the last bag I got, but maybe the* next *bag will do it for me*, you'd be like, *Hold up, do I really think that? Because so far that hasn't been true*, and reassess. (In that way, it's a great way to pump the brakes on lifestyle creep.) Either way, you're much less likely to spend mindlessly on stuff you don't really want.

Value-based spending also lets you calibrate what you buy as you live your life. The value of a dollar for you will change as you start to earn more, for one thing. Your life itself will change, too—you buy a house, you have a kid, and maybe two grand spent on new furniture or a bougie stroller now feels *way* more valuable to you than two grand spent on shoes. Even something as quick as a sudden rainstorm can change how valuable a purchase is for you—maybe you'd never pay twenty bucks for a rinky-dink drugstore umbrella ordinarily, but if you just got your hair done and it starts pouring rain, that twenty dollars is now money well spent. (Yes, you're allowed to consider convenience as something worth paying for! Promise!)

You can use the value-based mindset in the moment (to gut check your current spending habits when you do your audit, or to evaluate a potential major purchase), but you can also use it to plan ahead more generally (like when you're figuring out what to cut or keep as you adjust your budget for the future). When you give the cost of things a new common denominator (the work you do to pay for it) and understand what you're actually getting out of it, you'll have a much realer and more personal sense of the value of a dollar.

You Can Pry That Matcha Latte from My Cold, Dead Hands: Why Everyone Needs Nonnegotiables

Sometimes, we buy stuff just because we enjoy having, using, or eating it.

I know, right? SHOCKING.

Yes, this stuff costs money. But those little luxuries—I mean the ones that are basically meme-level villains of personal finance these days: your lattes, your avocado toasts, your hair treatments, your craft cocktails, whatever—aren't just black holes sucking the dollars from our pockets. They do something. They help us feel better. They make life nicer and more comfortable.

So guess what? It's okay to like spending money on them. (Or spending money at all.)

Trust me. We all do. (Rich people *definitely* do.)

I firmly believe that every single person has (and should have) some kind of fun, extra luxury or indulgence in their life, no matter what. They're what I call nonnegotiables.

For me, it's eyelash extensions. I get semipermanent lash extensions glued onto my eyelids every three weeks or so, and it's not cheap—$110 to $150 a session, depending on how much I've blinked off my eyes in between.

Now, some people would hear this and be like, "Wait. You're having someone glue synthetic lashes to your own lashes. Like, on top of the lashes that you already have. [confused pause] Literally what is the point? Does mascara not exist on your planet? How could that possibly be worth however many dollars it costs per year?!"

Well, I'll tell you however many dollars, because I did the math: it's about $2,500 per year. And yeah, that's a lot of money for some tiny eye hairs and glue!

But that's not *really* what I'm getting out of those lash extensions. What that $2,500 is actually getting me is daily confidence. I never feel like I have to put on makeup to leave the house. I don't have to waste time combing on mascara because my eyes naturally pop. I look good in person running to the grocery store, on camera in my videos, and at any events I may be attending. And *that* is something that money truly cannot buy: some extra time to sleep in and my daily dose of automatic confidence.

Of course, not everything in your budget can be a nonnegotiable, because unless you got those Bezos bucks, you're not going to have the budget bandwidth to spend on all of them.

The deal is this: *You can afford anything. You just can't afford everything.*

You might have to do some negotiating with *yourself* to figure out what's truly worth it to *you* (hey again, value-based spending!). For example, I gave up getting my nails done to be able to get my lashes done, a trade-off I was comfortable making. But you can (and should) prioritize at least one nonnegotiable as part of your budget planning—if for no other reason than it'll help you feel psyched about having a budget in the first place. Sure, what gives you joy and meaning might do absolutely nothing for some other rando. But remember: your budget is not their budget.

Every single person deserves to have one or two items that are nonnegotiable in their lives and not feel judged or ashamed about it. So as you review your spending, allow yourself to have—seriously, commit to it—those things that make you happy.

Being the Rich Aunt

In Chinese, there's a phrase, *yīnggāi*, that directly translates to "obligation" or "you should."

In many cultures, and in particular many immigrant cultures, there is a level of social expectation that kids will go out, make bank, and put a *lot* of that toward their parents and family. The idea is giving money to your family should *always* be your top priority—and that's a really tough idea to shake. I speak from true personal experience, not just my own upbringing as the kid of Chinese immigrants, but from my friends: I had coworkers who started with me at J.P. Morgan whose families were undocumented, and the expectation was that they would send their entire bonus home—even though they were struggling to get by themselves in their first years in NYC.

Why do I bring this up now? Because as you set out to follow your brand-new budget, you might feel this pressure start to bubble back up in a big way. A budget is ultimately just a set of boundaries for yourself—but it's hard to respect those if everyone around you is pushing, pushing, pushing on them. Even if you're not from an immigrant family, you might find that as you start "getting better with money," it affects your role in your family, *especially* if you come from a family or friend circle that may not have the best financial habits. Once you start making some money, or even just managing your spending so you have more cash for your non-negotiables, it may seem like everybody wants to be your best friend.

Here's exactly what you can say to set healthy boundaries around money and family, so that you can help lift up your loved ones without letting their finances drag *you* down.

"I don't loan money."

Seriously, just flat-out say it.

There is *huge* power in articulating your boundaries like this. And yes, the phrasing matters.

You don't want to say "I can't loan you this money." For one thing, it's not necessarily true: you might totally have the cash to do it. And if that's the case, you're just inviting the other person to push back. Getting into a "Yes you can!" "No I can't!" back-and-forth is going to be exhausting and pointless.

You also don't want to say "I can't loan you money *right now*." It may *feel* like you're softening the blow, but in reality you're just leaving the door open for them to ask again later, and then you'll be having the conversation all over again.

Saying "I don't do X" instead of these squishier alternatives articulates the boundary not just to the other person, but to *yourself.* It gets you to internalize your not-lending-money as a trait of your character.

To be sure, this isn't a magic phrase or anything. You're still going to have some hard conversations if your extended family is up in your grill for cash. But you can also leverage family dynamics to make this phrase work for you. If you're good with your parents, tell them to co-enforce this and help you set boundaries with your weird uncle Lester who's asking for money.

"This is what I can comfortably send home every single month. I am not able to do more."

That said, if the conversation about money is *with* your parents, it's a tougher one. These are the people who raised you, so it's a lot harder to say no.

But at the same time, I think it's healthy to say you'll help them *within* a certain boundary. After all, maybe you *do* want to help them out—you just don't want to clear out your bank account to do it.

If that's the case, you can work out in your budget how much you can send, and that is the number you will offer. You're being entirely truthful in saying that this is the most you can comfortably send—your needs (including savings, investing, and nonnegotiables) matter too.

If you get pushback, just repeat what you said: "This is what I can send, and I can't do more." Don't give more detail and open up a foothold for bargaining or cajoling. Don't fall into answering "Why not?" or "What else are you even spending on?" or anything like that—it doesn't matter. This is what you've budgeted and it's take it or leave it.

"I do not have room in my budget to gift."

Maybe your family isn't asking for regular checks home, but you know you'll likely be asked to offer a lump-sum "loan" at some point. In that case, you can set a yearly budget that you're comfortable giving.

Yes, *giving*, not lending. You need to budget for this as an expense because you must assume you're *not* getting it back. It is a gift.

You don't need to share your gift budget up front. It's for your eyes only. But odds are, if your aunt comes in asking for $500 and you give it to her, word will get around, and you'll be fielding more requests from cousins and nephews and the rest of the family tree. Eventually, you'll hit that budgeted number. And *that's* when you lay down the law. "I am no longer in a financial position to give money."

Almost certainly, they're going to say things like, "No, no, it's a loan, I'll pay you back! I just need it until . . ." blah blah blah. But you need to stand firm. Remind them of the facts as much as you need to: you don't loan money, you only give money, and you no longer have money for giving.

Of course, it's up to you to set the boundaries of how much your budget can handle giving—it might be $100 or $1,000 or more. Just remember, you *don't* have to reveal what your number is, only that you've gone over it and there's no more to go around.

"We can reassess this once I feel more stable in my financial security."

Alternatively, you can kick the can down the road. Again, maybe you truly do want to give back to your family, but you don't want to compromise your financial life this early when you've got a lot of foundation to dig.

No problem. Coming up with a milestone after which you'll be ready to give is a great exercise for yourself in terms of goal-setting, and also gives you a quick way to press pause on the requests.

When sharing this with others, you want to hit the sweet spot between too much detail and too little: avoid specific dollar figures and try to build in some flexibility for yourself ("once my student loans are more manageable" could mean when they're fully paid off, or just when you've tackled the biggest chunk of the debt) so that they don't have room to chip away at your logic or bargain you down.

This also isn't a guarantee with a delay. You're not promising that the money will come. You're only promising to reassess—which leaves the door open to hit that milestone and *still* say no if you don't feel it's a good idea.

"I don't mix business and family."

This is a great all-purpose phrase, especially for things beyond straight-up cash transactions. Family members might ask you to cosign a loan "because I won't qualify otherwise, but I can totally make the payments" or ask to be added as an authorized user to your credit card "to help rebuild my score" or otherwise hitch your financial wagon to theirs.

You don't want to do this. Period.

We'll dig into the whys later when we talk credit scores, but the quick version is that realistically, if a person needs a cosigner, it probably means they aren't actually qualified or able to pay back the loan they want, and your cosigning is basically you, personally, getting on the hook for that entire piece of debt. Similarly, adding someone to your credit card just lets them rack up charges that *you*, ultimately, will owe on. No good.

So, again, you can lay down the law. You don't mix business and family (or business and friends). Period, full stop, end of sentence.

"I'd love to do XYZ, but I need to be transparent about my budget."

This covers everything from small-time outings (weekend trips, concert tickets) to biggies (weddings, vacations abroad). When expensive, once-in-a-lifetime stuff like this is on the table, it sucks to be in the sticky situation of having to say no, but delaying your own personal financial goals for other people's life events is not sustainable *or* fair: you shouldn't go broke just to see your friends get hitched, and no reasonable person wants their pals to empty out their savings for a girls' trip. And since talking about money is hard, we tend to just avoid it . . . and rack up debt.

Instead, we have to learn how to have some tough conversations.

If you've been asked to be in a bridal party, or your bestie is throwing a lavish destination wedding that you simply can't afford to attend, don't dodge their calls or avoid them at happy hour. Grab coffee together (or write a nice email if you're nervous) and explain that while you're honored to be invited, you need to be transparent: you're under a lot of pressure with student loans, you're saving for a down payment on a home, you've already hit your travel budget for the year, or just plain "money is tight right now." If you have a budget you *can* swing, go ahead and name that number with the clear expectation that you don't want their vision for their special day to be restricted on your account. If you're completely okay just coming as a guest, say so. And be sure to let them know you're still super stoked for them and Future Spouse—if they're truly a good friend, they'll understand.

Now, what if *you're* the bride (or groom) to be and don't want to demand your friends pony up big bucks to celebrate you? Try sending this one as an email (either bcc'd or with a link to an online survey form, so that only you can see the results):

Hey, girlies, I am so honored to have you as my bridesmaids! I'm looking forward to an amazing time with you in May. I know that bachelorette weekends can get expensive, and I want to be up-front and let you know that it's very important to me to respect your budgets. I want us all to have fun and not feel pressure to overspend—what's most important is spending time with you all.

So, if you could each please let me know how much you're comfortable spending on this weekend, I will be able to plan accordingly and make sure we can all relax and have the MOST fun. Your answer is for my eyes only, and please don't hesitate to shoot me a text or call if you have any concerns. Xoxo!

"It's my expectation to be paid back on time."

Venmo is such a blessing and a curse. It's legit, fast, and convenient, but also a very easy way to *claim* you'll hit someone back with what you owe . . . and then never do it.

Personally, I am *hardcore* when collecting on Venmo. I do not let shit slide—not because I'm greedy or mean, but because it's not healthy for relationships. It's a one-way ticket to resentment. Ideally, I have everyone square up before we even call the Uber to leave the restaurant, but if people forget, or it's a bigger group expense like an Airbnb or a rental car, I will follow up firmly but politely the day after . . . and the day after that.

Are people busy, forgetful, chaotic in general? Sure. But that doesn't mean you can't say, "Hey, Maddy, I know you're busy, but transparently, when I agreed to front the payment for the bill, it was my expectation to get paid back. Can you do that as soon as possible? I'm happy to work something out with you over time if you need to." (And if they have to pay in installments, then help them do that—ask them to send what they can afford to send today, and let you know when they think they'll have the rest so you can follow up then.)

If someone basically ghosts you, though . . . well, short of pursuing literal legal action, you're SOL. Unfortunately, the only thing you'll get from someone power fading on a debt they owe you is an expensive teachable moment for you. Hopefully it's only a small price to pay for that wisdom!

The YOU Method (aka the Only Two Things Your Budget Needs to Do)

We've covered a *lot* in this chapter. But if there's one thing I need you to remember, it's this:

There is no one single "correct" way to budget!!

I truly cannot overemphasize this point. So if you're finishing this chapter feeling like there are so many rules and you're totally lost and oh my God oh my God—please please please, don't. I know budgeting can feel overwhelming, but let me reassure you. The only best method is the one that *you* can stick to and enforce without feeling super limited.

Plus, the only way to know which method(s) will work for you is to actually try them out. Test-drive them. Live them. Because budgeting does not happen overnight. It has to happen over time. If you're too freaked out to start, you'll never learn firsthand how fantastique a budget can make your life.

In all likelihood, you're going to have to trial-and-error one or two of the budget methods I mentioned, or mix and match, or invent your own system. All good, babe! That is totally normal and part of the process. You also don't have to do it exactly perfectly every single day—if you miss the mark, take that as useful info and see what you can change up to make things easier for you. Again, budgeting happens over time, and goof-ups are a part of that.

No matter how your personal plan shapes up, remember that a budget only really needs to do two things:

1. **Leave you feeling good about what you spent your money on.** Are your basic needs met? Are you happy with the value your dollars have brought you compared to the effort you put in earning them? Are you getting in some of those nonnegotiables to actually *enjoy* your life?

2. **Ensure you have some money left over to save and invest.** A good budget isn't just about not getting yourself in debt and zeroing out at the end of every month. It's about getting to that rich-person place where your money is what's making you money. Your ideal budget doesn't just allow you to save: it gets you maximizing those savings so you put your dollars to work, rich-AF style.

Does that sound good?! Excellent—because saving is how we're going to kick off part II.

**MONEY MANAGEMENT
TO-DOS FOR CHAPTER 3**

Here's the TL;DR for budgeting: take care of these and you'll be set for success.

☐ Prepare by grabbing all my fave budgeting resources at **richAF.club.**
☐ Find all your paperwork.
☐ Put it all in one place.
☐ Audit your spending using the red, yellow, green method.
☐ Select a budgeting method to test.
☐ Ensure your budget accounts for nonnegotiables.
☐ Refine your budgeting strategy over time.
☐ Practice enforcing your budget boundaries with any friends or family you think might push back on them.

PART II

Making Your Money Work Hard for YOU

4

I TAKE CARE OF FUTURE ME

The Saving Section

To illustrate the importance of having money saved, let me tell you two stories.

First, the story of how I chopped off part of my finger with a bread knife, how it grew back, and why you should have an emergency fund.

(TW: blood, medical debt, drunken mistakes)

For my twenty-fifth birthday, I booked out a private section of a fun bar so I could drink and eat tacos with my friends. I was psyched, and I wanted to go in ready to *party*.

So, that afternoon, I took a nap (didn't wanna be sleepy at the bar), and when I woke up, I was like, "Huh, I could use a snack" (didn't wanna get too drunk too fast, tacos notwithstanding).

So I grabbed a bread roll that I had picked up from Maison Kayser that morning, and a bread knife, and I started to make a sandwich. But as I'm trying to slice this crusty roll, the knife slips.

I look down, and all I see is a little nub fall onto the white kitchen countertop.

I look at the nub. I look at my finger. I look at the nub.

And all I could say was, "Oh no—I think I need to go to the hospital."

My boyfriend SPRINGS into action and grabs a paper towel. He immediately wraps my finger and squeezes it super tight. We take the elevator down from our apartment while my man googles "nearest hospital" on his phone while carrying my nub in some Tupperware.

In the most New York thing ever, we get into a yellow taxi, take the scenic ride up Eighth Avenue, and arrive at the Mount Sinai ER, where I was HYSTERICALLY SOBBING because the shock wore off in the cab, and my finger HURT. Your fingertip has a zillion nerve endings, and all of mine were straight-up not having a good time.

Then, after the nightmare that was getting to the ER, I had to go through a full metal detector, sit in the lobby, and pretend like there wasn't blood seeping through my now fully red paper towel. (Oh, and while I was sitting there, I literally heard the PA system go, "Custodial services to the lobby" and I realized they were talking about the puddle of blood now pooling at my feet.)

Fortunately, I was able to get in front of a doctor, who shot my finger full of lidocaine, took my X-ray, and bandaged me up. I was in the hospital for six hours or so. Worst birthday ever.

The happy ending is that over the next few months, my finger somehow regenerated. (Which . . . apparently fingers do?! Who knew.)

The *not* happy ending, though? The most infuriating aspect of this entire experience?! A month later, I got sent a bill for my little birthday party at Mount Sinai.

For $16,000.

Fortunately, I had good insurance, so I personally didn't owe nearly that much. But the bill for *my* portion was still $1,300, which is a legit chunk of change.

And that is why, my friends, I always advise people to have savings and an emergency fund before they begin investing. If my money had been tied up and I didn't have $1,300 in an account that basically said IN CASE OF EMERGENCY, I wouldn't have been able to pay my medical bill in a timely manner. That could've caused me to go into medical debt, and *that* would have had a negative impact on my credit score.

Okay, let's all inhale and recover from that. Here's a much more pleasant story.

My parents recently celebrated thirty years of marriage. (Which, I don't know about you, but that's relationship goals right there.)

So, being the grown-up, money-earning, incredibly grateful daughter that I am, I decided I wanted to do something nice for them.

Flowers? A card? A nice dinner out?

Hell no. I was going to send them on a *cruise*. We're talking lap-of-luxury, all-expenses-paid, don't-lift-a-finger-for-anything kind of cruise. Because they *so* deserved it.

After a little research, I found out that a cruise for two would set me back $6,500. And since I was timing it to their anniversary, I knew exactly what my time horizon was. From there, all I had to do was set up a dedicated fund (aka savings account), nickname it PARENTAL DREAM VACATION, and regularly set aside chunks of cash at a rate that would let me hit my target amount by the time the first deposit was due.

They had a *great* time. But honestly, so did I just giving it to them. It felt huge and amazing and Adult™, and with my savings strategy, it wasn't even that hard to pull off.

I tell you these two stories not to show you the Duality of Man, Your Rich BFF–style, but because these plotlines needed *savings accounts* to get a happy (or happy-ish) ending.

Saving will save your ass when you fuck up (or life fucks you over), and it will make your dreams come true when the time is right.

Saving will give you the abundance mindset and overall chill of a rich person, and it will give you the lifestyle of a rich person with all the bells, whistles, and all-inclusive cruises your heart desires.

Basically, saving is the foundation of financial security.

No, you're not going to be able to save your way to rich. But you *can* save yourself out of a paycheck-to-paycheck cycle. And *that* is the very first step to feeling truly confident in your personal finances—and to getting you out of a lot of really desperate situations.

Because the subset of people that make the shittiest, worst decisions with their money? It's not a certain gender. It's not a certain race. It's not a certain age group.

It's people who don't have options. It's people who are *desperate*. It's like grocery shopping when you're hungry—I don't know about you, but if I walk into the store when I'm hangry, I'm walking out with Doritos and Skittles, not kale and whole grains.

By having a good amount in savings, you don't have to make decisions from a place of desperation. You get to make decisions from a place of abundance. You get to make decisions out of a place of security instead of panicky problem-solving. You know that you have enough money to cover your basic expenses, handle any surprise bills, and gradually build up the cash to buy the stuff that you want. You feel secure, stable, and generally *chill*.

But it's not just that saving protects you from risk (although it definitely does). That sense of security changes your mindset.

I talked earlier about how rich people don't buy the latest shiny stuff just to flex, and it's true. Because they have so much money, and they're financially free, and they don't owe anybody anything—rich people are, in a sense, untouchable. And because of *that*, they don't feel the need to impress anyone, especially not the "common people."

The way that rich people *do* try to out-flex each other is by buying up money-generating assets: snapping up a great deal on a distressed multi-family home to rehab and rent out, maxing out their Series I bond purchase every year, beefing up their retirement portfolio.

Compare that to the regular person. Since they can't usually afford those big asset purchases, they settle for what is considered to be an affordable luxury, spending money on a little somethin' here, a little somethin' there. They think, *I have the biggest TV, I have the newest iPhone, I have the latest pair of Nikes,* and let that temporarily boost their sense of stability—the same way a bag of Swedish Fish at the grocery store will send your blood sugar rocketing up.

But these kinds of luxury goods are ultimately liabilities—stuff that just diminishes in value over time and will eventually *cost* you money—which means that, once the luxury sports car starts making a funny sound when you brake or the phone needs to be upgraded, you've gotten only a temporary value for your money instead of a lasting one. Worse, because you've been dribbling away that money, you never got around to saving up for that larger asset purchase that could actually *make* you money.

It all comes back to the fundamental truth of rich people: when you're rich, your money works for you. When you're broke, you work for your money.

Saving for stability will make you less desperate for short-term fixes. You won't be in panic mode. You won't have to stress over your basic needs being covered.

So, now that you've gotten your spending in a good place, it's time to add some building blocks onto your financial base. Without forcing you to turn into a cheapskate or an extreme couponer, this chapter will explain why saving helps to protect current you from any money mishaps life might chuck at you. I'll cover all those important (yet often confusing things) like picking a bank, getting your accounts set up to save, and how to seize *every* opportunity for saving and getting more bang for your buck, whether that's racking up rewards on a credit card or negotiating your bills way down.

Because when you're saving, and your needs are met, and you aren't stressing constantly about your bills, then you get to graduate and do other cool financial shit, like invest, fund your retirement, buy property, and all the other things that get your money making you money—aka living like a rich person.

How to Bank Like a Rich Person

When we're talking about "saving money," we're actually talking about two different things: (1) spending less money on stuff and (2) literally putting your money away into a designated container (i.e., a bank account). Unless you're stuffing bills under a mattress and somehow paying everything in cash (or, like, the barter system???), you probably already have a bank account. But be real: Do you actually understand how your bank accounts work—or if they're even the best ones for you?

I ended up with my first bank account the way most regular middle-class-ish people do: at college orientation. Right after dumping all my worldly possessions in my dorm room, I headed to the campus gym for the new-student fair, because I heard there was free stuff, and no one loves free stuff more than a broke college freshman. After that, the first bank to wave a trinket in my face basically got my business. All ABC Bank had to do was say, "Hey, free tote bag if you open an account with us!" and I was a customer.

Yes, this was a silly reason to pick a particular bank (even though I wanted that tote bag). I didn't research, I didn't optimize, I didn't do anything but fill out a form and take my new doodads. But, like I said, I know I'm not alone here. That's just how most of us do.

Rich people, on the other hand, are engaging with banks early in life, shopping around, and building a straight-up Avengers-level team of accounts. They are shamelessly in long-term relationships with multiple financial institutions: they keep savings at Bank A for the killer high-yield savings product, but do checking with Bank B because they get unlimited ATM fee reimbursements. They know that all banks want to reward and retain their loyal customers, so they figure why not be a loyal customer of several banks so they can choose from a bunch of insider offers? (Case in point: When my fiancé and I were getting a mortgage, we had relationships with multiple different banks, so we pitted them against each other. By asking them to compete with each other's rates, we ended up getting a better deal in the end—that has saved us *thousands* over the long run.)

Why? Well, partially because rich people are entitled. But they're not entitled without good reason. While most of us are just letting ourselves be acquired as customers whenever a bank happens to leap into our frame of vision, rich people know that *they* are what makes a bank money. They know they're worth a lot to that bank. And not in a "we're all family and *truly value* our customers" way. Like, in a cold, hard cash way.

See, when you put your money into a checking account or into a savings account, it does not just sit there. It goes out and makes money. Not for you—for the bank. Here's a very simplified version of how that works.

VIVIAN: Oh, hello there, bank! Can you hold on to this
twenty thousand dollars for me?

BANK: Sure thing, Vivian! I'll even give you a few pennies for letting me use your money.

VIVIAN: Ooh, pennies! [pause] Wait, what do you mean *use* my money?

BANK: I'm lending it out, obvi. I'll give it to someone who needs a mortgage and charge *them* an interest rate of, oh, seven percent? Maybe even higher if it's a personal loan or auto loan.

VIVIAN: But that interest goes to *you*.

BANK: Uh-huh.

VIVIAN: Even though it's *my* money that you're using to lend out.

BANK: Yep. But don't worry—when you need that money, I'll give it back to you. That's literally the law.

VIVIAN: Okay. But . . . what's in it for me?

BANK: Why, those nice shiny pennies, of course! And this free tote bag.

Maybe you're reading this and thinking, *Wait, what if everyone wanted our money from the bank at once?!* Well, that'd be a *really big fucking problem*, wouldn't it? And it's exactly what happened after Black Thursday—October 24, 1929—and precipitated the Great Depression. (It's also what happened more recently when Silicon Valley Bank imploded.) Everybody saw the market start to tank, panicked, and tried to pull their money from their banks—some of which was not there due to it being loaned out—and that led to an infrastructure crash.

So, no, at any given point, the bank does *not* have the cash to pay everybody out at once. They simply have so many customers that they're able to set up a cash flow that gets everyone money when they do need it. But the best part is when you bank with a reputable financial institution, your money is FDIC insured—basically, no matter what happens to the bank, the government will make sure you get all your money back (up to a certain amount).

In other words, when you put money into a savings account, you are essentially giving the bank or credit union a loan. They will then turn around and lend that money out to people, and you better believe they're charging those people interest. Then, to pay you for parking your money there, banks (at least traditional brick-and-mortar banks) will pay you on average about 0.07 percent in interest each year—meaning if you put $100 into a savings account, after one year you'd have a balance of $100.07. And since the bank is paying you literal pennies compared to the interest rates they charge when they lend out your money, they really, *really* need you as a customer.

Think back to that tote bag: Your bank paid to have those printed up and distributed, right? They do that because the cost of that tote bag is *less* than the profit they'd make off you as a customer. That tote bag is part of the *acquisition cost*, aka what a bank pays across freebies, commercials, influencer deals, and marketing campaigns to bring in a new customer. According to research by the consumer data firm FI Works, the acquisition cost on a financial services account can be as high as five hundred bucks per customer (which is *way* higher than acquisition costs for other consumer industries, incidentally). And since it's so expensive for the bank to get you on board in the first place, it's also really expensive to *lose* you as a customer. If you move all your money to a different bank, they're going to have to replace you with someone new—and there goes another thousand bucks in customer acquisition costs.

For rich people, this dynamic is crystal clear. That's why they have no problem not only shopping around for the best accounts to use in their "team" but also leveraging their worth as a customer so that banks won't push them around. They *know* that banks rely on *them* to make money, and when banks try to wring even more fees out of them—or cheap out on interest rates, or whatever the case may be—they have zero problem pulling a *Pretty Woman* and saying, "Big mistake. Huge."

Basically, banking like a rich person means always asking "What's in it for me?"

So here are two things to keep in mind to bank like a rich person. One, banks don't want you to switch banks. They're counting on you being lazy. They know you'd rather be on your couch and scrolling on your phone than finding a bank with better rates and fewer fees, and they are *more* than okay with that. Take advantage of that and *look around*. See what other, maybe better, banks you could move your money (or some of it) to. Just like your high school boyfriend or girlfriend, that first checking account may have been convenient at the time, but there's a whole big ol' world out there.

Two, banks will do so many things for you before they let you leave. They not only *can* waive that late fee or send you a free book of checks or whatever, they will do it *happily*, because it's *good business sense*. They would rather eat that measly thirty-five bucks than have to pay hundreds of dollars to replace you with a new customer. Got an overdraft charge? Slapped with an ATM fee? Call them up and just ask for it to disappear—you'd be shocked how easy this can be.

New Banks Who Dis: Banks, Neobanks, and Credit Unions

People seriously get stressed about just picking a bank. Seriously: here's a sneak peek into some of my DMs.

> HELP!!! Which bank should I put my money in? I can't tell which is best 😫

> Maybe a stupid question but I'm worried that it's not safe to use a small local bank??? Am I better off with a national one??

> What's a credit union tho . . . . is that like a credit card

I get it: there are a *ton* of choices out there, and banks are dropping serious marketing $$$ to make sure you know about how great *their bank* is. But every bank or credit union is ultimately giving you the same product: a bucket for holding cash. Size doesn't matter, either: as long as you go with a bank that is FDIC insured (or a credit union that is NCUA insured), then your money is safe,* and you're not going to pick *wrong*.

Both banks and credit unions are essentially buckets for your cash: they're places that hold your money. And both banks and credit unions offer a variety of ~consumer financial products~, including checking and savings accounts, as well as some investment options, loans, and credit cards. The main difference between a bank and a credit union is

---

*Meaning that should the bank or credit union fail, the Federal Deposit Insurance Corporation (FDIC) or National Credit Union Administration (NCUA) will reimburse your deposits. In other words, your cash is safe and you will *not* lose your money (with limits—the amount is capped at $250,000 per person per institution for both FDIC and NCUA insurance).

that a bank is a for-profit financial institution, while a credit union is a not-for-profit institution. In other words, banks are owned by investors, and operate to make money for those investors, while credit unions aren't. But let's go in-depth on what these places actually are.

Banks come in all sizes, from relatively small and local operations to the big names in the biz that you see in Super Bowl commercials. Many banks have physical branch locations, which can be handy if you need to deposit cash, have a cashier's check issued, or get a roll of quarters for the laundry machine in your building, but some nationwide banks are online only, meaning they have no storefront locations to set foot in. Large banks often have more branches and ATMs (handy if you're taking out cash away from home) and also tend to spend more on technology, meaning they'll have significantly better mobile banking tools (for stuff like depositing checks via a photo, transferring money to and from accounts quickly, budgeting, checking your credit score via portal, etc).

Neobanks—places like Chime, Current, and Varo—are a new crop of fintech companies that have recently popped up in the United States. They offer checking and savings accounts, *but* these aren't technically banks because they don't themselves have a bank charter—those are highly regulated and hard to get. Instead, the neobank builds a platform over an existing bank's infrastructure, the actual bank holds the deposits, and the neobank pays it out of the money it gets on things like interchange fees (which a merchant pays whenever you swipe your debit card) or ATM fees (when you withdraw cash). As you can probably guess, this means those fees tend to be higher as compared to a traditional bank so that the neobank can cover overhead costs. Plus, since they're tech startups, some neobanks are skating by on venture capital from investors—only to fold once that money runs out, as happened with Azlo and Simple. For both of these reasons, neobanks are, for the time being, *not* my recommendation. There are plenty of fully chartered online-only banks that offer equally good services *and* more peace of mind (and you can find my favorites at richAF.club).

Credit unions tend to be operated in a specific, smallish local area, meaning they almost always have physical locations and tend to have lower fees and better interest rates on savings accounts and loans. They're also known for providing better customer service since they're more localized, while large national banks tend to have less flexibility to make exceptions. That said, credit unions can only operate within certain customer bases, usually geographic areas, so whatever credit union you apply to, you need to make sure you're in their "field of membership" to qualify. They also tend to be lower-priority for certain outside suppliers (like the people who make microchips—remember the Great Debit Card Shortage of 2022?), so you might be waiting a tad longer for things like new cards or checks.

Honestly, though? The best bank is whatever is easiest for you: maybe the customer service is slightly better with one, or the app is slightly less buggy with another, but it's all the same core product. Here's a list of things to consider when you're evaluating a bank or a credit union:

- What fees does this place charge? Do I have to do anything annoying to *avoid* fees (like maintain a minimum balance or get a certain number of direct deposits per month)?
- Will my bank give me free paper checks (if I need them)?
- Do I care about having a physical location I can drop by, or am I good with doing everything online?
- Is there an app? If so, is the app actually usable?
- Are there options for online bill pay (a way to send a check in the mail to utility companies, landlords, etc.)?
- Is it easy to find in-network ATMs? Even better: Will they reimburse some or all of my ATM fees each month?

Setting Up Your Checking Accounts

Okay, you've scoped out your financial institutions, you've picked some faves, and you're ready to set up your checking accounts.

Yes, accounts—plural. Here's why.

Your checking accounts are the accounts that just pay for stuff. That's it—the money is not going to sit there for very long. Your rent payment, your grocery bill, your utilities, phone, Wi-Fi, whatever—all comes out of here. (A checking account is also what you'll use to pay your credit card bill.) With multiple accounts, each designated for a particular category of spending, you can save yourself *tons* of brainpower in the day-to-day of managing your money.

For example, I have about a dozen accounts across several banks. I have an account for paying my mortgage in New York. I have an account for paying the rent on my new place in Miami. I have different accounts for paying different credit card bills. I have an account for my business that holds all my business income. I have an account for keeping petty cash available to withdraw and spend. This means that I can see at a glance how much money I have available for any particular expense just by looking at the designated account's balance. I don't have to worry about my mortgage payment and credit card autopay hitting the same day and overdrawing my account, because they're kept separate. And I'm not paying anything extra for the setup because all my banks let me open unlimited checking accounts *FO' FREE.*

But that's just the beginning, because here's where it gets extra deluxe. Your checking accounts can automatically budget for you. And this is the incredible rich-person bank hack that saves you *so* much time and hassle.

Here's how. Way back when you started your job, there was a section of the employee portal (or your new-hire paperwork) that you probably never looked at again, which basically asked, "Where do you want your direct deposit deposited?" You probably entered the info for your checking account and then forgot about it forever.

However, you can redo that direct deposit selection whenever you want. You can actually set it up so that X dollars, or even X percent, of each paycheck goes to one bank account, then another Y percent or Y dollars go to another bank account, and so on and so forth. In other words, you can make your paychecks and your checking accounts budget *for* you. Literally while you sleep.

Even better, these accounts can be all with the same institution (for simplicity) or spread across a few different banks (to nab any good perks): for example, I keep my mortgage money with the same bank that services the mortgage loan, because they offer a monthly discount for paying out of the same institution, but my other checking accounts are elsewhere. Take a look at what bonuses or goodies your fave banks offer and see where they align with how you'll use your money (for example, if you want to have an account for petty cash, you probably don't want ATM fees).

As for how many accounts to use, that's up to you and your budget setup. For example, if you're doing 50/30/20, then maybe you have three accounts, one for each of 50, 30, and 20. If you're doing zero-based, maybe you have category-based accounts for rent, food, fun, and so on. If you're trying half-payment budgeting, you can have just two, one for each half. All you have to do is spend out of those accounts for their intended purpose and you'll never "get behind" on tracking your budget progress again.

This can sound complicated, but I highly, *highly* encourage you to give multiple checking accounts a shot, no matter your budget method.

It really does help you stay organized with where your money needs to go, it gives you relationships at different banks you can leverage in the future for things like mortgages and loans, and it just gets you comfortable with being HBIC of your own financial domain. If you need a solid place to start, head on over to richAF.club for my recommendations for the best checking and savings accounts.

Setting Up Your Savings Accounts

Okay, so rinse and repeat with savings accounts, right?

Yes . . . but also no.

We've already covered why you should investigate different banks and credit unions when setting up your team of bank accounts generally. But when it comes to *savings* accounts, there's an additional consideration you want to make. Because unlike checking accounts, where the money will just hang out in relatively small amounts until it gets spent on bills and expenses, your *savings* dollars might total up to thousands upon thousands, right? And we don't just want all that savings money sitting there *not* making us money, do we? Surely that can't be the Rich AF way.

No, indeed. We want that money earning us *interest*—and we want the most interest possible. Enter: the high-yield savings account.

Traditional savings accounts—the ones you get through your standard bank or credit union—typically pay interest, but as we've seen, it's often not very much (literal pennies on the dollar, remember?). Meanwhile, high-yield savings accounts (HYSAs) are out there being like, "This could be us but you playin'." A HYSA will pay up to ten times as much as a traditional savings account in interest annually. Right now (as

I'm writing this), HYSAs are paying anywhere from 4 to 5 percent interest—so four-ish dollars on every hundred dollars saved. And four bucks can buy you, like, a whole pack of gum!

No, but seriously, those four dollars help your money compound even faster, and obviously, the interest rate being a percentage means that the more you have saved, the more you earn in interest. Easy win.

So I'm asking—nay, *begging* you to actually sit down, get out your computer, and take the time to choose HYSAs when you set up your savings account. (Seriously, I'll throw this book in park and wait until you're done.) A HYSA may not be the one thing that makes you rich, but IMO, there is no reason *not* to have one: it is probably the easiest, quickest way to put yourself on a better financial path. You will literally just put money into the account and they will pay you interest, and that is free money you didn't have before. It's very, very, very simple.

There's no need to overthink which bank you go with, either. HYSAs came about when financial institutions that have not traditionally been brick-and-mortar consumer banks—SoFi, Goldman Sachs, American Express, and Ally, to name a few—decided to offer a new generation of savings account to build up their user base. This means they're (1) willing to pay up more in exchange for parking your money there and (2) set up with the exact same rules as traditional savings accounts (like you can only make six transactions a month, for example) and are FDIC insured (so your money is safe in the event the bank fails). As a bonus, since a lot of them are digital-first, and they're catering to younger audiences who prefer to do their banking from the comfort of their cell phone, they've invested in really solid apps and tech experiences.

Choosing a HYSA means that yes, your checking accounts and your savings accounts will probably be with different financial institutions. I promise you, it's *way* less hassle than it sounds like *and* it's worth it. (Although some banks now offer both high-yield savings and high-yield checking accounts, so if one of those suits your checking account needs, go for it! I've got a list of options at richAF.club.) Even a middle-of-the-pack high-yield savings account is still *so* much better than a standard savings account, so don't stick with your regular-schmegular bank just out of convenience—you're leaving money on the table!

WHAT'S UP WITH CRYPTO "SAVINGS ACCOUNTS"?

I'm *so* glad you asked. In case the BIGGEST AIR QUOTES EVER around "savings accounts" were not a dead giveaway, these crypto "savings accounts" are *not* what they're pretending to be.

You may have seen these getting hyped on your FYP or Twitter feed, but take it from me and *proceed with caution*. These so-called crypto "savings accounts" brag that they can give you interest rates of as much as 9 percent. Compared to maybe 4 percent for a HYSA, that *would* be dope . . . *if* that 9 percent was actually interest—which it's not.

In fact, that 9 percent is actually an investment return, which means it is *not* guaranteed—unlike actual interest from an actual savings account, which is. If you look in the fine print for these crypto setups, you'll see something to the effect of "Rewards rates can vary over time and are not guaranteed," "This is not a bank account," "We are not insured by the FDIC," or "This is not a risk-free product."

Basically, don't be fooled: these crypto accounts are not protected, not guaranteed, and—unlike a HYSA—not a good place to put your emergency fund. Legit savings accounts are usually insured by the FDIC, meaning your money is federally protected against theft or if the bank goes belly-up, and these "savings accounts" are nothing more than risky investments by another (deceptive) name.

And what are your savings accounts going to save *for*, you ask? Well, just like with checking accounts, we can give every savings account we have a job. For savings, an account's job will fall into either *emergency fund* or *sinking fund* territory. An emergency fund is a savings account with money set aside for covering unforeseen, uh, emergencies (like slicing off your fingertip). A sinking fund, on the other hand, is a savings account with money set aside for specific big expenses (like a fancy cruise for Mom and Dad . . . or yourself). Let's break down both of these in depth.

Emergency Fund

The very, very first savings account I want you to build up is your emergency fund. This is priority number one. It's pretty simple and requires only a little bit of math and a smidge of discipline. You're basically just stuffing dollars in a mattress (except the mattress is a high-yield savings account) and ensuring you have the cash to handle problems down the road.

You've probably at least *heard* of emergency funds before, and now that you've heard the sad saga of the Vivian Tu Mount Sinai Twenty-Fifth Birthday Party, you can see what they come in handy for. But emergency funds aren't just for the emergency *room*.

Emergency funds are essentially a way to make sure that you have cushion in your financial life. Whether it's a tire falling off your car or your roof caving in, or your dog eating a chocolate bar, life has a way of serving up situations that make you need money that you wouldn't typically spend. By having an emergency fund in a savings account that can be accessed at any time (instead of tied up in investments), you are able to protect yourself from the financial stress of covering those emergencies.

But e-funds are not just for one-off accidents, repairs, bread-knife mishaps, etc., either. They're there to literally keep you alive if your income suddenly vanishes. Maybe you get downsized, maybe your hours get cut, maybe you unexpectedly get hurt and have to go on unpaid leave—your emergency fund will keep food in your fridge and the heat on in your house.

This means that specific amount in your emergency fund will be personal to *you*. I typically like to recommend an emergency fund that's big enough to cover at least three months, but ideally six months, of living expenses (or even nine months, if the environment is looking recession-y). You can total this up using the monthly spending you figured out in chapter 2.

Oh, and to be clear, rich people *definitely* have emergency funds. In fact, e-funds are arguably even *more* important when you're a quote-unquote rich person, because the stakes are higher. Your monthly mortgage payment is higher, you reside in a higher-cost-of-living area, your kids are in private school with major tuition, and you might even have household staff you need to pay.

Because that's the thing about emergency funds: they grow with you. They get bigger as you get older—for a few reasons. For one thing, you've developed your personal life that much more. You have a pet, a partner, a few kids, and that fund now has to cover the vet bill for when your beloved dum-dum of a cat eats a sock or when your partner gets downsized and can't help cover expenses for a while.

For another, ideally, you're just making more money as you rise up the ranks in your career over time. In either case, I recommend doing a lil true-up on your emergency fund every few years, or whenever you have a big-ish lifestyle change.

For me, I did my first true-up when I was around twenty-six and moved in with my significant other. When I first moved to New York City, I was splitting a studio with another girl—truly horrendous, *except* for the rent, which was $1,600 a month per person and therefore *awesome* for New York. So my twenty-three-year-old emergency fund was based on that housing expense, plus all my other monthly necessities. But at twenty-six, I was out of the studio and now splitting a monthly rent payment of $5,000 with my partner ($2,500 him, $2,500 me), meaning my "three months" of living expenses saved up were now a month short. No big: all I had to do was prioritize filling up that e-fund a bit more with the savings portion of my budget, and after a few months I was back where I needed to be.

Long story short, there's no "perfect" amount for an emergency fund; you just want to make sure that money can cover you in true cases of emergency and that it is actually representative of the lifestyle you're living. Basically ask yourself: *If I were to lose my job tomorrow, would this emergency fund sustain me long enough to find a new job?*

Once you have a number in mind, reaching it can be seamless. Remember the trick of sending your paycheck to be direct deposited across several different accounts? You can do that with savings accounts as well as checking accounts. (Even if you're not doing the reverse budgeting method, I still recommend getting that e-fund money out of sight, out of mind with automatic deposits.)

This can end up being *so* seamless that you literally forget about it. I told one girlfriend to set up a savings account this way, and then a full two years later, we happened to be chatting about emergency funds when she said, "Oh, shit, I need to start one of those!"

I was like, "Girl, what about that money you've been setting aside automatically? What did you think that was for?"

Sure enough, she checked and had literally thousands of dollars safe and sound. "Wow, I feel a *lot* better about myself now!" she said. "Am I secretly a saving genius?!"

Yes! Because that's really all it takes to be a genius: do the math, set up the account, and *stop thinking about it.*

Sinking Funds

If your emergency fund is for when shit hits the fan unexpectedly, a sinking fund is a savings account you'll use to pay for costs, expenses, and purchases you are planning on. You don't plan to cut off part of your finger and have to go to the hospital, but you do plan to go on vacation, have a wedding, or buy a car. In other words, sinking funds are where you stash your money for big-ticket items or expenses—things you're opting in to.

Sinking funds are the best way to pay for things that you want to buy at some point in the relatively near future, for a few reasons. First of all, breaking up the amount you need to save into smaller chunks that you contribute to monthly (or however often) helps you see that you're making progress. When I was saving up for that surprise cruise for my folks, or even for my Prada bag, I felt *way* less sticker shock because I knew the final price ahead of time (precisely) and I felt like I was always making progress toward it even though it would take me time to get all the way there.

Second of all, sinking funds truly give your dollars a job. When you know that money is sitting in a savings account specifically for the purpose of surrounding you and your spouse-to-be with gorgeous floral arrangements at your dream wedding, it's a lot easier to leave it there instead of raiding the account to pay for smaller stuff you don't actually *really* want as much. Sinking funds operate based on a value-based spending mindset and roll it into a zero-based budget approach.

The math behind sinking funds is pretty simple: how much the thing costs divided by how much time until you plan to buy the thing. For big expenses with a firm start date, like a cruise or a wedding, that time horizon will be pretty well-defined. For purchases that you can make basically whenever, like a new bag, it's up to you to pick your "deadline" and then fine-tune it based on the amount you'd need to save every month—if socking away $500 every month isn't possible right now, but $250 would be manageable, then just plan on taking twice as long to save up. Alternatively, you can work backward from how much you're able to put into a sinking fund each month, then multiply that out to figure out how long until you'll have the dollars needed to pick it up.

Besides vacations, weddings, and designer accessories, sinking funds are a great way to set money aside for Big Adult Purchases like a car or even the down payment on a home. Generally, though, I suggest you pick expenses that are coming up in the next six months to a year. Longer than that and (1) it starts to feel so far off that you lose the sense of purpose you're getting by giving your dollars a job and (2) you might be better off investing to make that money earn more money (and we'll get to that).

Beyond that, though, you can have as many sinking funds as you want. This is, again, a fantastic place to create a team of multiple savings accounts, each with its own particular job.

Negotiation:
The Platinum Way to Save

On my very first TikTok, there was one kind of response I got over and over. Message after message came in along the lines of: "Okay, definitely into this, but can you *please* promise not to yell at me for buying five-dollar coffee or the new purse I have my eye on?!"

I will promise you here what I promised all those folks back in my baby TikToker days: I won't. I would *never.* As Your Rich BFF, I *love* to talk about spending less and stacking those dollars, but I am not about to yell at you over coffee. Life is too damn short.

But I do want to help you stack those bills, and I *do* want to help you save. So make a Starbucks run real quick if you need to, and settle in.

This "stop buying coffee" advice comes from a very traditional school of savings thought: that even though a few dollars here and there is not a lot of money per se, it can and does add up over time. It's the "death by a thousand papercuts" view of saving. Going back to that daily latte example, five bucks every day for coffee works out to be a touch shy of $2,000 at the end of the year. And two G's is a lot of money! It's a modest vacation, it's a not-too-shabby wardrobe makeover, it's a dinner out every other week.

So I do kind of agree here. This school of thought basically preaches that small habitual choices add up over time, and can small cutbacks to your daily budget put you in a better financial position than you would be otherwise? Yeah, duh! But does that make any *one* small purchase inherently problematic? No. It's just that making enough of those small purchases may prevent you from making major purchases down the line—ones that are much, much more valuable to you, and more important to your life. In other words, while one five-dollar coffee is not going to be the difference between whether or not you can buy a home, a daily five-dollar coffee over the course of twelve months *could* be the difference between whether or not you get to buy a new laptop at the end of the year.

But what's more, over time, that money could have been invested in the market. It could not only have held its spending power in reserve for a bigger purchase, but also generated additional income for you. Seen from *that* angle, the opportunity cost of spending that money five bucks at a time is actually quite high: you're missing the chance to spend a larger chunk all at once, *and* you're losing out on having your money make you money.

Now, think back to asking for a raise. Remember how I said you could make $5,000 for two hours of work? Well, the same principle applies to saving money as well as earning it. That's the other school of thought on saving—the platinum mindset that rich people use *way* more than us normies.

Every expense can be negotiated.

BUT: small expenses are less worth the *effort* to negotiate.

THEREFORE: focus on bargaining down the biggest expenses in life (housing, cars, bills, etc.), and you'll save the most money for the least amount of effort.

This is very much the "don't sweat the small stuff" attitude. According to this alternative school of thought, you don't need to do that day-to-day sweating over small stuff like daily coffees, but you'd better *bring it* when you're making large purchases—because this works only if you negotiate every single time, are very aggressive in your negotiation, and end up paying as little as humanly possible for those major expenses. Since those bigger purchases have bigger price tags, even a small comedown in price makes a big difference in dollars saved.

For example, say you're an average American looking to buy the average American home. Currently, the average sale price of a home in the United States is around $350,000. If you can negotiate with the seller to get the price down just 5 percent (which is completely feasible), you're instantly saving $17,500. Get them to come down 15 percent and you've just taken $52,500 off the top. That is over $50,000 (posttax!) you've just saved. You know how many lattes you'd have to give up to save fifty thousand bucks?!*

True, not every negotiation will get you everything you want, but the only way to get *nothing* of what you want is not to negotiate at all.

Remember: you can *always ask.*

You can negotiate prices: cars, houses, secondhand furniture on Facebook Marketplace. You can negotiate fees—I negotiated a real estate broker fee down from $8,000 to zero, simply because I felt strongly that *I'm not fucking paying this.* You can negotiate any telecom bill: TV, Wi-Fi, phone. You can negotiate all of your entertainment services. You can negotiate medical bills—holy shit, *please*, especially if you're low-income, negotiate your medical bills. (Most hospitals are nonprofits, and if you make below a certain amount of money—typically a certain multiple of the poverty line, depending on where you are—you are *entitled* to get charity care, which will wipe out a percentage of your bill . . . or even the entire thing.)

You can negotiate homeowner's insurance rates, realtor's commissions, title and transfer fees—in fact, you can negotiate *anything* when it comes to buying a house: you can ask the seller to repaint a wall, you can ask them to leave some furniture or appliances or the lawnmower, you can ask for an earlier or later move-in date, you can ask for a seller's assist, you can ask for a second appraisal.

---

*Rhetorical question, but let's do the math anyway: $50,000 divided by $5 per latte = *ten thousand lattes.* That's almost *thirty years of lattes* assuming you drink one per day.

Same goes for a car: you can negotiate many, many things when it comes to buying a car, not just price, but rates, lengths of terms, warranty limits, service fees. You can negotiate with vendors who offer services, especially for big parties and events like weddings: you can compare DJs and ask them to price match, you can tell the caterer, "Hey, we don't need dessert, can we lose that and knock something off the price?"

Now, it's unfortunate and unfair that all these things that you can negotiate are not made clear, but it's for obvious reasons: the people selling you stuff don't want you to know that you can negotiate these things, because if you *did* know, then everybody would do it.

But now you *do* know what you can negotiate—and now you're going to learn how to do it.

The art of negotiation ultimately boils down to those two key components of the rich-person money-saving mindset: be entitled and take your time. In other words, remember that your business has value to this company (because they spend serious $$$ to acquire new customers, so losing you would suck) and invest a little time in doing your research (because if you're informed on what the competition offers, you're equipped with #facts).

For the negotiation process itself, I'll break down the step-by-step and include a sample script for negotiating down something probably everyone has (and everyone is paying too much for): a cell phone bill. (Cell phone companies also happen to be a lot like banks, in that their model is to spend billions annually on advertising to try and gain new customers, but then churning through them by treating them like poo. Can you hear me now?)

Step 1: Research.

Figure out what other options are out there for whatever service you're negotiating. Find comparable offers from their competitors, and write down how much they each cost and the benefits. For example, if you're currently with AT&T, do some research on similar plans that Verizon and T-Mobile are offering, and compare what they offer in terms of data, talk, text, perks, etc.

If there are no alternative services to research, or it's hard to find intel on competitors, pull together some facts about *your* value that are on your side: how long you've been a customer, how reliable you are with your payments, even how much you like being with this particular company.

Step 2: Make your initial ask.

Call up the provider and start by simply asking if there's a better offer for you.

> "Hi, I was looking at my cell phone plan and it's getting pretty expensive. Could you tell me what other plans you have that would save me money?"

They *might* immediately say yes and offer you a discount, in which case, sweet deal! Just DON'T SAY YES YET. Skip to step 5.

Chances are, though, they'll tell you there isn't much they can do for you. No sweat. Go to step 3.

Step 3: Threaten (politely) to walk away.

"Okay, in that case, I'm thinking of switching to [XYZ competitor]. Can you transfer me to your cancellation department, please?"

A lot of folks are too nervous to go through with this part, because they don't actually *want* to cancel just yet. Don't worry! If you're dealing with a major corporation, your account will never get canceled until *you* say the final word. You can negotiate for hours and walk away, and the worst case there is that you're back where you started. The secret pro tip is that as soon as you say the magic word—"cancel"—you will likely be switched to customer retention (the department that will try to, well, retain you as a customer) instead of cancellations. They're not letting you go *that* easy.

If you're dealing with an individual seller or vendor, you can soften the approach by combining step 3 and step 4, emphasizing (again, politely) that unless you get a better deal from them, you're very well aware that their competition has a better offer waiting for you.

Step 4: Play hardball.

Don't be afraid to state the facts: pull out your intel on the competition and remind them of the value they have in *you* as a reliable, loyal customer.

"Hi [customer retention person], I am happy with my service, but I need to get a better deal to stay here. [XYZ competitor] is offering a similar plan for [X dollars] less, with added benefits like

[ABC]. Your customer acquisition cost is hundreds of dollars, and I've been with you for [#] years, so what can you do to offer me this plan for a lower rate?"

Pro tip: use the "What can you do . . . ?" form of the question to get the other person thinking about possible solutions instead of defaulting to a yes/no response.

Step 5: Ask for more.

At this point, they will hopefully say, "Yes, here's what we can do," and lay out the terms for you. (If they don't, jump to step 6.)

Now, most people would stop here. HUGE MISTAKE. Thank them, but be polite and ask for a few more things. Think beyond sticker price here: lock in the offer for longer, ask for fringe benefits or perks, or bundle in another service for a below-market rate.

"Thanks, I really appreciate that. I'm almost ready to reconsider canceling, but I also don't want to agree now only for my rate to go up again in a year. Can you lock this new rate in for two full years instead?"

If they say yes, then seal the deal and be sure to get some kind of written confirmation for any "off-menu" options they've agreed to give you. It also doesn't hurt to jot down the name of the customer service agent in case you need to call back and straighten things out later.

Oh, and SAY THANK YOU. Negotiating isn't the same as "being a dick," and these people are just doing their jobs. This twenty-one-year-old on the phone is not the reason your last three calls got dropped. Their job is to keep you happy, so if they're giving you what you need, it's also cool to be a decent person, show gratitude, and take the two-question survey at the end of the call!

Optional Step 6: Don't give up.

If you run into a dead end, don't panic. First, depending on the situation, the person you're talking to may not have the authority to sign off on what you're asking for. In that case, see if you can go up the chain:

> "I understand. Is there someone else who's authorized to make this happen? I'm happy to talk with a supervisor or manager if you transfer me."

> If the answer is STILL no, then STILL don't give up—just hit pause.

> "Thanks for the explanation. I'll have to think about this before I make a final decision. I appreciate your time." [click]

Remember, when you don't get the result you want on the first try, you can always just try again. Call back another day, try another point of contact, maybe go back and do some more research too. Different customer service people will respond differently, and at the very least, with more practice, your negotiation skillz will get sharper.

You Are Literally Worth It

I still remember this one message I got when I'd just started on TikTok. The DM read: *I'd really like to find a financial planner . . . but I'm middle-class. Is there anything you can recommend?*

What struck me as so strange is how this person said *middle-class*. Like a confession, or a disclosure.

Like *middle-class* was something to be ashamed of.

I wrote her this very long note back. "You know that being middle-class is an honor, right? That you still likely have thousands of dollars to put somewhere, that you're practicing responsible spending habits, and that your business is valuable. There is no shame in being middle-class, and if any financial advisor or financial planner makes you feel less than, they are not the person you should be working with."

After that, I told her to go speed date five different planners and see who takes her seriously, who treats her right, who speaks to her like an equal. (The first consultation should always be free, btw.) But the whole experience made me realize something. People think that if they are middle-class, they are not worthy of good service, like they need to be JLo walking in with three hundred million dollars to be taken seriously.

And that's just not true.

This brings me to a core principle of rich-people saving strategy: rich people are comfortable being entitled. Sure, this sometimes means entitled in the bad way, but it's more so in the "I know my worth" sense. They're just efficient, confident, and *well* aware of their own worth. They've been shown time and time again, from childhood onward, *You are worthy, you are good, you matter.*

When you grow up hearing these things, you get the confidence of that abundance mindset. You know there is always more where that came from and that *you*, personally, can go and get it.

If this bank won't give me a good offer, I can move on to the competition.

If this hair salon screwed up my balayage, I'm going to get them to fix it or else give me a refund.

If I don't get this job, another one will come along.

More than that, the reason rich people can *act* on this entitlement like this—by following up, insisting, going up the chain of command if they have to—is that they have the time to go out of their way. They can afford to be inconvenienced, not just in terms of cash, but in terms of time and effort. They are rich in money *and* rich in time. Maybe they are making a lot of their money from investments and therefore don't *have* to be at work with their boss breathing down their neck all day, and/or they're working a prestigious white-collar job that gives them max flexibility. They can literally walk out of their office at 1:00 p.m., say, "Hey, I'm going to step out for lunch, be back whenever," and then go harass the poor customer service person at some bank to inform them in no uncertain terms, "You should *never* have charged this fee to my account, and I expect you to make it up to me."

But when you've lived life with the deck stacked against you, when you grow up in a modest middle- or working-class community, when you *don't* get that positive entitlement from pampering and a "you're worth it, babe" environment that comes with being rich, when you've never really seen anyone who looks like you succeed and make a ton of money, of course you're going to doubt your ability to do it.

And when you're a broke-slash-poor person, you are likely poor in terms of money (duh) but also probably poor in terms of time. You're chained to your job that you probably don't like for most of "business hours." You spend a good chunk of your "free" time commuting and running errands. You don't have the freedom to leave your desk at 1:00 p.m. to go argue with someone at the bank. So when that surprise fee hits . . . you'll just suck it up and pay it, because figuring out how to fight it is going to take too much time and energy that you just don't have.

Bottom line, you're not going to live in that abundance mindset, and you're not going to exercise any entitlement, because that seems like something for other people. Other people who are not like you. Who are not middle-class like you—or, for that matter, who are not a woman, a queer person, or a person of color like you.

If that's you, then let me just reiterate: you're worth it.

Especially when it comes to saving and financial services. And I want you to keep this rich-person mentality in mind. Internalize it. Own it.

Your business is worth something. It's THEIR HONOR to work with you and for you.

You are entitled to the best service possible.

Your accounts—checking, savings, credit—are your personal team of financial specialists, and they each have a unique job to do.

Because *you* are the customer. *You* are the client. *You* are what makes these places have a business model in the first place. This bank or that credit union is not doing you a favor allowing you to have an account there—you are literally giving them a near interest-free loan every time you deposit a check there.

And no matter how big or how small that deposit, your business is *not* worth nothing.

Know that, be confident in that, be *comfortable* in that.

I want to be really prescriptive here because I *know* this is hard. Whether you're actively self-advocating or even just thinking "I am worth it," you need to literally go against your gut and do something that feels so terrifying for you to get in this mindset. So, sure, it's not gonna feel normal the first time. It's not gonna feel good. It's gonna feel scary. You're probably gonna have your heart beating out of your chest and your palms super sweaty and gross.

But try to remind yourself that whether you're interviewing financial planners or applying for mortgages, it's okay to do what you're doing. You're worthy of this product and this service—you're worthy of *good* service. You can stick up for what you're entitled to and be firm, *and* you can be polite. You can go for that win-win where they get the commission, you get the interest rate, and everyone's happy. You do ten minutes of googling to find a better deal or you can literally just ask for perks or upgrades or bonuses—sometimes that's all it takes. You can remember that negotiation is an option, even for you. You can trust that there's more where that came from for you—because there is.

When you can master that mindset, you won't just be enriching your bank account. You'll be enriching your whole damn life.

And that, my friends? Absolutely priceless.

**MONEY MANAGEMENT
TO-DOS FOR CHAPTER 4**

Ready to $ave? Here's your checklist:

☐ Do research into options for banks/credit unions and compare against your current bank—are you good where you
are, or could you get more for switching? Check out **richAF
.club** for my recs and faves.

☐ Review your checking account setup and strategize how
to use multiple accounts for a no-brainer budgeting
strategy.

☐ Open a high-yield savings account (or several) for your
emergency savings and sinking funds.

☐ Determine your emergency fund amount based on your
current living expenses and map out a timeline for hitting
that target.

☐ Set up any sinking funds for big near-future purchases or
expenses.

☐ Brainstorm what upcoming expenses you can negotiate
(bills, housing costs, car purchase, etc.) and prepare your
research for the big convo.

☐ BONUS: Download the Your Rich BFF mega-list of my top
hacks, apps, and programs for getting extra cash back, extra loyalty points, and other sweet freebies at **richAF.club.**

5

I WASN'T BORN RICH, BUT MY KIDS WILL BE

The Investing Section

When it comes to investing, I have three Your Rich BFF truths to share:

One: investing might *seem* complicated, but it doesn't have to be.

Two: investing does *not* require you to be a stock market genius (and if you think you are, you're probably in deep shit).

Three: investing—not saving—is how you get rich. Because you *cannot save your way to rich.*

If you think investing's way too complicated for you, you're not alone. Seriously. I have a friend who works in private equity—so, you know, a money guy. Literally does this shit for a career. Lives in Excel spreadsheets. And he did not open a retirement investment account until he'd been working for *four years.*

When me and the rest of our friends found out, all of us were like, "What the actual fuck? You just gave money away! Like, you literally flushed money down the toilet!"

And he was just like, "IDK, it was complicated and a lot of work to set it up, so I just . . . didn't."

Now, to be crystal clear, there does *need* to be a certain amount of clunky paperwork involved in setting up your investment accounts, but on the more "we aren't taught about this in school" level of things, the world of investment accounts feels complicated because no one in charge has an incentive to make it easier. In my friend's case, the process to set up his employer-sponsored 401(k) account was such a pain in the ass that he put it off basically forever. That sucked for *him*, because he was missing out on investment returns and tax benefits, but you know who it didn't suck for?

His employer. Because his employer had a 401(k) matching program—where they'd contribute a dollar to the account for every dollar an employee contributed. So why would they *help* people like my friend figure out how to do that—or explain why it was a good idea in the first place?

And if a little paperwork and financial lingo doesn't put you off, well, maybe you think you need to be brilliant at picking stock choices to make money investing.

No no no *no*. If my experience has shown anything, it's that the opposite is true: if you *think* you're brilliant, you are probably about to *lose* money. After I worked as an intern for ten weeks on Wall Street—where I wasn't even allowed to click any buttons because I didn't have my licenses—I thought I knew everything there was to know about investing.

See, during that summer, each intern was required to do a research project on good stock picks in a specific sector, which in my case was biotech, and admittedly I was a bit stressed about defending my trade ideas. Fortunately, there was a health-care specialist on the desk who took a liking to me, and after I showed up one morning with a donut and a coffee for him—you know, just cuz—and thanked him for all his help, he just so happened to offer me thirty minutes to practice my biotech presentation with him. And after drilling it, answering all his questions, and giving one of the—if not *the*—best intern presentations that summer, I felt like hot shit. I *knew* biotech.

After my internship ended and my employment contract was terminated until after graduation, I was finally allowed to trade in my personal account. And what did I do? I put $4,000 into one of the stocks I had pitched during my presentation, because I was *so sure* of my research and investment thesis. And on top of that—the guy who knew the most about health care on the entire team told me my idea was SOLID!

And you know what happened?

The company's new, exciting flagship drug—the one that I'd done so much research into—failed phase III trials. It could not go to market. The stock absolutely tanked. I lost half of my money in one day.

I was lucky that I didn't *need* that money to survive, but as lessons go, it was still a pretty expensive one. I had literally *everything* going for me—more resources than 99.99 percent of the investing public—and I *still* picked wrong. So, learn from my mistakes: even when you think you know what you're doing, you're *so* much better off investing in a diversified portfolio than trying to be a genius stock picker.

But none of this is to scare you away from investing. Investing is *critical* to your financial success in the future.

Which brings me to truth number three: you can't save your way to rich.

Yes, budgeting and saving are integral parts of getting your financial footing. But remember, rich people aren't rich just because they earn more money than you. They aren't rich because they're "more disciplined" or "less wasteful." They are rich because they use their money to make money—they invest.

And *nothing* can work harder to earn you money than your money itself. Money doesn't need to breathe or sleep or eat donuts and drink coffee. It can be out there grinding for you 24/7 and earning at a higher rate than you can *ever* get from a savings account, with *way* less effort than burning yourself out at your job.

Investing should be a system that you can do in the background, easy peasy, and will gradually snowball you to getting richer and richer as time goes on. It really can be that simple—I guarantee that regardless of whether you are an eighteen-year-old about to head to college or a forty-year-old who feels like you need to play catch up before retirement, there is an investment strategy that you can understand, you can implement, and you can use to get where you wanna be. Even if you don't have a ton of money to start with or you don't know a stock from a bond from a mutual fund, you're gonna be fine.

This chapter's going to cover all those nuts-and-bolts basics from how to open an account to what kinds of investments to buy to what (or who??) Dow Jones actually is.

And once I show you how your money will make you money, you'll be shocked that it ever seemed so impossible. (Seriously, the math? Easier than calculus. Arguably easier than algebra. And you don't even have to do any of it yourself.)

The Only Investing Breakdown You'll Ever Need

The biggest mistake finance education makes is trying to explain one concept at a time. It's like handing you a single puzzle piece and asking you to paint the rest of the picture. I've found it's *so* much easier to zoom out and see what's on the box, and *then* break down how the pieces of the puzzle work together to build it. Once you understand the big picture, you can get started on making it work for you—but you've got to get that big picture first.

With that in mind, I present to you this proprietary, extremely official, exclusive and deluxe Your Rich BFF Investment Flowchart.

This is it: a bird's-eye view on how you should think about investing. Once you've got a handle on this big picture, I'll help you dive into pre-investing prep, setting up your accounts, and buying your investments.

WHERE DO I INVEST?

Brokerages = institutions that help you buy and sell investments. Think of them like the grocery store: they sell all the stuff you want to buy, but they aren't in charge of manufacturing the products themselves. Instead, brokerages make money by providing the service that connects you to investments, the same way your grocery store connects you to delicious food. You don't have to know the president of Nabisco to get a box of Oreos, and you don't have to be an insider to buy investments—you just need a brokerage.

IN WHAT TYPE OF ACCOUNT?

Accounts = the containers that hold all your investments. These are like the tote bag you bring to the grocery store: you enter with money in the bag and leave with it full of food.

IN WHAT INVESTMENTS?

Investments/assets = the actual "things" that go in the account and earn you returns. These are the individual grocery items—the Oreos—that you store in your tote bag.

The rest of this chapter will be expanding on and explaining allllll the terms you see here, so feel free to bookmark this page to flip back to as you read.

Investing Like a Rich Person in Six Simple Steps

If that flowchart is the rule book, then this part is the strategy. Now that you've seen the overview of the whole system, I'm going to show you how to game it—rich-person style.

Step 1: Know what investing actually is.

Nonrich folks tend to have this misconception that investing means "trading stocks." They imagine it's going to be some *Wolf of Wall Street* inferno of watching tickers go up and down all day and yelling "Buy! Sell! Buy! Sell!!!" into a phone.

Good news: nope.

At its most basic, investing is simply putting your money into something that has the potential to grow in value over time. After enough time passes, you sell it, and pocket the profit. How do you know whether something will grow in value over time? Well, you don't—not 100 percent, anyway—but if you buy the right balance of different investments, you can essentially bet on the economy, as a whole, growing over time.

And guess what? That's a really, really, *really* solid bet. There has truly never been a time where we have gone into a recession and not come out of it. Yes, there are temporary downturns, but over a long period of time, *the market recovers*. Yeah, you might buy some stocks as part

INVESTING 101

WHERE DO I INVEST?

AT A BROKERAGE

SELF-DIRECTED

Fidelity
Vanguard
Charles Schwab
Robinhood

ROBO-ADVISOR

SoFi
Wealthfront
M1
Betterment

IN WHAT TYPE OF ACCOUNT?

FOR RETIREMENT

IRA

For retirement: Money goes in tax-free. Pay taxes when it comes out.

ROTH IRA

For retirement: Pay taxes when money goes into account. Comes out tax-free.

FOR KIDDOS

529

Tax-advantaged way to save for future education costs (college).

EMPLOYER-SPECIFIC ONLY

401K/403B

Employer-sponsored retirement (think IRA, but sponsored by your job)

ROTH 401K

Employer-sponsored retirement (think Roth IRA, but sponsored by job)

HSA

Health savings account: Used for medical costs, no taxes in or out!

GENERAL INVESTING

INDIVIDUAL BROKERAGE

An account where you can invest, but no major tax benefits.

IN WHAT INVESTMENTS?

If you have no idea where to begin, pick a robo-advisor OR stick to a diversified portfolio of index funds. Also, consider a target date retirement fund (associated year should be when you turn sixty).

NOTE:
Higher Risk = higher potential to lose OR make money.

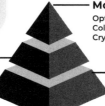

Most Risky

Options and Futures
Collectibles
Crypto

Medium Risky

ETFs/Mutual Funds
Stocks
High Yield Bonds
Real Estate

Least Risky

Government Bonds
Money Market Funds*
Certificates of Deposit (CDs)*
Cash

**Money market and CDs are basically cash that you agree to lock up for a set period of time, that earn you a slightly higher interest rate.

of your overall investment portfolio, but what you're probably picturing when you think *stock market* is *not* going to be your strategy.

Because that wild-ass stressed-out Wall Street scene you're picturing? That's *trading*, not investing. As my mentor explained it to me, when you're trading, you're in the moving business. When you're investing, you're in the storage business. Another term you may have heard of is *day trading*, which means buying and selling assets rapidly over the course of a trading day, while *investing* means buying something and holding on to it.

Rich people might buy and sell stocks, bonds, and funds and other Wall-Street-y things, but generally speaking, they are *not* day trading, which takes a lot of work and stress (both of which, need I remind you, rich people hate) and which, statistically speaking, is not a good bet (since 85 percent of day traders lose money over the long term). They are *investing*—making that bet that the economy will continue to average upward over time—and that's what you're going to do too.

Step 2: Have a stable financial foundation and budget.

As much as they love aggressive investment strategies, rich people are not going to put their asses on the line. They know that the market's gonna do what the market's gonna do, and while they know that short-term dips and drops aren't spelling doom for their long-term gains, they do *not* want that impinging on their cushy day-to-day lifestyle—in other words, they have that emergency fund ready to go.

Before you invest anything, you want to make sure you've set aside the cash to cover those three to six months of living expenses. This isn't just because there's a risk of losing money altogether once you've invested it, but because in many cases, investing will lock your money out of reach for a while—such as when you contribute to a retirement account, which you can't tap into (at least, not without a hefty penalty, or special circumstances that I'll get to later on) until you're at least 59.5 years old.

You'll also want to figure out how much money you should dedicate to investing each month: for example, if you're 50/30/20-ing it, then 20 percent of your income is going toward saving and investing, but where that 20 percent breaks down between the two is your personal judgment call, and in all likelihood you probably won't be putting that full 20 percent into investments 100 percent of the time.

That said, I want to make this crystal clear: investing is worth doing *no matter how much you're contributing*. You can't really go wrong following 50/30/20 every month, but you also can't go wrong putting in just twenty dollars every month.

That is how rich people invest. They do it no matter how much or how little they can put in. They do *not* miss a chance to toss even literal pennies into their brokerage accounts whenever possible. They're not hung up on any "you should be contributing X amount by the time you're X years old" kind of crap.

Step 3: Know your debt (and your delta).

Note that I did *not* say "pay off all your debt first." You can invest even if you have debt. Repeat: you can invest even if you have debt. Rich people certainly do.

Why? Because not all debt is created equal, and it all comes down to the *delta*.

The delta (if you don't remember from algebra class . . . or from chapter 1) is basically the difference between two rates of change. In this case, the two rates are "how fast your debt is accumulating interest" and "how fast your investments are earning you a return." If you have a positive delta—if your investment earnings are bigger than your debt interest payments—you'll *make money* over the long term. Yes, even if you're still technically "in debt." Think of it like a bucket of water with a leak in it: the water might be trickling out at the bottom drip by drip (your debt interest rate), but if you're pouring more water in from a high-powered hose (your investment returns), the bucket will still get fuller over time.

So, you *can* make money on investments while having debt *if* you can achieve that positive delta. And to do that—to keep the water level in your bucket steadily rising—you first need to know the hose rate: how fast water (aka money) will, on average, flow into your bucket (aka your investment account).

Fortunately, you don't have to guess how fast money will come into your bucket, because we have decades and decades of historical data that can show us how much, on average, the market tends to grow over time, in the form of a single handy number. That magic number? 7 percent. Seven percent is based on the average return on the S&P 500 over the past thirty years.* Why the S&P 500? Because the S&P 500 comprises the five hundred biggest companies trading stock in the United States, and is therefore considered a reliable measure of how fast the economy, overall, grows over time. How does that get us 7 percent? By calculating those five hundred companies' performance over a nice long chunk of time (like thirty years), accounting for inflation (ofc), and estimating averages on the low end of the range (just to be on the safe side), we arrive at a "hose rate" of 7 percent. In other words, some years the

---

*In other words: some years, it might have returned 25 percent, and some years it maybe returned negative 2 percent, but *on average*, over that thirty-year period, the earnings were 10 percent annually—which, when accounting for inflation, can range anywhere from about 8 to 10 percent, so 7 percent is a low-end, conservative (i.e., safer) estimate.

water (money) from your investments might trickle in around 3 percent, and other years it might dump in at 20 percent, but on average over time—because time is key!—you can reasonably count on 7 percent "inflow" per year.

Once you know how fast your metaphorical water is flowing in, you just take a look at your debts—the rate of leakage out of your bucket. You want to see which debt is losing you money *too* fast (the biggest leaks in the bucket) and which debt is trickling away slowly enough that you can more than replace it with your hose. In other words, you'll figure out which of your debts has higher than a 7 percent interest rate—and *those* are debts that you'll need to pay off before you can start investing.

Once that higher-interest debt is gone, you're in prime position for that positive delta—for your *net* rate of change (investment earnings minus debt interest payments) to be more than zero. At that point, just make the minimum payment on all your remaining debt *while also* investing and you've essentially created a money printer. The delta between those two rates is just additional money in your pocket: extra money to pay off your debt faster, or to help you invest more. Either way, extra money is a good thing.

I will say this: if your debt feels truly insurmountable, it's okay to pump the brakes on investing altogether. The mental load of debt management is real, and dealing with collections agencies or hits to your credit score are bigger priorities than investing for now. Jump ahead to the "Debt" section in chapter 6 for some strategies.

Step 4: Play by the government's rules.

Say it with me now: *rich people hate paying taxes.*

Investing like a rich person means giving the government the teeniest, tiniest percentage of your hard-earned investment returns as possible—and no, you don't have to commit tax fraud to do it, thanks to 100-percent legal tax-advantaged investment accounts. Put your invest-ment money in these bad boys and you can avoid paying taxes now, or later, or sometimes *both*.

"But wait," you might be thinking. "Isn't that basically free money? What's the catch? Why would the government *want* us to pay less taxes on something?"

Well, if you ask rich people, it's because the government sees us as a bunch of toddlers. We're stubborn, we don't listen, we need serious brib-ing to do basic self-care, and we're constantly at risk of wandering into traffic unless someone physically contains us in a playpen. When the government wants us to do something, they'll cajole us with a bribe. When the government *doesn't* want us to do something, they set up a big bad consequence.

And what does the government want us to do when we're investing? *Put money away for retirement.* Why? Well, think about it: if you stop work-ing, no longer earn an income, and have zero dollars to your name, you know who's gonna be on the hook for your food, rent, and medical costs? That's right: Uncle Sam, and he does *not* want to cut that check. No, the government would much rather you personally go HAM with saving for your golden years and retire with *plenty* of money for your arthritis meds and condo in Florida.

And since they don't trust us toddler-citizens to invest for our retire-ment *just because*, they're going to give us a bribe: a way to pay less in fed-eral taxes. The US tax code is crafted with a whole candy store's worth of tax-incentivized investment accounts. By using these special kinds of ac-counts to invest, you're agreeing to certain restrictions (as in, you can only use that money after you reach a certain age) but also stacking up deli-cious advantages (like paying less money to the government—score!).

The irony, of course, is that rich people are the least likely to actually need government assistance in retirement, and they'd *never* be so *igno-rant* and *backward* as to *neglect* saving for the long term! They don't *need* to be *incentivized*! But, like, they'll totally still take the tax break. Because free money. (That said, some tax-advantaged investment options—contributing to IRAs, for example—do have income limits and other restrictions, so it's not like the rich get a free-for-all, either.)

So, to invest like a rich person, you're going to prioritize those tax-advantaged retirement accounts first and foremost. Take that, Uncle Sam.

Step 5: Know Your goals, time horizon, and risk tolerance.

Retirement's not the *only* thing rich people are saving for, of course, tax bennies or not. They have a bunch of goals for their money, and depending what those goals are and when they want to achieve them, they'll calculate a different amount of *risk tolerance.*

It sounds complex, but we factor in our risk tolerance basically any time we have to achieve something by a certain deadline.

For example, imagine it's the day of a big gala and you *still* don't have an outfit. What do you do? Well, I don't know about you, but I am going to go to the nearest department store and picking out a classic little black dress. If there are just literal hours to go before I need to be at my event, I'm not wasting time browsing a bunch of places (because my time horizon is short) and I'm not picking something crazy or that's tailored weird (because my goal is to look nice). Sure, I could head to some hole-in-the-wall vintage stores on the day of the gala and potentially find something fabulous and one-of-a-kind, but I *also* might find absolutely nada. I don't have time for taking chances. In that down-to-the-wire moment, I'm *risk-averse.* So LBD it is.

On the other hand, if I'm just willy-nilly shopping on a Sunday in SoHo, I might go pick out a blue ostrich-feather top, because why the hell not? My goal is still to look nice, but there's no make-or-break moment I'm putting together an outfit for, so my time horizon is *much* more flexible: If I end up deciding I don't like the top, I can return it. If I end up wearing the top and loving it, I can go get another one. In this situation, I am much more *risk-tolerant*.

This example is risk tolerance in a nutshell: the sooner you need something to be accomplished, the more likely you are to choose a less risky way to get it done.

What does this mean for you and your investments? Well, when it comes to investments, generally speaking, the longer your time horizon is, the more risk-tolerant you can be. And you know what may be the *furthest* away goal, time-wise, you have right now?

Yep: retirement.

With decades to go before you'll need that money, you have plenty of time to recover if the market wobbles—so you can afford to be aggressive and tolerate more risk in your investment choices. As that time horizon shrinks and you get older, your risk tolerance will go down, and you'll rebalance your investments to something less risky (so that you aren't worried about losing the money that's going to sustain you literally until you die).

If you have shorter-term goals (like sending kids to college), that'll call for less risky investments: you still want that money to grow, but you don't have as much time to build back after a potential dip. As for *very* near-term expenses? Rich people will still invest—because, after all, *not* earning money on your money is out of the question for rich people—even when their risk tolerance is pretty damn low, and so can you. The cash you've earmarked for a new car or a wedding two years down the line can get invested in low-return, low-risk investment options with a shorter time frame. That way, the cash will be ready when you need it, plus a little extra on top.

Step 6: Just say no to YOLO and FOMO.

Last but definitely most important: rich people do not invest in random stuff just because people on the internet tell them to. Not the sickest new crypto coin and not the meme stocks that are "guaranteed to go to the moon."

Because they understand how investing works, and this ain't it.

Rich people know how the markets work.

They don't freak out over "timing" the market and buying things at the "right" millisecond, because they know that over time, it almost always tends to go up (remember that magic 7 percent number)?

They know when something's too good to be true, because value doesn't come from thin air, and a lot of those NFTs don't really . . . um . . . do anything useful.

And they know how to *wait*. They can delay gratification. They don't need to get rich quick—they want to stay rich forever.

**INVESTING LIKE A RICH PERSON:
THE TL;DR VERSION**

- Buy a diverse spread of investments that'll capture the growth of the economy overall.
- Aim for a consistent amount to invest in your budget . . . but *any* investment is good, even five bucks.

- You don't need to be debt-free to invest—just pay off all debt that's losing money to interest faster than your investments can gain it back.
- Prioritize investing in tax-advantaged accounts first
- The longer you have to invest, the more risk you can tolerate.
- Don't throw money into random internet meme-vestments, plz.

Girl, You've Got Assets: What to Buy When You Invest

Have you ever gone to a fancy restaurant for dinner and ordered something when you only half know what it is?

Like sweetbreads. *Ooh, dessert!*

Or Rocky Mountain oysters. *I mean, I love oysters, so that's* probably *fine, right?*

Then your plate gets there and surprise, surprise: turns out sweetbreads are slimy, gamey thymus-gland meat and Rocky Mountain oysters are bull testicles.

That's what can happen when you start investing. There's a ton of stuff on the menu that you've maybe *heard* of, but a little bit of knowledge can be a dangerous thing, and you can end up wasting your money on something that you actually have *zero* interest in.

So before you even break open your first brokerage account, let's slow down and see what's on the investing menu.

As we've just learned, investing is basically putting your money into something that has the potential to grow in value over time. That *something* is known as an *asset*: it's something you own that has value and can be used to make you money. Assets can be physical, like a house, a Picasso, a pile of gold bricks, etc., but they can also be intangible, like stocks, bonds, or cryptocurrency.

BUT. Just because something can technically be considered an asset doesn't mean it will automatically make you money—in other words, just because it's on the menu and *sounds* fancy doesn't mean it's a good choice. Some assets are more likely to appreciate (go up in value) over time, while others are more of a "maybe/maybe not" situation. And while different kinds of assets (aka *asset classes*) *tend* to change over time in the same ways, no one can ever 100 percent guarantee that X asset will have Y value on Z date (with, like, two exceptions—we'll get to those).

In other words, all assets are going to have risk involved (see: my baby trader story from earlier). HOWEVER. If you know what the different types of assets are, how risky they are and what *makes* them risky, you can pick the best ones for you—and start to understand what'll help you build that diversified portfolio that lets you profit on the simple prediction that "economy over time go brrrrr." So here's a list of some (but not all!) of the assets out there, in order of what you're most likely to be familiar with to the more abstract stuff you might not have encountered as much.

Luxury Assets

A Banksy painting, a Cartier ring, a Birkin bag: we casually refer to these kinds of high-end goods as "investment pieces" and *technically*, that's true: that Birkin bag is much more likely to hold on to its value over time than one from Target, and so yes, the odds of being able to resell these items at a profit is higher than for mass-produced versions.

But just because they *could* be resold doesn't mean that they *will*. The market for luxury assets is very *Project Runway*: you're either in, or you're out. Because your ability to cash in on something like a ten-carat sapphire ring or a hand-knotted Oriental rug will always be contingent on there being someone out there who wants to buy it (and wants to pay what you're asking), it's *way* riskier over the long term than more general-purpose assets. Plus, since luxury assets are just actual things, they can get lost, stolen, broken, dropped into the ocean by the old lady in *Titanic*, etc. Like, remember when Banksy sold that painting at auction and immediately had it run through a hidden shredder? The people who bought it thought they were making an investment . . . and Banksy did as Banksy does and basically bankrupted them on the spot. (JK, I doubt they spent their last dime on a painting, and I'm pretty confident someone out there would buy the shreds, but you get the point.) That's basically what can happen to any luxury asset: if your biggest "investment" is a diamond tennis bracelet, you're basically one house fire or sticky-fingered subway thief away from being financially screwed.

The Your Rich BFF stance is this: buy fancy shit because you *want* fancy shit, not because you expect to profit off of it. Nothing against luxury goods, but they aren't going to track with the overall growth of the economy (which is what we want, remember?) and they *also* can't be held in those extra-special tax-advantaged accounts (which is a bummer). Plus, since it's so hard to measure or predict the rate they'll appreciate in value, they're hard to factor into the debt-investment delta. Three strikes and you're out, buddy.

Real Estate

Real estate is like the flip side of luxury assets: not everyone needs a pair of Louboutins, but *everyone* needs a roof over their head. Owning houses, commercial buildings, or even just plain old *land* is one of the oldest investment strategies in, like, human history, simply because "space to exist and do stuff" is never not going to be something people need.

The most common version of real estate investing is one that might not even *look* like investing to you: buying a house, living there, and eventually selling it (or willing it to your kids). For generations, that has been *the* way that most middle-class folks preserve and grow wealth. As time goes on, housing prices tend to go up, and by the time you're ready to sell, your house is worth more than you paid—ta-da, profit.

The other way to use real estate as an asset is to be a landlord: to own a home, apartment complex, storefront, whatever, and charge other people to use it. This is a sweet setup because it essentially lets you double dip: not only are you holding on to the asset as it goes up in value over time, you're generating cash flow on the reg from the tenants/AirBnB guests/soybean farmers/whoever is using your property.

The beauty of real estate is that the investment almost never goes to zero—even a pile of bricks on the ground is worth something—and eventually, all real estate *tends* to appreciate. But what makes real estate a kind of supercharged asset—and why rich people *looooove* it—is that it lets you use *leverage*.

See, most property owners—even rich ones—don't pay the full value of the house up front in cash. Instead, they get a mortgage loan, where they pay a certain amount of money up front to secure the loan (most commonly thought of as the 20 percent down payment of the home price, but this can vary) and agree to pay it off over set a period of time (thirty-year mortgages are most common in the United States, but you'll also see fifteen- and twenty-five-year mortgages). With a mortgage, you can *leverage* a $60,000 cash down payment into $300,000 worth of property—and basically no other asset class has a loan setup that lets you do that.

Now, at the outset, this means taking on debt: you owe the remainder of the purchase price to the bank, plus a monthly interest charge. But if you hold on to the home long enough, the hope is that the increase in value of the home will outpace the total debt, so you still profit—and, in the meantime, you get to *use and live in the house.* Huge. And leverage works out even better with rental properties, because the rent payments from your tenants can cover your mortgage payments to your bank—so for that $60,000 down, you not only own that $300,000 asset, but your effective monthly payment is *zero* (and you maybe get to pocket a couple hundred each month too).

That said, while real estate is tried and true asset class, it's got a high-$$$ bar to entry (not just that down payment, but closing costs like taxes and fees, as well as ongoing maintenance) and it's overall just a bigger commitment (it takes longer to sell a physical house than it does to sell a share of a mutual fund, for example). So, honestly, if you're just breaking into investing, real estate is not the *first* place I'd start. If you're already considering homeownership just to, you know, have a place to live, then you can totally still pursue that, but if you've just got some cash in your monthly budget you want to start growing, you'll be better off with something you can buy in a brokerage account . . . like stocks, bonds, or funds.

Okay, I lied. There's a secret third way to invest in real estate, and it doesn't involve buying your own property: a REIT. *REIT* stands for "real estate investment trust," and it basically lets you own a piece of a bunch of different real estate properties all wrapped up into one investment product. REITs trade on stock exchanges, so you can buy and sell them the same way you would a stock, and they can be a great way to invest in real estate if you don't have a ton of money to buy a property outright (plus, they can also bundle together a variety of property types, not just residential, so you could put some of your money into apartments, shopping malls, office buildings, and more.

Stocks

Stocks allow you to own what is essentially a tiny, tiny sliver of a company. When a company is publicly traded on a stock exchange, they're basically selling up little bits of ownership stakes in the form of *shares*.

Let's think of a big, familiar company for an example—say a tech company called, uh, Banana. If you were to take every single penny of Banana's worth and compile it into a pie graph, then a share of Banana stock would be like a skinny slice of that pie. When you own that slice of the pie, you are essentially giving money to the company in exchange for the chance to participate in their success—but also potentially their downfalls. If Banana does well, and sells a bunch of new phones and earns a ton of profit, then the company pie gets more valuable, and so does your little bitty slice. You can then cash in on that success by selling your slice to someone else, or you can keep holding onto it because you think it'll go up even *more*.

But if Banana starts to falter, like their latest laptop explodes in people's faces and they're facing a giant class-action lawsuit, then their pie will suddenly be worth a lot less, and so will your slice. You *can* sell your slice, but since no one out there will pay top dollar for a piece of the exploding-laptop company, you're probably only going to get *some* of your initial investment back.

Stocks can also earn you money in the form of *dividends*, which are payments made from the company to all the shareholders on a regular basis (like every quarter). The amount you get in dividends is called the *dividend yield*, and is derived as a percentage of the value of the shares of stock. But, generally speaking, most investors make money with stocks by buying pieces of companies they expect to go up in value so they can sell the stocks for more money down the road.

But here's the thing.

When it comes to buying investments for yourself, I wouldn't recommend picking individual stocks. And I say this as someone who literally traded individual stocks on Wall Street for a living. (Do I have to tell you my sad biotech story *again*? Plz, no.)

That said, staying away from picking individual stocks isn't the same as "I'm too stupid to understand the stock market." It's actually the opposite: because you *do* understand how stocks work, you also understand that the gigantic risk of betting on just one company is way too much to bear. You can still take advantage of lower-risk ways to invest based on industries and areas of the economy you think are going to get big (and we'll talk about sector funds in a hot sec), and you can still put lots of time, thought, and energy into crafting your portfolio.

So if all this feels like I'm throwing a bucket of cold FOMO on you, I get it—but trust me, there's still plenty of hands-on investing for you to do.

Bonds

If stocks allow you to own a tiny sliver of a company and potentially make money off of its success, then bonds are you lending money to a company (or government) and making money off of them paying that debt back.

In other words, when you buy a bond, you're essentially issuing debt.

You become the bank. And you make money on that bond the same way a bank makes money when you pay it back with interest.

If you're buying a **corporate bond**, that means that you're lending money to a corporation, and the corporation will be the one paying you interest. This is less risky than buying stock in that company for the simple reason that if a company goes bankrupt, all the debtors get paid first—that's a contractual obligation. The shareholders (aka stock owners) aren't obligated to get anything.

But the cool thing about bonds is that you're not limited to buying *just* from corporations. **Government bonds** are issued by national governments as one way to raise money (because taxes can't cover everything, right?), while **municipal bonds** are issued by local governments (like cities and towns) to fund public projects like schools and highways.

The even *cooler* thing about bonds is that they have a built-in system to help you comparison shop. You know how when you're considering a new brand for your go-to mascara, you search for one of those Beautuber videos where someone has done an *exhaustive* deep dive into the ingredients, the applicator, the wearability, and whatever, so that you can decide if this is The One for you before just buying it and finding out for yourself? With bonds, you can find the *bond rating*, which is essentially a review of how risky a given bond is on a scale from AAA (v. v. low risk) to CCC (pretty high risk). The Beautubers in this case are the independent credit rating agencies, like Moody's or Standard & Poor's, who do the deep dive on all the particulars and sum it up for you in a nice little rating.

So, when you size up individual bonds, you can look at the type of bond, the rating, and the interest rate (how much money you'll be paid) to find one that fits your comfort level and earns you a return you're happy with.

That said, generally speaking, government bonds tend to be the surest bet risk-wise: they have a very high bond rating because they're backed by, well, a whole-ass government. Municipal bonds can be a great option if you like the idea of supporting your local community (slash maybe getting some local tax advantages, depending on the bond).

If you're okay with a tad more risk in your bond life, you can also take a look at **high-yield bonds**. These are issued by companies with lower credit ratings that are a bit riskier to lend to, *but*, as a result, they'll offer you a higher interest rate in return.

Because bonds are overall much less risky than other asset classes, there's basically no person that bonds *don't* make sense for—but unless you're five minutes away from retirement, you probably don't want *all* your investment money going into bonds. Yes, they're lower risk, but they're also lower *return*, and if you have a good long while for your money to grow, you're better off putting a larger chunk of your investment capital into equities with greater earning potential (and, yes, greater risk).

"But wait, Vivian," you may be saying. "Equities are stocks, right? I thought you said I *shouldn't* pick individual stocks myself? So if I'm not buying individual stocks, and I'm not going to be all bonds all the time, literally what else even *is* there?"

Friend, I am *so* glad you asked.

Funds

A fund is an asset essentially made up of little tiny pieces of *other* investments. Funds might have some stocks, some bonds, some other assets thrown in there . . . basically, if buying an individual stock or bond product is buying a box of Snickers for Halloween, investing in a fund is like buying a big multipack bag of assorted candy.

And that's what makes funds so awesome: you're diversifying your risk (buying lots of kinds of candy), but you only have to pick out *one* asset (the multipack). If Snickers don't end up being popular this year, your whole bag won't be a waste.

Now, just like there are different variety packs of candy in life, there are also different kinds of funds. There are two primary things that determine what kind of fund we're looking at. First is the obvious one, which is the contents of that variety pack: for example, an equity fund is just a basket of different stocks, while a bond fund is a basket of a bunch of bonds.

The other factor is whether a fund is an **exchange-traded fund (ETF)** or a **mutual fund**. Both ETFs and mutual funds are multipacks of investments, and they can have similar contents inside—the major difference is in how they're put together and how you buy them.

With an ETF, you invest by buying a number of shares of that fund, kind of like you do with a stock. Since *most* ETFs are pegged (aka tracked) to the performance of a particular index (like the S&P 500, NASDAQ, etc.), regional market (like the US, Asia, Latin America), or sector (like tech, energy, or real estate), they don't need a human person there to monitor them, and they trade all day just like a stock, with the price fluctuating constantly.

With mutual funds, you're investing with a minimum dollar amount—so no matter what the share price is, you have to buy in with at least X amount of money (usually a few thousand bucks). Most (but not all) are actively managed, meaning that there's a person at a desk somewhere responsible for monitoring the investments in the basket and swapping stuff in and out to try to beat the market. This means mutual funds are only priced once a day, after the market closes (and the human person monitoring is done for the day).

> ## ETFS VERSUS MUTUAL FUNDS
>
> **PROS OF ETFS**
> - Minimum investment is cheaper
> - Lower fees
> - Great for beginners with less to invest up front
>
> **PROS OF MUTUAL FUNDS**
> - Can schedule automatic investments every week/month/whatever (not possible with ETFs)
> - Includes set-it-and-forget-it target-date funds (more on this on page 212)
> - Also great for beginners who meet the minimum buy-in

Cryptocurrency

Let me say this up front: You should not put anything into crypto that you aren't willing to lose. It is not a good place to put 100 percent of your money. If you're a pretty regular-schmegular investor who isn't raking in tons of bucks at your day job, you probably have *many* more investment options to exhaust before the thought of crypto should even enter your brain. You don't get any tax breaks for buying crypto, you don't get any employer match, and unlike real estate, you can be left with zero value if your coin holdings plummet.

Now, with that out of the way: What actually *is* crypto?

Well, at its core, cryptocurrency is just virtual money. It's based on a network of computers that keeps accurate records of transactions—called a *blockchain*—which allows it to be sent in peer-to-peer transactions with no banks butting in (or charging fees).

However, while you *can* use crypto to make payments online, most people buy crypto coins not to spend them, but to hold on to them as they go up in value—in other words, as an investment. You can buy them on exchanges using either standard currency or other crypto coins—and in that sense, investing in crypto is like investing in any other asset class. But that's kind of where the similarities end.

Stocks, for example, are heavily regulated by government agencies and must follow certain rules and disclosures. Crypto, on the other hand, is largely unregulated and operates in a decentralized manner. There are no third parties in the way to charge fees, but there are *also* no third parties in the way to throw on the brakes if something fishy (or illegal) happens.

Crypto is also much more volatile than traditional asset classes. Yes, stock prices go up and down, but they rarely swing as dramatically (or as quickly) as crypto does, which makes crypto a riskier investment.

The Your Rich BFF take? Basically, it's totally possible for a healthy investment strategy to include crypto, but it should not be at the top of your priorities list for investments, and it should *definitely* not be your only asset class. I'd recommend crypto being 1 to 5 percent of your entire portfolio. And if a crypto investment seems at all fishy to you? RUN.

Brokerages and Investment Accounts

Okay, you're pumped to put your dollars to work, you've learned all about asset classes, and you've got some money you want to put into the market to make more money. But, like . . . how?

Well, if you recall the beautiful flowchart on page 168, you're going to open up an investment account, and you're going to do it at a brokerage.

A **brokerage** is a company that basically acts as a middleman to help you buy and sell investments. You'll open up an account with one of them, contribute some cash, and then pick out the investments you want to buy with that cash. Your brokerage will handle making that transaction, keeping the actual assets you've invested in (stocks, mutual funds, etc.) in your account, and tracking how much those assets go up or down in value. Your brokerage can also give you advice on what investments might be a good fit for you based on your financial goals and risk tolerance. Basically, they're where all the investment magic happens.

Traditionally, brokerages used to charge customers *commissions* on every trade they made, as well as offered a ton of services like research, access to trading ideas, and a wide variety of investment accounts to choose from. All of which was fine if you wanted those things, but otherwise just kinda made the cost of entry pretty expensive. If you were only investing small sums of money, those commissions and other costs could basically wipe out your gains.

With the introduction of no-cost brokers like Robinhood, however, those legacy firms got ~disrupted~. The new kids on the block weren't charging commissions, but were offering access to buy and sell the same things. Suddenly, average people could start investing way easier *and* cheaper, and the old guard was *shooketh*. The legacy brokerages were forced to cut their commissions to zero (so that their smaller-dollar customers wouldn't jump ship), while keeping the benefits they previously offered (so their big-boy investors wouldn't make a stink).

So the TL;DR on brokerages is that you can now pay Spirit prices and get first-class service. There's basically no reason you should be paying money to make a trade anymore—and if you're not paying for trades anywhere, you might as well put your money where you can get access to the most resources and tools to help you learn. That said, I don't want you to get paralysis by analysis—there's no such thing as the best brokerage, only the best brokerage for *you*, so poke around on their user interfaces, apps, and websites, and just pick the one that you feel most comfortable navigating. And if you'd like my recommendations, or don't know where to start, head to richAF.club and take my handy-dandy Which Brokerage Should I Use? quiz.

Once you're signed up with a brokerage, you're going to open up an **investment account**, and that's probably where you're going to be hit with all this nonsense: 401(k). 403(b). IRA. HSA.

If reading that list makes you go OMG WTF, then *welcome*. I don't know a single person who looks at the alphabet soup of investment account options and instantly is like, "Ah, yes, these make complete and utter sense and are named exactly for what they are and do." But it's also not *that* complicated once you get down to what these all actually mean.

First off—again—all the fancy numbers and acronyms up there are just different kinds of *investment accounts*. If your investments (your assets) are your wallet, phone, lip gloss, water bottle, etc., then your investment *account* is the tote bag that holds them all in one place.

Second, each kind of account serves a slightly different purpose and has slightly different advantages—again, kind of like tote bags. Like, yes, a cute cotton tote from an indie bookstore and an ugly reusable grocery bag both *technically* hold things in them, but only one of them is a reasonable swap-in for a purse, right? You know which one to grab depending on what you're planning to do with that bag.

And how do you do that? Welp, each kind of investment account is used for a specific purpose, scenario, or type of person, and I'mma outline the benefits of each.

This is far from an exhaustive list—but these are some of the *most* common options that will be available to and make sense for beginner investors. And with that in mind, everyone can get some kind of tax break by investing for retirement, so everyone should have a retirement investment account. Period. (Remember how the government will basically bribe you with lower taxes if you're a responsible little citizen and invest money for when you're older? Yeah, that's this!) The kinds of retirement account you personally can open will depend on a few factors, specifically whether your employer offers retirement accounts (more on that in a sec), but at a minimum you should be eligible for an individual retirement account.

So, with that in mind, let's run down these bad boys. (For accounts that are tax-advantaged, you'll see the money emoji next to the name.)

401(k) and 403(b)

401(k)s and 403(b)s are investment accounts you get through your employer and use to save money (and grow your money) for retirement. The major difference between the two is that 401(k)s are available to employees of private companies, and 403(b)s are for public-sector or nonprofit employees like teachers, government workers, and so on. (The letter-number names come from the parts of the US tax code that governs how these accounts are administered.)

If your employer offers one of these, you should *absolutely* have one.

First off, these accounts save you money. The way it works is that all your contributions to your 401(k) or 403(b) are made *pretax*. Those dollars can go directly from your employer to your investment account, and they *won't* count as money you earned for the year—meaning you're paying taxes on less money overall, and therefore landing a smaller tax bill at the end of the year.

Granted, this comes with a few slight catches. You can't withdraw from your 401(k)/403(b) until age 59.5 without paying a steep penalty—that's the government's way of saying *no touchy*. And you can't just dump *all* your money in every year (the government still wants you paying *some* taxes, after all): there's an annual contribution limit of $22,500 (the limit as of 2023; the limit often increases annually to keep up with the cost of living). But as we'll see, compared to other tax-incentivized accounts, that limit is *preeeeetty* high.

But the tax savings are just the beginning. 401(k)s and 403(b)s have the potential to be the *best* type of retirement accounts, thanks to two little words: *employer matching*, aka *free money*.

Here's how employer matching works. Say you make $100,000 a year, and your company offers a dollar-for-dollar 401(k) match on any contributions you make, capped to 6 percent of your salary (this is what my employer gave at my first job, FWIW). That means if you put 6 percent of your salary—so $6,000—away in your 401(k), at the end of the year, your account will have your 6 percent contribution *plus* a matching amount from your employer—so $12,000 total.

That's a 100-percent risk-free return before you've even invested a penny, and *that* is hard to beat.

Employer matching came about as a way to hit the sweet spot in retirement benefits for employees. Quick history lesson: back in the day, companies used to give out pensions and pay for *everything* for their employees once they retired. But it wasn't really working out for the companies, because they were bearing all the risk for paying that out (and if one VP lives to 105, they could be on the hook for a *lot* of hefty pension payments). Gradually, more and more companies were like, "Hey, what if we had our *employees* take most of the risk? They're the ones retiring, after all!" and switched to 401(k)s, where the burden is on *you* to take action and contribute. But, because they (and the government) are still trying to incentivize you to save for retirement, companies will typically give you some free money to put in that investment account in the form of an employer match.

Granted, not every employer offers matching contributions (and some employers still offer pensions!) but even if yours doesn't match, you can still get that tax break. Plus, 401(k)s and 403(b)s are generally protected from creditors in case you find yourself in some kind of financial hot water, and some company plans allow you to take a loan out from your retirement investment account under certain circumstances (such as buying a house), which will be penalty-free as long as you repay it within a set time frame.

The other thing to know about 401(k)s and 403(b)s is that, when it comes time to fill this kind of tote bag—aka invest the money you contributed—you'll be limited in your options. Again, this is a way to incentivize Good Choices: because these investment accounts are designed, regulated, and administered with an eye toward *getting people to retire comfortably*, it's in no one's best interest (least of all yours) to be able to chuck the money at whatever super-risky investment you feel like and potentially lose all of your money. Going back to our tote bag metaphor, think of these accounts as big grocery bags that you can fill up to the brim—but only with decently healthy food. (And employer match is like buy one get one free!)

Practically speaking, this means that you typically won't be able to do things like buy individual stocks or trade options in your 401(k)/403(b). Instead, you'll most likely be picking from a prospectus—basically a menu of all your investment options—that your company provides. (I highly suggest, if you have a 401(k) or 403(b), digging up that prospectus to reference when we get to talking types of funds in the next section. That will help you understand what's best for *you* to pick!)

BUT I'M A FREELANCER . . .

If you're a freelancer or self-employed and all this talk of "employer-sponsored" this and "matching funds" that has you bummed out, HOLD THAT THOUGHT.

Did you know that you can actually set up your own 401(k) *and* put away more money than your traditionally employed friends?!

It's true! A *solo* or *individual 401(k)* is a special type of retirement account for self-employed people or small-business owners who don't have any employees besides themselves or their spouse. It works pretty much the same as a regular 401(k) that you might get through your employer, but since *you're* the boss, you can contribute both as an employer *and* an employee, up to a total of $66,000 (for 2023). Which is . . . ridiculous and amazing?!

You can open a solo 401(k) (see page 207) with many online brokerages. You'll need to have an employer identification number (EIN) for your business to do so, so if you don't already have an official business entity (like an LLC or a DBA), you'll need to set one up, which will cost a little money—but given how huge that contribution cap is, it might be well worth the effort to be able to live like a "boss" (hehe, get it) in retirement.

Traditional and Roth IRAs

Let's start with that acronym: IRA stands for "individual retirement account."

Individual means that unlike 401(k)s and 403(b)s, IRAs aren't sponsored by an employer: you're the HBIC here, so you're the one

opening the account, contributing the dollars, and choosing the investments.

Retirement means . . . uh, retirement. Like when you're old and not
working. And account is account. So, ta-da?

Seriously, though, IRAs are accounts specifically intended to stash
and grow your money for when you retire. Like 401(k)s and 403(b)s,
there's a yearly contribution limit ($6,500 as of this writing, with a
"catch-up" contribution limit of $7,500 if you're over fifty years old) and
you can't withdraw your earnings from an IRA until you reach age
59.5—or, rather, you *can* withdraw those earnings, but you'll pay capital
gains tax on that money, and an early withdrawal penalty to boot. Remember how the government taxes stuff it doesn't want you doing? It
super does not want you touching this money until It's Your Time. But
by the same token, you also get a tax advantage to sweeten the deal . . .
and that's where we get to this traditional versus Roth situation.

There are two flavors of tax advantage you can choose between when
opening one of these accounts: traditional and Roth. I like to explain the
difference using a universally relatable metaphor: pizza.

Your traditional IRA is like a pepperoni jalapeño slice. It's going to be
so delicious when you eat it, amazing and enjoyable from the very first
bite . . . but it might be a little, um, spicy coming out. (As in when you
poop. Just to be clear.) That's because a traditional IRA lets you take
advantage of all the amazing tax benefits up front. The amount you
contribute to a traditional IRA is deducted from your taxable income
for the year you make those contributions. So, for a very simplified example, if you make $70,000 this year but put $6,500 into a traditional
IRA, your taxable income would go down to $63,500 ($70,000 − $6,500).
Less income counted = less money paid to the IRS.

That said, the tax benefits of traditional IRAs do have some limits and restrictions . . . and here they are.

- If you're a single filer (i.e., not married or head of household) with a modified AGI of less than $73,000,* or married with a total modified AGI of less than $116,000, you can deduct the full amount you contribute to your traditional IRA, up to the contribution limit for that year.
- If you're a single filer with a modified AGI of more than $73,000, but less than $83,000, or married with a modified AGI of more than $116,000, but less than $136,000, you can deduct some of your traditional IRA contributions.
- If you're single with a modified AGI north of $83,000, or married with a modified AGI north of $136,000, you can't deduct any traditional IRA contributions.
- HOWEVER. If you (and your spouse, if you're married) don't have the option of an employer-sponsored retirement plan (like a 401(k)), then you're exempt from these income limits and there is no phase out. You can deduct all your traditional IRA contributions up to the contribution limit for the year.

So no matter what, you're going to need to know your individual situation to figure out what works best for you. (Sorry it's so annoying but, uh . . . welcome to the US tax code!)

---

*All numbers shown for 2023. Visit irs.gov and search for "IRA deduction limits" to get the latest figures.

However, you *will* pay taxes on the money earned by the investments in your traditional IRA—you'll just do it later on. You'll pay income taxes on your withdrawals (aka when you start taking distributions from the account in retirement), so that's when things get spicy.

A Roth IRA, by contrast, is like a slice of veggie pizza. It's a healthy, nutritious choice right now that maybe isn't as bursting with deliciousness, but will come out *much* easier when the time comes (if you know what I mean . . . apologies because I am taking this metaphor *way* too far.) With a Roth IRA, you don't get to deduct your contributions from your income this year and save on taxes today. *But*, when you start taking distributions from the account in retirement, those distributions will be 100 percent tax-free, baby.

For whatever reason, people tend to get hung up on the word *Roth*, but it's just a fancy way of saying "you pay taxes now, not later." (It's also the name of the guy who invented it, not an acronym for anything, FYI.) So even if you don't remember all of these different definitions, if you can tattoo it on your brain that "Roth = tax at the front, not at the end," you're good as far as retirement account wisdom goes. (401(k)s can also come in Roth varieties, too–whether or not you have access to one will depend on your employer.)

The other thing to know about Roth IRAs is that in addition to an annual contribution limit, they also have an *income* limit—basically, if you make over a certain amount of $$$ annually, you're not eligible to contribute to a Roth IRA.

> When you hear "income limit," rich people hear "loop-hole," and Roth IRAs are no exception. Even if you earn over the income limit, there is something called a back-door Roth IRA (not as gross as it sounds, I swear), which

is basically just a fancy workaround to get money into that pay-NO-tax-later account. It works like this: every year, I contribute posttax dollars to a traditional IRA. I do *not* invest this money, but instead, as soon as it hits the traditional IRA, I roll over the funds to my Roth IRA. Since I contributed posttax instead of pretax dollars, I pay no additional taxes.

So aside from making you want pizza real bad rn (just me?), what does this all *mean?* A traditional type of account may make sense for you if you make more money now, and think you'll make less money closer to retirement: it makes more sense to take advantage of that up-front tax break when your taxes are likely to be higher relative to your income, aka when you earn more money. If the opposite is true—that you think you'll be earning *more* money when you retire than you are now—a Roth type account may make sense for you, because you'll get to skip paying taxes on your distributions when your tax rate is relatively higher.

Obviously, you can't just know which of these will be the case for you. None of us can just be like, "Yes, I'm def going to be rich later!" and pick a flavor of IRA with 100 percent confidence based on that one factor alone. There are lots of other factors that might influence which one you pick—for example, reducing your taxable income with a traditional IRA might make sense if you're on an income-based student loan repayment plan and you want to get your annual income as small as possible to reduce your monthly payments, or if you're on health insurance under the ACA and want to maximize the premium credit you get.

IMO, at the end of the day, the decision between a traditional account or a Roth account is not going to make or break you. What I *do* know is that if you don't use either, you are *way* more likely to stay broke. So don't sweat it so much that you don't do *anything*—it's better just to pick one and get started.

> "But Viv, I already have a 401(k) through work—do I *also* need an IRA?" *Great* question. The short answer is that you *can* have both an IRA and a 401(k), but there's an order of operations to maximize your take: namely, if you have a 401(k) through your job *and* your employer offers matching funds, you should prioritize putting your investment dollars toward getting that max match *first*—because that's free money, baby—and *then* branch out to an IRA. **For a more in-depth step-by-step of the order of operations, check out the chart on page 206.**

Health Savings Accounts (HSAs)

Are you ready for the CROWN JEWEL of the tax-advantaged investing world? Allow me to introduce you to Health Savings Accounts, or HSAs.

Yes, you heard me right. Technically, yes, an HSA is part of your health benefit package, and its stated primary purpose is to help you pay for medical costs. It is, in short, an *account* to *save* for *health* spending. But nevertheless, they are a fantastic way to cover medical costs tax-free *and* can be used as an awesome retirement savings vehicle.

> Because acronyms are the worst, it's super easy to mix up an HSA (health savings account) with an FSA (flexible spending account), either of which might be of-

fered to you depending on your health insurance options. Here's the diff: FSAs can save you a lil bit on taxes, but they are *not* investment accounts. They're a chunk of change you can set aside at the beginning of the year (pretax!) and spend on qualified health expenses over the course of that year . . . and only that year. After that—*poof*, the money is gone. So FSA money = use it or lose it, can't be invested. HSA money = yours forever *and* investable. Hope that clears things up!

To qualify for an HSA, you need to be over eighteen and be covered by a qualifying high-deductible health plan (or HDHP). That HDHP has to be your *only* medical insurance, and you also can't be claimed as a dependent on anyone else's taxes (like your parents'). With that HDHP as your only health insurance, you'll become eligible to fund money into an HSA. (Even better, a lot of times your employer will also match your HSA contributions, either as a lump sum up or as a percentage of your contributions).

Now, all your contributions to that HSA account will be made tax-free, which is nice enough in and of itself—every dollar you contribute lowers the annual income that you report to the IRS, which means you'll owe them less money in April. But this is what makes this account special is that once you get to a certain threshold of dollars in that account, you can start investing them. This means you're not just socking away money like you would in a sinking fund: you can actually let your money grow in that HSA. And while it's growing, it's growing *tax-free*.

Of course, you may need to withdraw money from that HSA to pay for a medical expense, and if you do, no sweat—that withdrawal is *also tax-free*. But if you end up not using it for medical expenses right away, it'll just keep on growing and growing and growing. If you can manage to hang on to it until you're older (and are likely to have more medical expenses), then you could actually end up paying for those costs with purely investment returns—dollars that *your* dollars earned just by hanging out and going to work in investments.

This is what makes HSAs the crème de la crème of retirement investment accounts. HSAs are a triple threat of tax advantages: you put money into the account pretax, the money grows tax-free, and you can withdraw from it at any point to pay medical expenses . . . and that's *also* tax-free.

But here's the really big kicker. Even if you're maxed out on contributions to your retirement accounts (like an IRA or 401(k)), you can *still* contribute to your HSA—because it is, after all, *technically* a health savings account, not a retirement account, and has its own contribution limit (in 2023, that's $3,650 for individuals, plus an extra $1,000 if you're fifty-five or older). But that extra few thousand you can put into your HSA can effectively be retirement savings too: if you don't end up using that money for medical expenses, you can take withdrawals and distributions out starting at age sixty-five for *anything*—not just medical costs—and just pay regular income taxes on it.

To be clear, HSAs aren't for everyone: not every insurer and employer offers an HDHP option, and if you have lots of medical expenses and need Cadillac health insurance coverage, a high-deductible plan is likely going to cost you more (or make you put off getting the care you need), neither of which is worth getting an investment return (because your health is an investment too!). But if your employer offers one, and you're cool with a high-deductible plan, HSAs can be huge for growing your wealth long-term. (Why is one of the best investment vehicles out there tied to health care, which is tied to employment? IDK, AMERICA.)

Individual Brokerage Account

Sadly, not *every* kind of investment account has a tax benefit to it, but that doesn't mean you have to just stop there: if you've invested as much as possible in your tax-advantaged accounts, you can still open an individual account for all the rest of your investment $$$—and that's what an individual brokerage account is for.

If traditional and Roth IRAs are the pepperoni jalapeño slices and veggie slices of the investment account world, then an individual brokerage account is the cheese slice.

It's pretty good. It's great, even. (Because, you know, it's pizza.)

Is it the *best* piece of pizza you ever had? Probably not.

Is it the worst? Definitely not.

Is it still worth having? If you're still hungry—then hell yeah.

Individual brokerage accounts are pretty simple. These are your standard retail investment accounts that you'd get by signing up with a brokerage like SoFi, Fidelity, Vanguard, or Charles Schwab. Anybody can get an individual brokerage account. Anybody can have it. There are no tax benefits to be had, but there are also no limits—no limits on how much money you can put in every year, no limits on how much you earn in order to qualify, and no restrictions on what kinds of actual investments are allowed to be held in this account. While you definitely want to prioritize your retirement accounts first (because tax bennies), there ain't nothing wrong with grabbing a slice of cheesy goodness if you're still hungry (aka you still have money available to invest). Individual brokerage accounts can and do help grow your wealth.

How to Invest,
the Your Rich BFF Way

Okay. You understand what brokerages are, what the different kinds of investment accounts (aka the tote bags) are for, and the various kinds of assets you can buy and throw in there.

Now it's time to *literally actually invest*. It's time to Buy a Thing and put it in your tote bag. Are you pumped?! I'm going to walk you through e-v-e-r-y step of the way.

Step 1: Look at your budget.

We've gotta start somewhere, and that's with the actual cash. Revisit your budget and look at your saving/investing category—again, make sure your emergency fund is taken care of first—and make sure you've got some money that you can afford to invest.

Ideally, you'd be able to invest all of this category in your budget, but there might be some sinking funds that you need to beef up in the short term (saving for a wedding or an already booked vacation, for example), so crunch those numbers real quick so you know what you're realistically able to contribute. That's the amount that you'll set up to automatically transfer into your investment account every month.

Step 2: Sign up with a brokerage, open your investment accounts, and fund them.

Now you're going to find a place for that budgeted investment $$$ to go.

For your employer-sponsored accounts, you are stuck with whichever brokerage firm is contracted to handle your company's employee accounts, so that's taken care of for you. (But honestly, this can be great: it saves time and cuts out any decision fatigue or analysis paralysis.) Otherwise, do your research and find one that suits you and makes sense—keeping in mind that most of them offer *verrrry* similar products in the end.

Signing up is almost exactly the same process as signing up for a bank account. You'll fill out some paperwork (or online forms), give them your SSN and contact info and the whole bit, and link a bank account that you'll use to contribute funds. With that, you'll set up a login account (as in, username/password combo) and you're all set to open up whatever investment accounts you desire.

As with bank accounts, you not only *can* have more than one investment account, but you should. I talked earlier about how all the different account types serve different purposes, and while there is no one "best" combination account for everyone, when it comes to *funding* those accounts and investing those dollars, there is an order of operations that is the most *efficient* for maximizing tax benefits: Basically, you want to prioritize accounts that give you the biggest tax benefit (and/or employer match) first.

In practice, this means you'll contribute your monthly budgeted investment dollars to one account at a time, starting with the one that gets you the most in tax breaks and employer match. When you hit the limit on that account, you move down to the next account on the list and start filling that one up. From there, just rinse and repeat. By doing this, you'll make sure you're not leaving any free money on the table *and* get the maximum possible tax benefits for your investing.

And fortunately, I have a handy step-by-step guide to help you do it.

There are two versions: one if you have access to employer-sponsored retirement accounts (Checklist A) and one if you don't (Checklist B). Start at the top and then work your way down, choosing the columns that apply to you as you go and following the checklist beneath it.

CHECKLIST A:
If Your Employer Offers a 401(k) or 403(b)

Set up your employer-sponsored account and fund it until you hit your company's match limit.

... AND YOU HAVE AN HDHP/HSA		... AND YOU DON'T HAVE AN HDHP/HSA	
IF YOU EARN LESS THAN $153,000* ANNUALLY	**IF YOU EARN MORE THAN $153,000 ANNUALLY**	**IF YOU EARN LESS THAN $153,000 ANNUALLY**	**IF YOU EARN MORE THAN $153,000 ANNUALLY**
Fund your health savings account up to the federal limit. Once you hit the $1,000 investing minimum, begin allocating to investments. ↓ Open a Roth IRA, fund it to the federal limit, and allocate to investments. ↓ Fund your 401(k)/403(b) to the federal limit and allocate to investments.	Fund your health savings account up to the federal limit. Once you hit the $1,000 investing minimum, begin allocating to investments. ↓ Open a traditional IRA, fund it to the federal limit, and allocate to investments (and consider rolling into a backdoor Roth IRA—consult with your brokerage for more details on how to get this process in motion). ↓ Fund your 401(k)/403(b) to the federal limit and allocate to investments.	Open a Roth IRA, fund it to the federal limit, and allocate to investments. ↓ Fund your 401(k)/403(b) to the federal limit and allocate to investments.	Open a traditional IRA, fund it to the federal limit, and allocate to investments (and consider rolling into a backdoor Roth IRA—consult with your brokerage for more details on how to get this process in motion). ↓ Fund your 401(k)/403(b) to the federal limit and allocate to investments.

WITH ANY REMAINING INVESTING DOLLARS BUDGETED FOR THE YEAR
Open an individual brokerage account, fund it through the end of the year, and allocate to investments.

OPTIONAL: IF YOU'RE PLANNING ON KIDS AND WANT TO SAVE FOR THEIR EDUCATION
Consider opening a 529 account, funding it, and investing the money. While there are no federal tax benefits, many states offer incentives!

---

*The $153,000 figure is for single filers in tax year 2023, but if you're filing jointly (or as a head of household) or in a different tax year, this number will vary. Consult irs.gov for the latest figures for your situation and tax year.

CHECKLIST B:
If You Don't Have an Employer-Sponsored Account

YOU WORK FOR YOU*		YOU WORK FOR SOMEONE ELSE	
...AND YOU EARN LESS THAN $153,000†ANNUALLY	**...AND YOU EARN MORE THAN $153,000 ANNUALLY**	**...AND YOU EARN LESS THAN $153,000 ANNUALLY**	**...AND YOU EARN MORE THAN $153,000 ANNUALLY**
Open a solo 401(k), fund it to the federal limit, and allocate to investments.	Open a solo 401(k), fund it to the federal limit, and allocate to investments.	Open a Roth IRA, fund it to the federal limit, and allocate to investments.	Open a traditional IRA, fund it to the federal limit, and allocate to investments (and consider rolling into a backdoor Roth IRA—consult with your brokerage for more details on how to get this process in motion).
↓	↓		
Open a SEP IRA,‡ fund it to the federal limit, and allocate to investments.	Open a SEP IRA, fund it to the federal limit, and allocate to investments.		
↓	↓		
Open a Roth IRA, fund it to the federal limit, and allocate to investments.	Open a traditional IRA, fund it to the federal limit, and allocate to investments (and consider rolling into a backdoor Roth IRA—consult with your brokerage for more details on how to get this process in motion).		

WITH ANY REMAINING INVESTING DOLLARS BUDGETED FOR THE YEAR...
Open an individual brokerage account, fund it through the end of the year, and allocate to investments.

OPTIONAL: IF YOU'RE PLANNING ON KIDS AND WANT TO SAVE FOR THEIR EDUCATION
Consider opening a 529 account, funding it, and investing the money. While there are no federal tax benefits, many states offer incentives!

---

*This checklist works best for freelancers and sole proprietors. If you are a small-business owner with multiple employees, this process gets a lot more complicated, so if that's you, I highly recommend you speak to a financial professional (check chapter 6 for tips on finding one) about including retirement benefits as part of your employment package!

†The $153,000 figure is for single filers in tax year 2023, but if you're filing jointly (or as a head of household) or in a different tax year, this number will vary. Consult irs.gov for the latest figures for your situation and tax year.

‡A special kind of IRA available to self-employed people who do not have an employer-sponsored retirement account: it has higher contribution limits than standard IRAs, but does not prevent you from having your own personal IRA as well.

Remember, as soon as you've transferred funds into an investment account, go allocate that money to investments. Even if you're still working up to hitting the max, you don't want your money just sitting in the account—you want to buy assets!

Step 3: Pick out your investments and buy.

Time to put your money where your brokerage account is and start investing in those assets!

There are three basic approaches to asset allocation, aka picking what investments to buy, depending on how much you want to DIY. You can think of them like a salon mani, nail wraps, and painting your nails yourself: all three options can leave you looking bangin', so the real question is, what *process* is best for you—how much time do you want to spend on this, how interested are you in learning all the ins and outs?

> If you're investing in your employer-sponsored account, you will almost certainly have a limited range of options. (You can't, for example, buy individual stocks in almost any 401(k) account . . . which, given the risk, is probably a good thing.) You'll want to get ahold of your retirement plan's *prospectus*, which is a list of available investment options, and read it over to see what's on the menu.

THE SALON MANICURE: Financial Advisors

At a salon, you are in good hands—literally. It's the most expensive option, but you're going to get the spa experience in exchange, and professional-grade tools, skills, and attention lavished on your look.

So if you want a pro to handle all of the messy work of your investing life, good news—that's what a financial advisor does.

Well, that, and charge a bunch of money.

Okay, I'm not *anti*–financial advisor (in fact, there are some good reasons to hire one, as we'll get to in chapter 6), but they are *not* cheap. If you're just starting out and your net worth isn't that high yet, I don't necessarily recommend hiring a financial advisor right up front. (TL;DR, if you don't have a seven-figure net worth yet, I personally don't think you're going to get enough bang for your buck.) Seriously, just by virtue of having finished almost all of this chapter, you now know *so* much of what financial advisors try to teach beginners (go you!). Plus, independent financial advisors can leverage such high fees that any gains you make on your investments will get wiped right back out, so . . . sort of pointless.

Some brokerages (like Vanguard) will offer financial advisory services for a certain percentage of what you have invested with them, and while that's cheaper than finding and hiring someone on your own . . . well, it will depend on *your* individual scenario, of course, but from what I've seen, they don't go much deeper or more personal in customizing your options than a DIY option like a target-date fund does. (They do make the fees higher, though!)

The one exception that might be worth looking into is if you're able to consult (or just chat) with a financial advisor who works with your employer-sponsored retirement account. If there's anything you don't understand about how your company's 401(k) system works, what investments are available, or even what makes sense for you personally, then it's worth seeing if there's someone available to talk to you—and this should typically be made available to you for free.

THE NAIL-WRAP OPTION: **Robo-Advisors**

With nail wraps, you don't have to worry about much: the colors won't smear, you won't flood your cuticles, and you won't smudge your look when you go to sleep. You're not getting that professional touch, but you're saving majorly, and they're almost entirely foolproof.

That's basically a robo-advisor for you. Robo-advisors are online platforms offered through your brokerage that use computer algorithms to analyze your financial situation and automatically recommend the investments and allocations that are best for you. They're simple, completely legit, and an amazing way to get tailor-made investments in your account without having to do any of the heavy lifting yourself. Not all brokerages offer robo-advisors, but many of the major ones do (and if this is the option you think you'll go for, then be sure that your brokerage of choice has these when you sign up).

A robo-advisor will start by giving you a quiz to figure out a picture of you, your life, and your goals (with questions like "How old are you?" and "How much money do you make?" and "When do you want to retire?"), and with that picture they determine a risk tolerance. Then, based on that risk tolerance, they make investment decisions on your behalf. You give them the money and they automagically divvy it up into stocks, bonds, mutual funds, or whatever combination of investments they've calculated make sense for you.

And what's *extra* wonderful about robo-advisors is that they will never forget about you. They'll periodically bug you to fill out a questionnaire every so often so that their picture of you is as up-to-date as possible. As you get older, or as things in your life change, your robo-advisor can rebalance your portfolio accordingly.

Brokerages with robo-advisor platforms do charge a management fee for using the service (0.25 percent is usually pretty standard). That's much less than a human flesh-and-blood advisor would cost (about 1 to 1.25 percent), but also more than just doing it yourself (free). (You can also head to richAF.club to find my favorite robo-advisor recommendation!)

THE PAINT-IT-YOURSELF: Self-Directed Portfolios

Painting your own nails *can* be risky (you might spill that whole bottle of OPI on your carpet) and it *can* take a while to get the hang of (it takes practice to get your dominant hand not looking super janky, right?), but it's ultimately doable and not *too* hard to learn.

Same goes for picking your own assets. If you've been following along so far this chapter and picking up what I'm putting down, there is *very* little chance of you completely exploding your entire financial life (because you're not going to dump all your money into a meme stock, right?).

That said, it doesn't have to be all-or-nothing. You can have most of your investments managed by a robo-advisor or through your employer's program *and* have a separate brokerage account where you invest a few bucks a month in a self-directed portfolio. As you feel more confident, you can keep going—or call it quits.

When you buy individual assets, you'll look them up using a symbol of a few letters—this is true for ETFs and mutual funds as well as stocks!—which you can also use to research the makeup of the assets ahead of time on websites like Yahoo! Finance. You'll log in to your online portal with the brokerage and select how much you want (either in shares, for a stock or an ETF, or in dollar amounts, for a mutual fund), and the brokerage will take it from there.

"But *what should I buy, Vivian?*!" Okay, deep breaths! Here are two solid options for beginner investors that give you a sensible place to start investigating.

- **Target-date fund:** Probably my number-one pick for a self-directed account when you're just starting out, these guys are an incredibly beginner-friendly option for buying your first shares of something, while still knowing that you're making a solid choice. Target-date funds are mutual funds that are regularly rebalanced to a mix of stocks, bonds, and other assets tailored to someone retiring in a given year. To find *your* target-date fund, first off, calculate what year you'll turn sixty—that's your target date. Next, log in to your brokerage and search "target-date fund" and look for the one with your target date (or the closest one to your target date—if you're equally distant between two, just pick whichever one: the difference won't be big enough to really matter). Some target-date funds do have minimum investment amounts, so check with your brokerage to see if that's the case.

- **Index fund:** If you've scrolled through #richtok, you've probably heard index funds mentioned more than a few times . . . and you're probably like, "Okay, I get that they're a good idea or whatever, but WHY. WHAT IS THIS WITCHCRAFT." So here goes: an *index* is just where certain companies' stocks trade: things you've heard of like NASDAQ, the S&P 500, and the Dow Jones Industrial Average. An index *fund* is a basket of investments that replicates all the companies in a particular index. So, if you've got an index fund based on the S&P 500, that'll be a basket full of bits of those 500 companies. The index fund then acts like an annoying little brother and copycats whatever the index does: if big bro S&P 500 goes up, lil bro index fund will go up. S&P goes down? Index fund will go down.

This makes index funds, generally speaking, pretty good long-term investments, especially for beginners, because they're an easy way to bet that the largest and most influential companies within our economy will go up over time. What you *won't* get, compared to target-date funds, is that age-specific asset allocation—and the copycat action of index funds is less optimal when the economy, um, *temporarily* tanks. (Remember 2008? March 2020?) Index funds are available as mutual funds and as ETFs. Many index funds can be purchased as fractional shares (with less money overall) if you want too.

Now, if all that made you super nervous, don't be! Take a deep breath and remember that a robo-advisor is always an option.

Step 4: Wait and watch.

Everyone's favorite part of investing—waiting. But seriously, you don't have to monitor these things like a hawk. It's fine (and a good idea) to pop in every so often and see how your investments are doing, but mostly so that *you* get comfortable with using your brokerage platform and seeing the (very normal) ups and downs that your investments will take. What you *don't* want to do is see a dip, panic, and pull all your money out of investment accounts entirely. Temporary dips—even bigger "market corrections"—are going to happen, and you are going to have to be mentally ready in order to stick this out for the long term. Remember, you have a diversified portfolio, not 100 percent of your money in Shitcoin or Beanie Babies Incorporated. You're betting on the *overall economy*, and sometimes the economy takes a lil spill. And so long as you're doing that, you're in good shape: In fact, according to a recent market simulation study by NerdWallet, if you invest in a fund that simply tracks the growth of the economy (such as an index fund), you have a 99 percent chance of at *least* keeping your initial investment over forty years, and a 95 percent chance of *tripling* that initial investment.

You might have heard people buzzing about *market corrections* when stocks take a dip—that just refers to a rapid change in the price of a specific security or index. There's actually not one specific definition for a correction, but generally you'll hear a decline of 10 percent or more in the price of a stock or index referred to as one. Corrections can last between a few days to months, or even longer. And while they can be scary, corrections are also a healthy part of the financial ecosystem: they help adjust asset prices from getting *too* overvalued, which keeps us out of bubble territory (aka the moment of major hype preceding a crash).

**MONEY MANAGEMENT
TO-DOS FOR CHAPTER 5**

☐ Review your budget and make sure your emergency fund is solid and you have accounted for investing $$$ as part of your budget plan.

☐ Find out what investment account options are available at your employer ASAP. Enroll and set up your accounts if you haven't yet. Figure out what the annual match (if any) is.

☐ Map out your investing plan based on the Your Rich BFF checklist and start funding your accounts. Go to **richAF .club** for my recommendations on brokerages and robo-advisors.

☐ Make sure your investment dollars are allocated into assets. (Pick investments to buy, or use a robo-advisor.)

☐ Sit back and observe! Over the next few weeks, check in on your investments and see what they do. Remember, do *not* panic if the line does not go up right away—dips and market corrections happen. If you've allocated wisely, you have very little to worry about long-term.

6

I AM READY FOR
FINANCIAL DOMINATION

When I first moved to NYC, I was twenty-two, fresh out of school, single and ready to ~mingle~. So, naturally, I spent a decent amount of my free time dating. One night, I ended up on a date with this one guy, and it was going pretty well—like, not love-at-first-sight level, but not fake-a-phone-call-to-escape level, either. He was cute enough, the drinks were good, it wasn't a total waste of an evening.

Now, I couldn't help but notice that homeboy was dressed *up*: we're talking Rolex, Ferragamo loafers, Hermès tie. And I was kind of surprised, because he was around my age, and he'd said he worked on Wall Street. Of course, I, too, worked on Wall Street at that point—which meant I had a rough understanding of what he was probably making. And it was not Ferragamo-and-Hermès money. At least, *I* was not making that much money: I was splitting a 600-square-foot studio apartment with another girl to save on rent and still buying those cheap drugstore pantyhose. So, you know, maybe a little sus.

See, I've talked a lot in this book about all the stuff rich people do to get rich, get rich-*er*, and stay rich. But I want to be absolutely clear: being rich doesn't automatically make you good at money. In fact, some rich people? Terrible with money. And I didn't quite appreciate how true this was until I started hanging around them.

Like on this date.

As it turned out, this dude spent the rest of the evening talking about how he just traveled to Mykonos, how he bought himself this Rolex with his bonus, blah blah blah. You know—tacky. I was kind of losing interest. But somewhere between tequila shot six and seven, he let it slip.

HE HAD FIVE-FIGURE CREDIT CARD DEBT.

Yes. My drunk ass almost fell on the floor when I heard that. Like, SIR—YOU ARE WEARING YOUR DEBT ALL AT ONCE RIGHT NOW. I'M LOOKING AT IT. YOU ARE A WALKING BILLBOARD FOR BAD DECISIONS.

Needless to say, there was not a second date. (Hot take, but if someone's finances and financial goals don't jibe with yours, that's a big red flag.)

My lil outing with Wish.com Chuck Bass here just goes to show that even people who work in finance, even people who are literally born rich (because did I mention this guy's dad was a big-time CEO too?), aren't always good with their own money. This guy was about as one-percent-y as it gets, and yet he still didn't understand why it might be a bad idea to rack up thousands on a credit card he had no way of paying back on time.

Understanding the fundamentals of earning, budgeting, saving, and investing is all well and good. But there's also some next-level shit that you need to get in order to truly achieve financial domination. Things like credit, debt, and even taxes can all be used to your advantage *if* you know how they work—or screw you right over if you wing it.

Luckily, you've got a Rich BFF ready to show you allll the ropes. This chapter is all about that more meta stuff that comes with money: borrowing it, paying it back, giving the government its cut (sob sob), and making those big financial plans that'll let you do exactly what you want with your life.

(Unless that involves going into debt for designer loafers. Can't help you there, bro.)

Cash versus Debit versus Credit: When to Spend with Which

What's the difference between cash, a debit card, and a credit card?

I know, it sounds like the setup to a dad joke. But it's a legit question, right? Why *do* we have these so many forms of money to use, anyway? Does it really make a difference to pay with a wad of bills versus an AmEx? If a credit card is swiped in an empty forest, *does it make a sound?*

Okay, we're not in a freshman philosophy seminar, but still. There are pros and cons to each of these methods of paying for things, and knowing the difference will seriously level up your ability to spend wisely.

Cash

Generally, I am very anti-cash.

One, there's no protection. If you have twenty dollars in your pocket, and you trip and the twenty dollars falls out on the sidewalk, well, that's not your twenty dollars anymore. The next person who walks by? It's their money now. Don't really love that for you.

Two, it's really easy to spend cash. It's not going to show up on a statement except as "ATM withdrawal," so you can easily get into this weird headspace of lying to yourself because *Future Me will never know, ha ha ha!*

Three, you're not getting anything for spending cash. You don't get credit card rewards. You're not getting bonus points. You're not getting cash back.

So there you go. Unless you're just trying to pick up a Gatorade from the neighborhood bodega, I just see no reason to be using cash.

THAT SAID.

There are certain perks to using cash. A lot of places—restaurants, salons, other service providers—provide a discount for paying in cash, and that discount may be worth more than the amount you would make in rewards from a credit card. That's a very case-by-case basis, but if it makes sense, then it makes sense.

Other places have a minimum spend for credit card purchases, or are straight-up cash only. Not my fave, but if you truly just want *one* bodega Gatorade and not *five*, then you're better off paying in folding money.

Finally, cash is king for tips. Unfortunately, credit card tips don't always make it back to the service industry folks in charge of your order, for whatever reason, and if you like the peace of mind knowing that your awesome waitress gets all of the $$$ you're tipping her, you're better off handing her a twenty.

All things considered, the best strategy for cash is to withdraw it only when you know you'll need it for something specific, so you're not tempted to spend it freely (or lose track of it). Personally, I get out cash to pay my housekeeper and my lash technician, but that's pretty much it—for everything else, there's a credit card.

Debit Cards

Your debit card is directly linked to your checking account. It allows you to spend the money in that account either by swiping the card at a merchant or by withdrawing cash out of your bank for no fee, or getting cash out of an ATM for a small fee.

And that should be its primary purpose in your life: getting you cash.

Yes, your debit card might be emblazoned with a Visa or Mastercard logo, and yes, you can swipe it at the register or punch the number in online just like it's a credit card.

But I seriously don't recommend it. Too often, people tend to think of debit cards and credit cards as "basically the same thing," but that's just not true. They don't see the point in having a credit card because they already have a debit card, and that lets them swipe for stuff instead of using cash, and isn't that the point?

Noooooo. No no no. Buying with a debit card is the same as buying with cash: you're not getting anything for it. If you're already handing over a card or typing in a number, why not use a credit card and earn something in return?

Also, as with cash, there's no protection. But in the case of debit cards, that lack of protection is actually potentially much worse than the finders-keepers nature of cash. If you drop twenty bucks, you've just lost twenty bucks—that's it. If you drop your debit card, you've potentially lost everything in your bank account. Whoever finds it can swipe and tap and order on Amazon to their heart's content until you realize and have the bank freeze the card.

And, unlike with a credit card, that money is likely *not* coming back.

This is where debit and credit cards really diverge. A debit card is access to your money. A credit card is access to a financial institution's money. With a credit card, you're basically spending the bank's money for a month, and then a month later they'll say, "Hey, we lent you this money a month ago, so pay up," and you replenish their coffers with your credit card payment.

Now, if your debit card gets stolen, that thief is spending your money, and you're fucked. The bank is going to say NMPYP—not my problem, your problem. Think about it: if it's your money that gets stolen, your bank is not that incentivized to help you get it back. Of course they'll freeze the card, but other than that, they're just like, "Oh, sorry, that really sucks for you!" They're like a friend patiently listening to your story about a terrible Tinder date: there's nothing they can do to fix it, and they're really just replying to be polite.

But if your *credit* card gets stolen and spent on, that person is spending the bank's money. And when a thief is spending the bank's money, the bank is *very* incentivized to get that money back. They will call merchants. They will scan security cameras. They will figure out who is using that card and go full Liam Neeson to track them down. They'll also close the card right away and make sure that those charges are taken off, because since you reported it right away, they know it isn't you, and you're not liable to pay up. (Similarly, if you buy something with a credit card and it never shows up? You can issue a chargeback, get a refund, and make your bank argue with the merchant about why it never arrived. Debit card? You're just going to eat the cost.)

So not using your debit card for everything is just thinking about where incentives lie, recognizing your value as a customer, and knowing that you can tap into those private security forces that will be *on the case* if your card gets stolen.

The one other thing to keep a debit card on hand for is verifying your identity at a physical branch of your bank: if you need to go in for any reason, the teller can just ask for the debit card linked to your checking account and instantly pull up your profile.

But besides that and cash withdrawals, there really isn't any other reason to use a debit card on the reg. For all those checking accounts I have, I keep one (1) debit card in my wallet, and that is the one that I pay no ATM fees on.

Credit Cards

I think everyone should have a credit card.

At their most basic, credit cards let you purchase something now and not have to pay for it until later. Instead of drawing the money directly from your checking account, like a debit card, a credit card essentially fronts the money to the merchant on your behalf, then sends *you* a bill later in the month.

So that's pretty convenient to start, right? But there's so much more to credit cards than just an IOU.

Credit cards offer fraud protection, so they'll make you whole if someone steals your Visa and goes on a shopping spree at Walmart. They'll let you earn you perks like travel points and cash back, so you can get free shit dot com for zero extra effort. They help you build your credit score, so you can qualify for better terms on things like mortgages and auto loans down the road.

Basically, they take something you're doing anyway—spending money—and give you something extra in return.

Which basically makes credit cards the greatest thing ever . . . IF you understand how they work.

See, credit card companies aren't fronting you cash out of the goodness of their hearts. They want to make money, and they have three ways of doing it. One, they might charge an annual fee for the privilege of holding that card (usually if it's one with a lot of perks). Two, they make money off of charging merchants interchange fees: whenever you swipe your card, the store is paying a 1.5 to 3.5 percent fee to process the credit card payment, which goes right back to the CC company. And three, they make money from people carrying a balance.

Remember my broke-little-rich-boy date and his five-figure credit card debt? People like him represent a major source of revenue for these companies. They use a credit card to buy stuff they can't pay back by the bill due date. Instead, they just make the minimum payment each month—whatever the card company asks for to keep the card open, usually *far* less than the total balance. Whatever's left over after that drop in the bucket payment rolls into next month—with interest. Sometimes *hella* interest. And when you focus on just that minimum payment, it's easy not to realize how much the APR (the annual percentage rate, which is how the card company will determine how much to lump on to your total every statement period) is jacking up your total debt month after month. This means my rich-broke date and people like him are not only still on the hook for their initial shopping charges, they're paying for what they bought *and* for the fact that they didn't pay it off right away (aka interest).

Good news for the credit card companies. Bad news for Prince Alarming and his Rolex.

The thing is, though, that situation is completely avoidable. If you know the rules your credit card has, you can not only play safely within them, but beat those suckers at their own game.

Because you know who credit card companies *don't* make money off of? Rich people.

Rich people know how to use credit cards so that they can not only avoid getting dinged with interest charges, but they can actually *profit*. They know if they play their cards right (lol), they can get much more value in rewards—in the form of cash back, luxury perks like hotel status and airport lounges, and other freebies—even if they're paying a three- or four-figure annual fee. And all they have to do is simply use their credit card regularly and pay it off in full every balance period. That's it. They aren't shook by cards with massively high APRs because they know that when you pay the bill in full, the interest rate has literally zero effect on you.

> The other thing about paying off a credit card correctly is knowing the difference between the statement closing date and balance due date—which most people don't. Every month, your credit card will issue you a statement of all your purchases, ending on the statement closing date. The balance due date (or payment due date) usually falls about twenty-one to twenty-five days *after* that statement closing date. So if your statement closing date is May 21, your balance due date would be on or around June 18. This means that in order to avoid getting charged interest, all your purchases incurred from April 22 to May 21 must be paid off by June 18.

So that's why credit cards are the best thing ever. Learn the rules, don't break them, and you can make the money you're *already* spending work for you. Whatever expenses you put on your credit card should have a dollar in your checking account already assigned to cover it, and then the credit card statement should be paid off on time. That's how you hit that sweet spot between "earning rewards" and "avoiding interest payments"—and score stuff like resort stays, travel insurance, and first-class tickets to St. Tropez along the way.

FINDING THE BEST CREDIT CARD FOR YOU

Yes, we'd all love to be able to pop a shiny new Centurion Card in our wallets, but unless your first name is Jay and your last name is Z, you're not going to get a one just by asking. For one thing, credit cards are something you need to *apply* and *be approved* for (if not hand-picked for, like that schmancy black AmEx), and for another, just because a card is fancy doesn't mean it's best for *you*. Here's some cost-benefit analysis you'll want to do when sizing up your options.

- **What's the rewards system like?** The simplest reward setup is **cash back**: a certain percentage of whatever you spend is credited back to your account every X months. Next are **points**, which are earned at different rates depending on the card and the purchase, and can be redeemed for things like travel or purchases. **Perks** are things you can't "spend" per se, but still have value—stuff like waived DoorDash fees, hotel status upgrades, exclusive discounts or other benefits (like travel insurance in case your flight home for Christmas gets canceled . . . again). Make sure you understand how each potential card's setup works—rewards are worth zero if you can't figure out how to use them.
- **Where do you spend money?** Cards will often offer different amounts of points or cash back for different purchase categories (like dining, gas, groceries, travel, etc.). If you don't own a car, then 5 percent back on gas is probably useless for you . . . but if you charge a lot of reimbursable work travel on your own credit card, then 3 percent back on airline tickets could be sweet.
- **If you get points from a card, *where* can you use them?** The more partner programs (frequent flyer, hotel loyalty, etc.) you can transfer to, the more options you'll have (*espe-*

cially if your card issuer offers periodic transfer bonuses that throw in a few extra points when you transfer out). If you're locked into spending *just* at Amazon or Target, you've got not only fewer options to spend on, but fewer chances to get mega-huge-outsized value for your points. For example, 85,000 AmEx Membership Reward points might get you just $850 in cash back, but transferred out to Air France's frequent flyer program, those 85,000 points can score you a *$5,000* business-class ticket to Paris if you time it right. Champagne, anyone?!

- **What kind of rewards would you *actually use*?** Take a realistic look at your lifestyle (your lifestyle *right now*) and see where and when those bonuses (like subscription credits, free memberships, cash back, etc.) might take a bite out of your existing expenses. Also be sure to note how those credits are issued. Are they use-it-or-lose-it once per month, or counted up over the year? Are they subject to additional approval?

- **What about APR?** Trick question!!! When people ask me "Viv, what's a good APR on a credit card?" my answer is basically "There's no such thing." Remember, you're paying this card off in full every month, so the APR will not matter. You're just gonna spend responsibly like you always do, pay your statement in full on time, and hop on that next flight to France.

- **Want to know my favorite credit card picks?** Meet me at richAF.club and I'll give you all the options I love.

Finally, there is one last aspect of credit-card-having to discuss here: your credit score. Remember how credit cards are basically you using the bank's money? Well, the bank has to deem you worthy of using its money before it turns you loose to buy stuff. And it's not going to trust just *anyone*. It's like when a girlfriend of yours is going to a black-tie wedding and asks to borrow a dress from your closet: are you automatically going to give her the nicest gown you own, the one you absolutely love and would cost a fortune to replace?

No, right? Because it depends on how much you *trust* this particular girlfriend of yours.

If you've been friends since, like, Girl Scout camp, and remember that she won a merit badge for "tidiest tent," you probably trust her to take good care of your dress and probably even get it dry-cleaned after. If she's a newer, more casual friend you don't *really* know that well, maybe you'll lend her that nice, replaceable dress you got on sale so that you won't lose sleep over if she never gives it back. And if you met her in college when you were holding her hair so she could barf up a Long Island iced tea . . . maybe you don't risk giving her anything.

The same is true for financial institutions giving out loans or lines of credit. The more trustworthy they find you, the higher a spending limit or the bigger a loan they'll be comfortable giving you. And *that's* what your credit score represents—and what the next section is all about.

"Wait, don't banks, credit card companies, and mortgage lenders make money off interest, fees, and penalties? Why do they *want* me to pay back on time if they get more money when I'm flaky?" Good question—but fees and interest are only going to provide income for lenders up to a point. If you're rock-bottom broke and have zero dollars, they're not getting paid no matter what. Sure, they can make your financial life hell by sending you to collections or to court, but you could default on your debt, claim bankruptcy, and never pay it back—which is their biggest nightmare.

Credit Score Goals

The biggest mistake I ever made with my first credit card? It wasn't overspending. It wasn't losing it and having some rando max out my limit on Amazon.

It was CLOSING THE ACCOUNT.

Why? A little thing called *my credit score.*

Your credit score is a number from 300 to 850 that essentially grades you on how "creditworthy" you are as a consumer. It's the "how likely are you to pay back debt" score, so the higher the credit score, the better you'll be to potential lenders—basically, it's a grade, but for real life.

Now, in my defense, I thought I was being responsible. My thinking was somewhere along the lines of *Something something it's bad to have too many outstanding lines of credit something.* I had certainly heard this piece of wisdom from more than one "financial guru": I'd been in the workforce for a few years, I was finally making some real money, I had gotten some more "elite" credit cards, and when I looked at the entry-level card I had gotten at the end of college, I just figured, *Eh, I don't need this anymore.* Basically, I thought what I was doing was total A+ student behavior.

But that starter card also happened to be my *oldest* credit card. And what I failed to realize in that moment is that one of the things I was being graded on was my *credit history*—aka how many years I'd been a solid, reliable credit card owner making regular payments in full. When I canceled that card—*poof.* My credit history was cut in half, from eight years to four. It was the equivalent of writing the world's best term paper only to delete the first half of it off my hard drive forever—doesn't matter that I *did the work*, because I didn't have the proof anymore.

This whoopsie dropped my credit score a full sixty points, and the only thing I could do was wait and keep on top of my payments. At the time, I was royally pissed (okay, ngl, I'm still *slightly* pissed) but in hindsight, if I had actually known what credit scores were (beyond just some random number), I probably could've saved myself a lot of stress.

So please: learn from my mistakes, and learn what the hell this real-life grade is all about.

Why are credit scores even a thing?

No one likes being graded, but credit scores do have a purpose.

As we saw in the last section, credit scores are how credit card companies will determine whether you're worthy of a Super Mega Diamond Elite card, or if you're more of a Super-Simple Cash Back kinda person. Same goes for things like mortgages, car loans, or even leasing an apartment. And given that our economy is now a literal worldwide web of banks, lenders, and consumers, a numerical score is kinda the only practical way to do this.

See, back in the day, when banks were small-town affairs and everything was old-timey, lenders could rely on knowing who you were, knowing your family, and knowing that your barrel-making shop or whatever was doing pretty steady business and decide that you were loan-worthy. But nowadays, lenders need something less based on village gossip and more based on facts. (This means that the credit score *itself* is actually pretty modern: the first standardized credit scores came about in 1956, and the system we use today has only been in play since 1989.) For all their issues (and we'll get to those), the number grades of modern credit scores solve that problem.

Now, you may ask: "Okay, so they're grades . . . but I don't remember taking a test??? Was I supposed to apply for something?"

Nope. Broadly speaking, everyone who has a social security number in the United States is eligible to have a credit score. There are three major credit bureaus in charge of credit scores—Equifax, Experian, and TransUnion—who do all the collecting, analyzing, and providing lenders information about consumer credit. Whenever you first take on credit, or are somehow associated with debt or loans, you'll start getting graded by these guys (technically, credit "score" is a misnomer and you have multiple "credit scores," one from each credit bureau, but because all three bureaus are drawing on the same information about you, they'll usually fall within a relatively similar range).

Until you do that, however, you won't have a credit score. And, unfortunately, *no* credit score can be just as tough as a *bad* credit score, because until you've proven you're good at paying things back, the creditors have nothing to go on.

This is one place where rich people *love* to work the system. What savvy rich parents do is put their child on their credit card as an authorized user, meaning their kid's social security number is associated with that line of credit. Even if the kid doesn't do any of the buying or repaying, as long as those parents pay their credit card bill on time, the kiddo will be recorded as a Responsible Credit-Using Person. The more time passes, the longer the kid's *credit history* gets, and the more their score goes up. They get an A+ without even having to study.

For those who *weren't* born to ultra savvy parents, though, we're talking basically starting from square one. That's why it's so important to understand what's on these invisible tests that are grading your credit and what the best possible grades are.

How are credit scores calculated?

The credit bureaus are looking at five major factors when they score you—you can think of these like a class syllabus that lays out which assignments count the most toward your semester grade:

1. Payment history (35 percent of your score): Basically, how often have you paid on time? The more, the better.

2. Credit utilization (30 percent of score): This is evaluating how much you owe, but grading it on a curve. It's not the flat dollar amount that counts, it's how much of what's *available* to you that you've used that matters—the percentage, in other words, which is your credit utilization. So if you have a credit card with a $10,000 limit, and you owe $2,000 on it, your credit utilization is 20 percent.

3. Length of credit history (15 percent of score): How long have you had your current lines of credit? The longer that history, the less risky you're considered, because there's more data to show your payment history.

4. Types of credit (10 percent of score): There are different kinds of credit out there, and lenders like to know that you can handle every variety. This looks at the mix between your installment (your mortgage or car loan), revolving (your credit card), and open credit (a charge card like the AmEx, where you need to pay the full balance each month) and grades you on how well-balanced the mix is.

5. New credit (10 percent of score): This grades you on how often you're applying for and opening new lines of credit. Frequently asking for more loans can be a red flag ("Why does this b keep needing more money?? She broke???"). This is also known as the number of recent credit inquiries, or "hard pulls," on your credit score.

What's a good credit score, and what's *my* credit score?

As for the actual A, B, C, D, E, and F breakdowns, the overall range of credit scores goes from 300 to 850.

Unfortunately, unlike letter grades, the threshold to "pass" is a lot higher than just "not getting an F." Even though 300 is the minimum, once you hit 500 or lower, you're much more likely to be refused point-blank for any loans or credit. To get the best terms on any money you may need to borrow, you're going to want a score in the Very Good or Excellent category—what constitutes "good" (or "good enough") will vary from lender to lender.

That said, the general breakdown is usually this:

- 800–850: Excellent
- 740–799: Very Good
- 670–739: Good
- 580–669: Fair
- 300–579: Poor

To check your score, you can go to AnnualCreditReport.com once per year for a free credit report (including the score, as well as the de-tailed reporting that went into your scoring) that won't count as a "hard inquiry." If you discover you're at the bottom of the class, *don't freak out.* Just like with school grades, you can do makeup work and do some extra-credit assignments to bring your grade up. With time and some smart money moves, credit scores are very fixable.

(Also, I am begging you—learn from my mistakes. Don't get rid of your starter credit card!!! I don't care if it's the rinkiest, dinkiest card giving you negative one points for every dollar you spend—don't close it. You can always look into upgrading it to a fancier card you'll use more, or downgrading it if there's an annual fee you don't wanna pay anymore, just DO. NOT. CLOSE. IT. Thank you for coming to my Ted Talk.)

Extra Credit: Five Tips for Acing Your Credit Score

1. **Make payments on time.** For any loans, credit card statements, car notes, or other lines of credit you have, don't miss payments—even by a day, and even if you can only swing the minimum. If you're a bit of a space cadet with deadlines, then keep a cash cushion in your bill-pay checking account and set your bills to auto pay every month. And if you're accidentally late with a single payment? Call your bank and ask if they'll remove it from your record as a one-time courtesy.

2. **Know the credit utilization sweet spot.** The magic numbers here are 30 percent and 10 percent. 30 percent is the red-flag number: once you start using more than 30 percent of your available credit, your credit score will take a hit. (So, for example, if you have a credit card with a $10,000 limit and carry more than $3,000 on it.) Ten percent, on the other hand (so, carrying about $1,000 on that card) is more what lenders like to see: this shows that you're actively using the card (which is good) but not going crazy and racking up charges. Keep your utilization in that friendly zone for a few months and you should see your score increase.

3. **Move the goalposts.** This is my absolute favorite trick in the book. You might *think* that the only way to decrease your credit utilization is to pay down that debt . . . but it's not. Remember,

credit utilization is a percentage—a fraction. So if you make the bottom number (your credit limit) bigger, you can magically shrink your utilization, even if the top number (how much you spend and owe) stays the same. Every six to twelve months, call your credit card company and ask for a credit limit increase—*especially* if your income has increased since you opened your card. Many times, if you're in decent standing with them, they'll bump you up on the spot.

4. **Scrub your record.** Credit bureaus make mistakes. Incorrect personal info, accounts that don't belong to you, and even accounts that are marked as delinquent when they're not can all show up on your credit report and ding your score. Get a copy of your full credit report (not just the score) and look it over carefully. If you see anything fishy, that you don't recognize, or that's wrong, contact the credit bureau ASAP and let them know what's wrong. They'll investigate, make sure your report is accurate, and hopefully fix your score. (This is also a good way to spot identity theft—someone using your name and SSN to rack up debt.)

5. **Get a secured credit card.** If you have no credit or low credit, it doesn't mean you can't get a credit card. It just limits you—temporarily—to a certain *kind* of credit card. A *secured credit card* is sort of what it sounds like: it's essentially a card with a security deposit, where you send the company a cash deposit up front as collateral. Lots of secured credit cards will also charge an annual fee—usually somewhere between twenty-five and ninety-nine dollars annually—in addition to that security deposit, but that can be a price *totally* worth paying: with a secured credit card, if you are able to spend wisely, don't max your limit, and pay it off every single month, that responsible pattern

will, over time, boost your credit score—and eventually you'll be able to upgrade your secured card to a more lucrative credit card with better benefits.

Net net, credit is your friend if you are responsible, read the fine print, and can play the rules of the game correctly.

Debt

If just reading the word *debt* makes you want to curl into a ball, I get it. Maybe you have student loans of infinity dollars, maybe your credit card debt is teetering on six figures, maybe you're paying out the ass for a car you've already totaled. For something as straightforward as "money borrowed and owed back to the lender over a period of time," debt sure can make us feel like shit.

So let me reassure you: This section? It's a shame-free zone. The *last* thing I want is for you to skip this section just because it makes you feel uncomfortable. I know debt can be scary, but it doesn't have to be. If you're drowning in debt, I got you: there are some solid, doable strategies to help make debt more manageable—and I'm going to walk you through those.

But also, debt shouldn't make you feel like shit because debt isn't inherently evil, and you're not a bad person for having it.

Debt is a tool, the same way that shovels are a tool. It's value-neutral, and can be used for very practical, constructive purposes. The same way shovels can help you plant a beautiful garden and save you time and effort, debt can let you achieve your goals faster and with less work on your part.

But tools can also be used for evil. You can dig a hole with that shovel and then turn around and whack someone over the head, murder, and bury them (for legal reasons, we need to make it clear—Your Rich BFF DOES NOT ENCOURAGE MURDER).

In either case, shovels aren't inherently evil and debt isn't inherently bad. But *sooo* many finance reporters, educators, and money gurus out there are *super* judgmental about debt. They're *very* absolutist. Their argument basically breaks down to two points:

1. "Having debt means you'll be poor forever."
2. "Having debt comes from making bad financial choices."

THEREFORE: Having debt is bad, and you should feel bad.

To which I say, *Swing swong, you are wrong.* Both of these are not true, because, again, *debt is a tool*—and no one knows this better than rich people.

Truth #1: Rich people absolutely *do* have debt.

I mean, I'm rich and I have debt.

Rich people with holdings in real estate and rich people running huge businesses have debt.

Hell, even Notable Rich White Man™ Warren Buffett? Guy had a mortgage.

But I have to hand it to my fellow rich people on this one: they have given debt one hell of an Extreme Makeover. Seriously—the people who did this were also behind the brand relaunch of mayonnaise into aioli.

All debt is just borrowing money, right? We know this. But what most of us don't know is that the way we treat debt—the way we think of it, judge it, view its usefulness—is entirely different depending on your socioeconomic class. That's why it's so easy to assume that "rich people don't have debt." They've covered their tracks *pretty* well.

See, when rich people borrow money, we don't call it debt. Ew! No, we call it *leverage*. A multimillionaire takes out a mortgage, invests the rest of their cash into a startup and makes bank, and we applaud their business brilliance and put them on the cover of *TIME* magazine.

When poor people borrow money, though, that's debt. That's *bad*. Shame!

A single mom of three children goes and puts groceries on her credit card—groceries that she unfortunately cannot afford with the money in her pocket—and we point the finger and say, "Look at how irresponsible you are, racking up *debt* like that." A person between jobs puts a smartphone on a layaway plan, because they don't have a computer and need *some* way to send out résumés, and we get all judgey for them "buying luxuries they can't afford."

A *lot* of the time, we're borrowing money as a way to do our best with the resources we have, rich *or* poor. But rich people have managed to distance themselves from *debt* as *that kind* of four-letter word and repackage *their* money-borrowing as something savvy.

So let me be clear: rich people *love* borrowing money. They live by that line from the *Moulin Rouge* song, "Why spend mine when I can spend yours?" and they use leverage to do it.

Now, strictly speaking, not *all* debt is leverage, but all leverage is essentially debt. It's just borrowing money for the purpose of making *more* money. Leverage lets you use a little bit of money to control a lot of money, and get that much more spending power while only actually putting in a fraction of the total from your own pocket: like how you can put down just 20 percent of the purchase price on a house up front but still get to live in 100 percent of the house right away.

But here's where the *real* infinite money loophole of debt comes in. Rich people are always thinking back to that delta—the difference between interest rates.

Take Kim Kardashian, for example. Love her or hate her, you need to give credit where credit is due: she is a fierce businesswoman and doesn't play when it comes to her money. When she bought a new house in Malibu, she had a net worth of over $1.2 billion, and likely had the cash for a $70 million mansion.

But she would never make such a foolish business decision. She has ways to put that cash to work that will get her *much* higher returns than just the appreciation of a single piece of real estate. She has private equity opportunities, startups begging her to invest, not to mention Skims, SKKN . . . the list goes on. Basically, she has ways to put her money to work, and if that money can earn her money faster than the interest on her mortgage adds up, then voilà, instant money. Therefore: she got a mortgage.

So rich people don't hate borrowing money. Hell, they're *excited* to take on debt that's growing at a slower rate than their investments, because they get to pocket the difference. (Even better, if they can take out debt that grows slower than the rate of inflation? They don't even have to *do* anything and they're effectively profiting.)

Bottom line here is that rich people understand that sometimes, borrowing money is a *great* idea. They already know that their money can work harder than they can. Borrowing money to get leverage is basically just saying, *Okay, but how much harder could my money work if it could be in two places at once?*

There is really no way you can call yourself a financial expert and say that "rich people don't have debt." Rich people *do* have debt, and it's how they get rich and stay rich. And when rich people find that they are able to get leverage on the cheap they do not walk. They run.

So *this*, besties, is why *debt* is not a four letter word. (I mean, technically, it is . . . but not a bad one). Again, debt is just something that can be used as a tool in your life, and it can help you become *more*, not *less*, financially empowered.

Truth #2: Unmanageable debt is a solvable problem, not a character flaw.

Now, maybe you're like, "Okay, dope, thanks, Viv! But, like . . . I would *love* to take on some cheap debt in real estate and get leverage and all, but I owe major bucks to my credit card company and the interest rate is a gazillion percent. I'm screwed, right? I'm too bad with money to play this game."

No! First off, you're not screwed. There are strategies that you can use to pay down your debt and get on the good side of interest rates so you can start earning money with your money.

Before we get into those, though, having debt doesn't mean you're bad with money.

Even if it's consumer debt, high-interest debt, a payday loan.

So many factors way, way beyond our control affect our relationship to debt: how much debt we have, the types of debt we have, and the re-sources we can use to help pay it off. Maybe you grew up low-income, maybe you live paycheck to paycheck, maybe you've faced housing in-security, maybe you have to support your parents and family members, maybe you're from a marginalized background and not making as much cash as your white male coworkers.

It's important to address these socioeconomic nuances because no one should feel like they're behind, or bad with money, or doomed, just because they have debt. All of us are just using the tools and resources available to us to the best of our ability. Beating yourself up over past decisions won't change what happened, it'll only change how you feel about yourself, and in a not-great way.

Fortunately, now you have a new resource: me, Your Rich BFF!

So let's talk strategies for paying down that debt.

Like I mentioned earlier, mindset plays a huge part in being able to get a handle on your debt. It can feel really overwhelming, especially if you have creditors constantly blowing up your phone.

STRATEGY #1: The Snowball Method

The biggest block to getting debt under control is *mindset*. Seriously, people just don't tend to organize and rank their debt in a smart way. Yes, even smart people—because debt is *emotional*, in a lot of ways, and we're psychological creatures, driven by the need to feel like we're making progress.

Enter this first strategy, known as the debt snowball. This strategy is relatively simple, pretty popular, and it plays on that desire to see the needle moving and feel good feelings about your progress.

For this strategy, you'll take a piece of paper and list out your debt: name/type of debt (and/or who is owed that debt), how much you owe, and the interest rate. The order doesn't matter, you're just brain-dumping here.

So, for example, you might have:

1. Credit card #1: $10,000 at 24% interest
2. Student loan: $7,000 at 3% interest
3. Mortgage: $270,000 at 5% interest
4. Car loan: $20,000 at 7% interest
5. Credit card #2: $2,000 at 22% interest

You then take this list and re-order it. Rank your debts by how much you owe, from the smallest to the biggest amount.

1. Credit card #2: $2,000 at 22% interest
2. Student loan: $7,000 at 3% interest
3. Credit card #1: $10,000 at 24% interest

4. Car loan: $20,000 at 7% interest
5. Mortgage: $270,000 at 5% interest

Then you take action. Every month, you'll make the minimum payment on all of the debts (to keep you in good graces with the credit bureaus). With the minimum payments made, you'll put any additional funds you've budgeted for debt paydown toward the account at the top of the list—the one with the smallest balance. As time goes on, you'll tick off debts from smallest to largest, and you'll reduce the number of accounts you owe on relatively fast.

The snowball method works really well for people who want positive reinforcement to stay motivated, and it's a great way to see early results. But . . .

Look, I'm an Aries. I'm impatient. I'm hot-headed. I want to get things done *fast* and *efficiently.*

And the snowball method? It just isn't the fastest or most efficient way to pay down debt. Don't get me wrong: it's *huge* to be able to close up an account. It feels good. But me, I'm just not going to pay more in interest over time for the privilege of doing so.

So let me introduce you to *my* favorite method: the avalanche.

STRATEGY #2: The Avalanche Method

This method still has you rank your debt, but this time, instead of ranking from smallest to largest sum owed, we're going to rank from highest to lowest interest rate.

So if you start with the same list:

1. Credit card #1: $10,000 at 24% interest
2. Student loan: $7,000 at 3% interest
3. Mortgage: $270,000 at 5% interest

4. Car loan: $20,000 at 7% interest

5. Credit card #2: $2,000 at 22% interest

Ranking by interest rate, from highest to lowest, you'd get:

1. Credit card #1: $10,000 at 24% interest

2. Credit card #2: $2,000 at 22% interest

3. Car loan: $20,000 at 7% interest

4. Mortgage: $270,000 at 5% interest

5. Student loan: $7,000 at 3% interest

From there, the process is the same: you make the minimum payment on all of the debts, but put any additional debt paydown funds toward the account with the highest interest rate.

This is why I love this method so much. By tackling debts in order of interest rate, you get to pay down your debt on the fastest possible timeline while paying the least in interest.

And if you'd love a little spreadsheet calculator to see your debt mapped out under both the snowball and the avalanche method, check out richAF.club to download my Excel workbook.

STRATEGY #3: Debt Consolidation

With both the snowball and avalanche method, you're ultimately changing the same thing about your debts: the total amount you owe. The only difference is the order you tackle the pieces that make up that total.

This strategy, on the other hand, can allow you to tackle the *interest rate* on your debt.

Debt consolidation is when you take out a loan and use it to pay off multiple debts. You still owe the same total amount of money, but now it's in the form of a single loan. The idea is that this new single loan will have a lower interest rate than your previous individual debts, so you're paying less overall.

With your debts consolidated, you don't need to do any ranking, snowballing, or avalanching because they're all rolled up into one package. That convenience, plus the savings on interest, can be a huge help in keeping your debt feeling manageable.

This strategy makes the *most* sense if your debt is mostly high interest rate debt, such as credit card debt. If the bulk of your debt is on the lower-interest side of things, like federal student loans or a low-rate mortgage, you probably won't be able to beat those rates by consolidating.

The other thing to consider with debt consolidation is your payment history and credit score. To qualify for a loan, and to get an interest rate that makes the numbers work, you're going to need a solid credit history so that a lender feels good handing you the money. But if you do qualify, the savings in interest can be huge: depending on the bank, of course, your solid credit score could help you get your overall interest knocked down to a single-digit percentage (instead of the 20 to 25 percent on credit card debt, for example).

To set up a debt consolidation loan, you reach out to a financial institution like your bank or credit union and apply. They'll want to know the amounts of your debts and the current interest rates on those debts, as well as all the basics like your personal info and credit score. If they approve you for the loan, they're essentially agreeing to pay off your multiple different debts, and you're agreeing that you now owe the total of all those loans to the bank.

CREDIT CARD DEBT RELIEF

Credit card debt can be uniquely overwhelming—not only are the APRs much higher than other types of loans (like mortgages) but it's relatively easy to get a credit card compared to getting a loan to buy a house or get a degree.

If you are straight-up drowning in credit card debt, here are three credit-card-specific relief options you can try.

Credit counseling: A nonprofit credit counseling agency can help with your budget, debt management, and credit by setting you up with a personalized repayment plan (sometimes with lowered interest) at NO COST TO YOU. Look for an agency that's a nonprofit and accredited by the National Foundation for Credit Counseling.

The upside is that you get organization, accountability, and *help*. The downside? You'll probably have to give up credit cards entirely for as long as you're in the program, and you have to be *super* on top of your payments—miss one and lenders might revoke those waived fees and lower interest rates.

Balance transfer: This is basically the credit card version of debt consolidation: you bundle all of your credit card balances together and transfer it over to a new credit card with a limited-time interest rate of 0 percent. You'll have to have a good credit score to qualify, though, and you have to be prepared to pay off fast: usually you get around eighteen months before the 0 percent disappears and a standard APR kicks in.

Negotiate: The ultimate rich-person move! Call up your CC company and ask them to give you more favorable terms. You'll have the most success with cards you've had the longest and where you've been the most reliable about paying your bills. Depending on what you can pay off now, and where you're getting dinged the most on fees and interest, your ask will be different, but here are some starters:

- "Will you waive my late-payment fee as a one-time courtesy?"
- "Will you lower my interest rate? What about a temporary rate reduction for the next year?"
- "Can I skip or defer a payment this billing cycle with no penalty?"

Taxes and Tax Bracket$

"Vivian, how do I pay taxes like a rich person?"

Pssshh, more like how do you *not* pay taxes like a rich person?

I've talked a lot about how rich people *loathe* paying taxes, and it's still very true. But the sum total of rich people's knowledge about taxes does not start and end with "taxes bad." In fact, there's a lot more that most people should understand understand about how taxes work in order to *truly* navigate the IRS like a rich person. This section is going to break down how tax brackets work, what taxes are for, and how you can legally do everything in your power to minimize how much money you give away.

Tax Brackets

Most people do *not* understand how tax brackets in the United States work. Like, is it just me, or is everyone's Facebook full of people telling everyone to turn down raises or not take overtime because "it'll bump them up into the next tax bracket and you'll end up paying it all to the government anyway."

Good news, friends: The conspiracy theorist from your high school is wrong. You will never be worse off if you make more money. That's because our tax brackets in America are marginal—and I know, you're already falling asleep, but stick with me here, because I can explain taxes to anyone.

Imagine that you no longer get paid in money. Instead, you're getting paid in pizzas. For the first 11,000 pizzas you earn every year, you get pesto pizza. (Ick.) This is how *everyone* gets paid—doesn't matter if you're Richie Rich or Broke Becky, we all start with pesto flavor for those first 11,000 pizzas. The government is like, "Ehh, we don't like pesto so much, so we only want ten percent of those guys." They take a pretty skinny slice out of each pesto pie—so far, so good.

Once you start making more than 11,000 pizzas a year, though, you level up to the next flavor—mushroom! The government likes this a little more, but just a little (because let's be real, it's still mushroom) so they want 12 percent per pie.

Now, at this level, nobody has gotten any good pizza toppings yet, because we all upgrade at the same thresholds—and, unfortunately for Broke Becky, that's it for her: she's not getting any other flavors because she's not earning any more pizzas for the year. This means that overall, the government's not taking too much of her pizzas because they're like, "If all you got is pesto and mushroom, then we really just wanna take the bare minimum."

But you're still earning pizzas, and you hit the next level: after about 45,000 pizzas, you start getting sausage. Now the government's like, "YUM, yes please! We want twenty-two percent of those bad boys." So they take a pretty thicc slice of all your sausage pizzas, and they do that until you hit the next level at about 95,000 pizzas, when you start getting pepperoni. Government's still into it, obviously, and they're gonna take 24 percent of each pepperoni pizza.

Now, you stop there—that's all the pizza you get for the year. But

Richie Rich keeps going, and he earned 600,000 pizzas last year. So he's hitting a *lot* of flavors along the way: he's getting barbecue chicken, buffalo ranch, and even Hawaiian. (Do not fight me on this. This is a hill I am willing to die on.) The government *loves* those pies, so they'll be taking 32 percent, 35 percent, and 37 percent respectively of each.

That's what *marginal* means. When you move into a higher tax bracket, you aren't suddenly giving away a bigger percent of every pizza you got—you're only giving up more of the newest flavor. It doesn't suddenly mean you give up more of your total income.

So when accountants or other financial pros ask "What's your tax bracket?" what they really want is, basically, a rough indication of the max you'd *ever* give up in your top pizza flavor.

Now, when people *don't* understand marginal taxes—like our pals on Facebook—they panic and make stupid decisions based on bad math. They see those tax brackets start at 10 percent and 12 percent, then take a big jump to 22 percent and 24 percent, and then from there jump vastly again to 32 percent, 35 percent, 37 percent, and they start to freak out: "Well, if I'm between twenty-four percent and thirty-two percent, I'd rather earn less and stay in that twenty-four percent bracket, because then I take home more, even if I earn less!" They don't realize that they're only losing 24 percent of each *pepperoni* pizza, because the government doesn't want that much pesto and mushroom or even sausage pizza. Their *effective* tax rate—the average amount taken per pizza, across all flavors—will *always* be lower.

Which ultimately makes sense if you think about it. Like, yes, sure, the government definitely does things that are sometimes not in our individual best interest or are even totally illogical, but they are not going to set up a tax system *that* broken, right? If tax brackets worked the way people thought they worked, nobody would be incentivized to have

Marginal Tax Rates, Visualized

All figures based on 2023 tax brackets.

These dollars taxed at 32%

$182,100

These dollars taxed at 24%

$95,375

These dollars taxed at 22%

$44,725

These dollars taxed at 12%

$11,000

These dollars taxed at 10%

Salary A: $60K   Salary B: $103K   Salary C: $197K

a high-paying job, *ever*. There would be no heart surgeons, because why would you be a heart surgeon when you could be an underwater basket weaver for the same amount of money . . . I mean pizza?

This is all to say: always take the raise, and don't be afraid to work overtime. You'll end up with more money in your pocket. Every incremental dollar you earn is good for you. That said, you *will* see diminishing marginal returns, because past a certain point in your earnings, the government starts to take a bigger chunk—but only of the dollars earned above that threshold, not of every dollar. But your *effective* tax rate (the percentage of your income you actually pay in taxes) is *never* going to be as high as your marginal tax rate (the tippy-top percentage you're taxed at for *some* of your dollars). Being in a higher tax bracket means you're earning more money, and *that* is a good thing.

Tax Returns and Tax Refunds

Let's get something cleared up real quick.

The stack of forms you send in to show how much money you made that year and what you owe the government?

That's your tax return.

The money the government sends you if you overpaid on taxes?

That's a tax *refund*.

Not a tax return. A tax *refund*.

You send your *return* to the government, and the government sends a *refund* to you.

We good?

Cool. Because I'm not just bringing this up to be petty. See, in some countries, the government basically *does* send you a return. They prefill it for you. For example, the Australian Tax Authority literally just sends everyone Down Under a form that's like, "G'day, mate, does this number look right to you? Check yes or no."

So when I hear people say, "Oh, I finally got my tax return from the IRS," all I can think is "Yeah, if only."

Instead, it's more like:

> **TAXPAYER:** Tax time, cool cool. How much do I owe?
>
> **IRS:** Uh, that's on you, bud. Gotta figure it out on your own.
>
> **TAXPAYER:** Seriously? But don't you guys already have all the forms and stuff?
>
> **IRS:** Oh, yeah. Yeah, we totally do.
>
> **TAXPAYER:** So . . . ?!
>
> **IRS:** Like we said, bud. It's on you.
>
> **TAXPAYER:** But, I suck at math! What if I get it wrong?
>
> **IRS:** *Prison.*

In the United States, we primarily pay our income taxes to the federal government, plus state and local governments where applicable, via deductions from our paycheck. Then, at the end of the year, our employer gives us a form that's like, "Here's how much we paid you, and here's how much we withheld in taxes for you." You use that to fill out your tax return, send it to the IRS, and then either pay up what you owe (if you came up short) or get a refund paid to you (if you *over*paid).

Or, you know, prison.

(No, I'm kidding. Penalties for filing incorrectly on accident are not as severe as people make them out to be. Minor good-faith mistakes are not going to get you locked up. Worst case, you'll just owe the government the money and worst WORST case you'll pay a small penalty on it.)

It sounds so simple in practice, but as we've seen with tax brackets, the math isn't that straightforward. People often just don't understand the forms they're filling out, they make mistakes, and they don't pay the right amount over the year.

And while owing money on April 15 sucks, because, well, now you're out a few more dollars you maybe weren't expecting to pay, getting a refund? That also kind of sucks.

People treat their tax refunds like free bonus money, but it's not: It's just *your* money. Money *you earned.* Money you essentially loaned to the government, for *zero interest,* for up to a year.

That is *not* getting your money to work for you. So it's in your best interest (lol, get it) to get all those forms filled out correctly, get your withholding as dialed-in as possible, and not give *anyone* money for nothing.

Fine-tuning your withholding will look different depending on whether you have a traditional salaried/hourly job, or whether you're a freelancer/self-employed.

If you work for an employer, you'll have filled out a form W-4 when you're first hired, which basically asks, "Who are you, how much do you make, how married are you, and how many kids do you have?" and uses that to determine how much tax to withhold.

This means that if, during the year, you become more or less married, you have a kid, or you get a new source of income from outside your job, you should go to HR and update your W-4 on file. You want to make sure that your spouse's income (if you're going to file jointly) or your $$$ from your side hustle is accounted for when payroll figures out your withholding rate, because *all* the money you earn affects your tax bracket, not just salary bucks.

Plus, if there's anything that you're ever uncertain about as it pertains to your day job, you should actually have a benefits manager on the staff that can help you with this. It's literally their job to get the paperwork correct, so ask them for help.

If you work a sales job or any other commission-based job, you'll see that your commissions are typically taxed at a higher bracket than your standard salary. People get upset about this, but it's essentially to protect you. If you get put into a higher tax bracket because of your commission earnings, you'll owe a bigger portion in taxes, which could mean a hefty surprise bill come tax szn, and that would suck.

If you're a freelancer, then taxes are an extra pain in the ass. You're the boss, which means you're *also* the payroll department, and instead of waiting until the following April to deal with taxes, you need to pay estimated taxes every quarter—that's the freelancer version of payroll withholding. You don't get a single W-2 from your employer, but instead get a 1099 form from every client you worked with.

Paperwork aside, the sucky part is that unlike a paycheck, which is the same amount every time, freelance income can be wildly variable from year to year . . . and because income tax is progressive, it's not as simple as just paying twenty-two cents of every dollar you earn. You have to guess how much money you'll have made by the end of the year, and use *that* to determine how much to send the IRS every three months. These payments are typically calculated on your previous years' income, which is at least a starting point—but, again, freelance income varies. It's so easy to either under- *or* overpay.

You don't want to give the government a free loan, but you *also* don't want to end up with a bill for several grand. So here's the life hack: open up a dedicated high-yield savings account just for your tax money. Every payment you get, put a generous chunk in that account—I'm talking 30 to 40 percent. Pay your quarterly taxes as usual based on last year's income out of that account, and then leave the rest there. At the end of the year, if you do your tax return and discover you owe more money? No problem: it's right where you left it in the HYSA. And if you *don't* owe more money? Then the money is yours—*and* it's been earning you interest.

Personally, what I like to do now is just set aside 40 percent for taxes, because I know that at the federal level, I'm going to be in the highest bracket of 37 percent.

"Wait, Vivian, didn't you just say that the effective tax rate isn't the same thing as your tax bracket? What gives??"

Yes, that's still true. But I also live in New York City, right? My local taxes are going to be steep, and I need to set aside a healthy amount for those too.

Finally, if you're a freelancer? Get a bookkeeper and an accountant. Seriously, they will likely save you *so* much time and money compared to DIYing your taxes (and, of course, all the money you pay them is a business expense, so . . . tax deductible, baby). They can also help you get deductions or credits where you could actually get money back, and that's free money on the table.

WHY YOU SHOULD NOT JUST GOOGLE "FILE TAXES FOR FREE"

If you make less than $73,000 a year (this number might fluctuate slightly depending on what year you're reading this book), you should not be paying money to file your taxes. But you should also *not* trust the internet to help you do that.

See, at one point the government was talking about creating its own free-filing tax software for taxpayers below a certain income threshold. Sounds nice, right?

Well, not if you're TurboTax or any other tax-prep software company. They got wind of the IRS's plans for free filing software and panicked, because that would eat up a huge chunk of their customer base.

So in 2002, these tax-prep companies put their lobbyists to work. They told the IRS, "No, no, don't worry about it! Let *us* create free filing software. We already have the technology, after all!"

The IRS, who is a total cheapskate, was like, "Cool, sounds good," and that was it. Because while these major software brands *did* say they'd create free filing software, they *didn't* say they'd make it easy to find. Their lobbyists all had their fingers crossed behind their backs when they made their promise. Obvi.

So while all the tax filing companies *do* have true free-filing programs, they do everything they can to prevent you from finding them and make their flagship paid programs *super* misleading. For example, TurboTax "Free Edition" is riddled with booby traps where you will be forced to pay to file if you did things like collect unemployment or pay student loans— basic stuff that does *not* disqualify you from free filing if you're under that income threshold. Even worse, they'll push these booby-trapped apps to the top of Google results using targeted ads and hope that anyone searching for "file taxes for free" will just get too confused or too frustrated to realize they're in the wrong place and end up paying after all.

For a list of Your Rich BFF's favorite free (and low-cost) tax filing software options, hit up richAF.club.

Tax Deductions and Tax Credits

So how *do* we not pay taxes like a rich person? We can maximize our deductions and credits, which even regular, non-billionaire people can still do. Tax deductions and tax credits aren't anything fancy: they're just the government's way of incentivizing us to do stuff, whether that's owning a home, driving an electric vehicle, donating to charity . . . the list goes on.

Here's the difference between the two. Tax credits are like a coupon for your taxes. A credit reduces the amount of taxes you owe, dollar for dollar. So if you have a $1,000 tax credit, you'll pay $1,000 less in taxes.

Tax deductions, on the other hand, don't subtract directly from your final tax bill, but from the income that determines what your tax bill will be. Basically, if you spend money on something that makes the IRS happy, the IRS goes, "Nah, it's cool—we'll just pretend like you never even earned that money, *wink*."

One major deduction is something we've already covered: retirement savings. If you contribute to a 401(k) or a traditional IRA, you can essentially subtract the amount that you contributed to those accounts from your income before you do the math on your taxes. Retirement contributions, along with certain other expenses, like student loan interest and alimony payments, are what's known as "above-the-line" deductions, meaning you can take them no matter what (as long as you meet the income requirements, like I described on page 197).

Other deductible expenses, however—things like charitable donations and mortgage interest paid—will apply only if you *don't* take what's called the *standard deduction.* Basically, everyone gets a certain amount deducted from their taxable income no matter what in the form of the standard deduction. This is just the government's easy-peasy way of saying, "Most of y'all are regular people, and regular people usually spend about X amount on deductible stuff, so we'll just assume that you spend that much on deductible expenses this year. You don't have to prove it or anything, even—we cool."

The amount of the standard deduction changes every year, but it's usually a decent chunk of change ($13,850 for single filers and $27,700 for married couples filing jointly in 2023), so unless your deductions total up to *more* than that number, you should take the standard deduction.

Finally, if you run your own business, have a side hustle, or do freelance work, you should *definitely* be deducting eligible expenses. You don't need to itemize to take these, either (since they're deducting from your business's income, not your wages from an employer) so definitely make sure you're not missing out.

Financial Advisors, Tax Pros, and Building Your Money Management Team

Even when we *can* DIY something, sometimes we just want professional advice. Like, sure, you can go around Sephora trial-and-erroring foundations by swatching on your wrist, and you'll probably find a good match eventually . . . or you can let the consultant come over and scan your face with the little color-matching undertone-detector gun and get an *exact* match.

Or maybe we want to save time and keep as many of our precious non-work hours as free as possible, so we let Instacart do our shopping. The upcharge, fee, and tip might be *well* worth the convenience.

The same is true for our financial lives. Whether we want to get tailored advice from a pro beyond our expertise, or just want to save ourselves the hassle of money-related chores, there are people who can be hired to make that happen.

Now, we already know that rich people *love* themselves a good team, and money management is for sure at the top of the list for them: book-keepers, accountants, tax attorneys, estate planning attorneys, investment managers . . . the list goes on.

But for those of us who *aren't* high-net-worth individuals (yet), it might not make sense to shell out for every single expert out there—especially if you don't know what each of them really does. It's easy to either jump the gun and pay for services we don't need at this stage in our money-making lives, to shell out for someone who's not actually act-ing in our best interests . . . or both.

For example, one of the most common FAQs that I see popping up in my DMs is "Viv, how do I find a financial advisor?!"

But real talk: most people don't need a financial advisor yet. If you're not at the point where you're maxing out all your tax-advantaged ac-counts every year, you more than likely don't need any expert advice. The only thing you need to do at that stage is keep on investing and in-creasing your income as much as possible.

The thing about these financial pros is that they're best for dealing with money situations that are complex, but complex doesn't have to mean "involving tons of capital." See, the reason rich people build up these teams isn't just because there are tons of zeros on their account statements. It's because their setups are complicated: multiple proper-ties across different states, college savings and trust funds to set up and manage, maybe some alimony payments to work out or business struc-tures to formalize . . . it's just A Lot.

But just *having money* doesn't automatically mean you need to run to get a bunch of people telling you what to do with it. If you're a rich per-son working a regular W-2 job, maxing out all your retirement accounts, and putting the rest of your investment dollars into a straightforward portfolio of index funds and high-grade bonds . . . there might not be that much you need to change. Seriously, I don't care if you're pulling down $400K a year, if your budget and investment plan is working for you, then there's no pressing reason to hire someone to tell you what to do.

That said, there are some financial professionals it's worth getting on board sooner rather than later.

Here's who you might want to hire, when you might need them, and why—plus where to find them.

Certified Public Accountant (CPA)

When it comes to dealing with the IRS, CPAs are the real MVPs.

A certified public accountant is someone who helps people prepare and file their personal and/or business tax returns. If you have a CPA, you can basically dump all of your forms on their desk (or upload them to a secure file share) and then sit back and wait for your draft return to be ready.

That's the across-the-board benefit of CPAs: they save you time. But CPAs aren't just bean counters or human TurboTax machines. They can also help you take stock of your individual situation and make sure you get all the credits and deductions you're entitled to (slash explain the ones you *could* qualify for with a few tweaks). They also do something that no computer screen can do, which is pick up the phone and answer your questions, no matter how "stupid" those questions are. Hire an accountant and your days of googling "what is my adjusted gross income" are over.

Plus, if you've got a major change in your financial life on the horizon (or recently in the rearview mirror), hiring a CPA can also make sure you properly cross all your t's and dot all your i's when navigating your first tax return after marriage (or divorce), setting up the right with-holding at a new job, or claiming any health insurance premium credits after going on Obamacare.

To be sure, not *everyone* needs a CPA. For the vast majority of folks, especially those people who are younger and don't own property or have kids, you are fine just using DIY tax software and filing on your own. You're not missing any super-secret tax benefits, promise (espe-cially now that you've read this chapter), and you're not at any increased risk of an audit (because even if a CPA preps your tax return, *you're* re-sponsible for making sure it's accurate—so you can't just blame your accountant).

> If you're self-employed (or otherwise make the bulk of your income from freelance work) and are considering applying for a mortgage (soon or even just eventually), I highly rec looking into a CPA. Mortgage lenders can be *very* particular about income documentation for freelance folks (because it's not like you can just sub-mit a pay stub), so being able to say "Of course I'm le-git, and here are three years of professionally prepared returns to prove it" can go a long way to reassure them. CPAs can also send an additional "comfort letter" to your lender that attests, basically, "This bitch is for real and I know cuz I've seen her shit."

Estate Attorney

Look: rich or poor, we're all gonna die. (Sorry to break it to you.)

I know I said earlier that most financial pros are best utilized when your situation gets complex. Estate attorneys are the exception. I think everyone should have one, because I think everyone should have a professional and legally binding will and testament.

Like I said, we're all gonna die.

And while we may not like thinking about doing stuff like setting up our wills because confronting mortality sucks, having an expert help you do it can bring you huge peace of mind.

First off, everyone has an estate, not just rich people—an *estate* just means "all the stuff you're leaving on earth when you bite it." This means the money in your bank accounts, the assets in your retirement or investment accounts, any property you own (and not just houses, but cars and *things in your house,* too).

Second, even though we think of wills as "the document that leaves all my stuff to my kids," you can and *should* have a will even if you don't have kids. If you were to suddenly and tragically die *intestate*—meaning with no will—your surviving family would have to go through probate court (and probably pay a lawyer for help) to chase down all of your assets and figure out where they should properly (and legally) go.

> What's the deal with living wills? Living wills are also called advance directives and are basically a document that spells out exactly what medical procedures you do or don't want performed in the event that you're in a serious accident that leaves you unable to advocate for yourself. I also highly rec getting one of these—even if you're young and healthy, you could still be hit by a bus tomorrow (sorry, Regina George) and you probably don't want your family stressing out over "what [your name] would want" when it comes to things like risky surgeries or feeding tubes.

Financial Planner

If you googled something like "person who can help me with my money," you would get an avalanche of so-called money professionals in your results. And sorry not sorry, but not all of them are legit.

People who call themselves things like financial coaches, budgeting consultants, money mindset experts, or whatever are basically just making up titles. Sure, they might have a slick website, a chill vibe, and maybe even some high-quality social media infographics, but that does *not* make them a legally qualified professional who can help you 1:1 with your situation. There's a huge difference between posting helpful finance videos online versus digging through your individual financials to create a plan. So I'm begging you: before you slap down a fee for a consultation, look up if your fave has any actual credentials.

Or, alternatively, start your search by looking *only* at qualified, bona fide pros. For the vast majority of people, a *certified financial planner* is a solid go-to. In order to become a CFP, a person has to pass an accreditation exam, complete a required amount of education and hands-on experience, and comply with a strict set of ethical rules and codes of conduct. I don't think I need to explain why all of these are green flags, but, basically, yeah, you want someone who knows what they're doing and isn't going to scam you.

That said, I want to state again that you don't automatically need to hire a CFP once you hit six figures in annual income or a quarter million in net worth or any benchmark at all. If you feel good about how you're spending, saving, and investing, and everything feels on track to your goals, you don't necessarily *need* extra advice.

But, like CPAs and estate attorneys, CFPs can be hugely helpful as a resource for any and all random questions, vibe checks, and basically asking, "Am I good?" Like I said earlier, as much as I'd like to cover every individual possible financial scenario in this book, I do *not* have the pages, and although I love being everyone's Rich BFF, no matter how fast I post on social media, I cannot realistically explain everything to everyone.

But most importantly, a CFP is a *fiduciary*, which means they must *always* act in the best interests of their clients. While *some* financial planners might push certain investment products hard because *they* earn more of a commission, a fiduciary (like a CFP) will advise you to do only things that benefit *you* the most—and that is obviously what you want.

FU Number

So you're rocking those credit cards, you're paying down your debt, you're paying taxes like a champ and you've got a killer team at your back for all the tricky stuff.

Now how much money do you need to have to kick over your desk, quit your job, and tell your boss F U?

The answer is your FU number. (Also, not *literally* suggesting you do that.) It's the amount you need to, essentially, never worry about working for money again. It's the *ultimate* achievement for financial domination—and it's more attainable than you think.

The FU number is my personal Your Rich BFF spin on what is often called the FIRE number. *FIRE* stands for "financial independence, retire early," and personally? Not a fan of the term.

In principle, I am all for people living happily ever after entirely off the passive income of their investments. In practice, though . . . FIRE people are just a little intense. They love to evangelize. And look, if you love FIRE, then great. No shade. But I have a few issues with the movement.

First of all, there's a lot of shame in FIRE-related discussions. A lot of the biggest names in the FIRE community have these extreme lifestyles. For some people it's straight-up going off the grid, *I hunt my own food, I live in a log cabin, I have composting toilets.* And that's great for you, but I don't think I have to explain why that's not for everyone.

Except these hardcore FIRE personalities who live in Airstream trailers and don't buy shoes are only too happy to point out that *their way* is the best way to FIRE. (Meanwhile, I'm like, "Do you ever want to go to a grocery store? Because you have to wear shoes. IDGI.") For whatever reason, FIRE purists like to shame others for their choices, especially any "wastes" of money.

And, as you know, your girl loves her some nonnegotiables, so I find that attitude to be incredibly unhealthy—because seriously? Just live your life how you want to live it and don't judge other people for living differently. If you're not buying shoes, hey, live your dream. I couldn't make it work, but you do you, boo.

The other thing is that FIRE is often kind of a misnomer. Like, the whole premise of "financial independence, retire early" is that you get to a savings number that's large enough that you can live off of the investment returns annually and you can literally never work again. But for a lot of FIRE people, what ends up happening is that they hit that FIRE number, and then they become a FIRE guru. They set up a blog or a course and teach other people how to hit their FIRE numbers.

But this directly contradicts what FIRE is supposed to be about. Speaking literally, FIRE means you've retired early, right? You are no longer working, you are not making income through labor because you are living off of investment income. So if you quit your job as an accountant because you've hit financial independence, but then you start teaching a "How to FIRE" course... IDK, but that doesn't sound like retirement to me. That just sounds like you found a new job that you like better.

To be clear, there ain't nothing wrong with teaching people finance—
I say this as someone who literally quit my day job to teach finance for a
living—but call a spade a spade. If you're "FIREd" but actively taking
dollars from people in exchange for your sharing FIRE wisdom, you're
still making money by working. You're making money differently, and
maybe you now have a job that has a lot more work/life flexibility, but
you're still working. You have *not* retired early.

But beyond that, I don't think most people even *want* to stop working. Rich people don't. Sure, their work is stuff like running the Junior League Thrift Shop or serving on the board of the Metropolitan
Museum of Art, but they are not all just sitting on their asses sipping
martinis. They are putting in effort and keeping busy, but it's on *their*
terms—because rich people have the opportunity and the optionality
to do whatever the fuck they want.

That's why we need to reconceptualize what this number is and
chuck this idea of retiring early. Getting to that number ultimately has
zero to do with retirement. It literally just means you are no longer tied
to a job that you don't want to do. Personally, when me and my partner hit our number, I will definitely downshift in my creator/influencer
career. I'd likely pick up a lot more philanthropic work, or do a job I
couldn't live off of without the supplemental income from my investments. For example, there's a tiny piece of me that's always wanted to be
a social worker, but, transparently, social workers in New York City get
paid jack shit, unfortunately. It's not really a job you can take on if you
are the only daughter of two immigrant parents whose retirement plan
is you. But when I hit a number I'm fully comfortable with, I can do a
job—like social work—that I'm just really interested in doing, *without*
having to stress about covering my expenses.

So I have basically rebranded the FIRE number as the FU number,
because when you hit this number, you can tell your boss F U and go do

whatever you want. You do not need to retire, but you are not *obligated* to do a particular kind of work any longer. In other words, hitting this number means you are now able to live solely off of investment returns. You've stockpiled enough assets in cash and investments to sustain your needs until you croak.

Getting to your FU number is awesome for a multitude of reasons. One, as we've established, is that you get to pick a job that you want to do. If you don't want to work a job, you don't have to. Lots of folks choose to focus on raising their family, or trying out a passion project and becoming a photographer or an interior designer or whatever.

More than that, though, it's awesome because after that FU number hits, money is no longer a factor in how you make choices. Because, let's be really honest with ourselves: money is a factor in everything we do. Whether it's picking up brand-name organic milk versus store brand, or whether it's "Do I take this job nearby or move across the country for that job?" we are always, on some level, running the numbers. That limits our choices *and* it's a lot of mental energy to expend.

But hit that FU number and money is no longer a factor in your decision-making.

And *that* is huge.

That is being truly Rich AF.

The beauty of the FU number equation is that it will be different for everyone. There are people who want to live childfree in an Airstream with no shoes, and there are people who are like, "I want to own my home, I want to have two kids and put them through college, and I want to have a vacation home in Naples so we can go to Florida every winter." Both are valid dreams to have. These two people living their two different dreams will have *vastly* different FU numbers. And the numbers can change over time, too—like, say you want to have the vacation home in Naples, Italy, instead of Naples, Florida? NBD, just adjust that FU number accordingly.

The math to figuring out your personal FU number is pretty simple. Here's the formula:

FU number = annual spending ÷ average annual rate of return

In other words, your FU number is the amount you need to have invested in order to "earn" your required annual spending in investment returns.

With that in mind, start by figuring out your annual spending. How much money will you need to sustain yourself every year? To make the math easy, let's say your required annual spending is $100,000. Your FU number will be the amount you need to have invested in order to get $100,000 per year in investment returns. We can plug in the number to look like this:

FU number = $100,000 ÷ average annual rate of return

As you can see, we still need to plug in one more number to complete the calculation: the average annual rate of return. True, no one can see the future, but you *can* safely assume your investments will give you, on average, a 4 percent annual rate of return. (I'll explain why you can assume this in a sec—let's take care of the math part first.)

We can render that 4 percent here as .04. This makes our equation:

FU number = $100,000 ÷ .04
= $2,500,000

Ta-da, your FU number! If your annual required spending is $100,000, then you can bounce out of that rat race forever once you have $2.5 mil invested.

"Okay . . . but how much should my annual spending be, though?"

Your annual required spending should be whatever you need to sustain yourself and your family.

But when I say "sustain," I mean this in a very loose sense of the term. For Airstream people, sustain literally means "cover enough expenses to not die," so maybe paying for the parking of the airstream, basic food, and maybe a pair of flip-flops to wear to the store. Whereas for this other person, "sustain" could mean covering tuition for their kids, paying all the mortgage payments on those homes, and spending on travel. It could mean taking care of parents or having a budget to go out to eat and entertain yourself and buy nice jewelry. Basically, if you think it's money that you intend to spend, then it should become part of that number.

However, since this is all so personal and values based, there's no cut-and-dried way to approach calculating this number. There's no "should," in other words. It's very much a soul-searching expedition as much as it is researching what your dollar-figure expenses will be. You have to think about what these things are going to cost every year *and* what's important to you. (Also, it's okay if it's a rough estimate to start—you're probably going to change it a few times over the years, which we'll get to in a sec.)

"But Vivian, investments can be volatile! How will I know what my returns will be in the future?!"

Well, you won't know *exactly*. But you can make a good guess. More importantly, you can make a good *conservative* guess, so that you're intentionally lowballing and giving yourself a cushion.

With that in mind, I recommend calculating that FU number by assuming an average 4 percent return on investments, and here's why.

Four percent is an incredibly conservative investment return. (Lower than the 7 percent rule we saw earlier, remember?) Even high-grade, low-risk bonds can yield you 4 percent annually (and at the time of this writing, even 100 percent risk-free high-yield savings accounts—where your money is FDIC-insured up to $250,000—are paying 4 percent or more). But assuming your asset allocation isn't totally unhinged (like 100 percent in crypto), you can almost certainly count on making 4 percent annually on average—some years you'll get 15 percent and some years you'll get negative 9 percent, but *on average*, you'll hit that 4 percent, if not more. (Obviously, the hope is that you'd be making more than 4 percent, on average, to account for things like any capital gains taxes or unexpected sudden jumps in cost of living, but again—if you *plan* for 4 percent, anything above that is a pleasant surprise.)

This very conservative number will also help to account for inflation: if, over time, you're only making a certain return, and that return is *less* than as inflation is, you're going to end up with less money than you initially started with, and as that number gets smaller and smaller, your returns may not be able to cover your annual costs.

"Uh, my FU number seems huge. Is this even remotely achievable?"

Here's what's great about the FU number: it's flexible.

First off, I'm not saying you need to retire early and stop earning money with work, remember? Again, rich people love doing more of a gradual fade-out. Instead of quitting the working world forever, they just change the job they do. They get to that point where they don't need to be hustling trying to make a million dollars a year, but having

$50,000 come in the door when you're just leisurely working or doing something part-time? It's not a bad gig at all.

So even if you hit your FU number, who's to say you don't want to sign up to, for example, walk dogs on Wag? You can go for your thirty-minute walk in the morning, your thirty-minute walk at night, and happen to hold somebody's dog's leash at the same time, *and* continue to have money coming in the door. It's money that you don't need, but it's nice to have, especially if you were going to go for that walk anyway.

To get more nitty-gritty, you can do this FU calculation for a few different flavors of effing off. You can have your bare-bones number, the one where you'll be able to say, "When I hit this, I'm going to downshift in my career and pick a job that I actually like, but I'll def still be working." You can have your no-more-work-period number, where you're saying, "At this number I'm going to retire fully, and instead of working I'm going to focus on my family." And then you can have a number that's literally like, "When I hit this number, you hoes will never hear from me again, I'm moving to the south of France, peace, goodbye."

I actually suggest having all three of these numbers in the back of your head. Because that way, when you go to work every day, you know what your goals are, and how close you are to each of them—and those goals essentially give you something to work for. Just figure out those tiers of annual spending and redo the calculation the same way.

The other thing to keep in mind is that your FU number will probably go up as your life evolves. If you decide to expand your family, if you move somewhere more expensive, if you adopt a pet, if you develop a long-term condition or suddenly need to care for a family member, that number will get a lot higher. Those kiddos and golden retriever mean you can't drive that Prius into the ground anymore; you're gonna have to go for the Toyota Sienna and make sure you're budgeting for Champ's heartworm meds.

You can get a bit ahead of these life changes by estimating—again—conservatively to start. If you highball your projected annual expenses and lowball your expected investment returns, you're planning for the worst, but will in all likelihood get something better than the most dire situation when it all shakes out.

But the best approach here is to treat your FU number like your budget and give it that periodic true-up. Reevaluate what you want out of life, what you need to stay stable, and what that's all going to cost, and recalculate your number accordingly. Do this whenever you have a major life change (marriage, kids, new job) or at least once a year. (Easy rule: review your FU number whenever you're reevaluating your health insurance, whether it's for a qualifying event or just your annual confirmation of coverage.)

And even with the numbers defined, keep a flexible attitude. For me, I feel very, very fortunate that I love my job, I love my work, and I wake up every day legit *stoked* to get to whatever's on my list. I'm not jonesing to retire basically ever. Still, my partner and I sat down for an honest conversation about what our FU number would be: basically, if we want to have two children, pay for them to get the best education possible, have a beautiful primary residence and one, maybe two vacation homes, what are we talking here? We figured that to be really super on the safe side, we'd need about $1 mil annually, so our FU number is sitting at $25 million.

But does that mean we're going to be going HAM at work straight on until then? No, lol.

Certainly there will be a downshift when we hit $5 million, and another when we hit $10 million—there's nothing magical about those milestones beyond their being nice round numbers and a good place to reevaluate. As we keep getting closer, there will be mental shifts, too, weighing out things like "Do I need to squeeze in one last meeting or am I ready to just chuck it all for a happy life and go on vacation with my kid?"

Do I know the answer to that question now? Also hell no. I don't know how forty-five-year-old or even thirty-five-year-old Vivian is going to feel about life, and I'm fine with that. Because these questions, pauses, and reflections? They aren't things you do once. They're a practice you're going to do basically from now on.

TL;DR: the math behind the FU number is simple, but it's also not set it and forget it. You want to be constantly checking in with what you're getting out of your life situation and whether your money is going to get you the most value possible.

**MONEY MANAGEMENT
TO-DOS FOR CHAPTER 6**

- [ ] Check out your credit report. You can check your full report (not just your score) for free at AnnualCreditReport .com. Pull yours and review for anything that looks shady or wrong (and contact the credit bureau if you do see something).
- [ ] Rank your debts and figure out a repayment plan that makes sense for you (either snowball or avalanche method). You can use the Your Rich BFF Debt Calculator spreadsheet to make the calculations automatic: find it at **richAF.club.**
- [ ] Look over your most recently filed tax return (if you used software like TurboTax, get the full PDF or printout of the IRS forms, not just their dashboard summary) and look for where your income, above-the-line deductions, standard or itemized deductions, and total tax bill are listed and calculated. Just get yourself familiar with all the different aspects of how much you're paying in taxes and why.
- [ ] Figure out which financial pros make sense to add to your team, then reach out to a colleague or mentor for recommendations and set up intro calls. Remember, that first call should *always* be free (and if they're a dick to you, don't keep working with them).
- [ ] Figure out your three annual spending levels (bare-bones, leisurely working, and completely retired) and calculate your FU numbers.

Conclusion

The True Secret to Being Rich AF: Solid-Gold Habits

When I was applying to colleges, my dad told me that I was not allowed to complete the FAFSA—the Free Application for Federal Student Aid. Not because my family was ultra wealthy, or anything—we were solidly middle-class. My parents had big expectations for me in college, and loans would've made that massive education bill a lot easier to stomach.

No, this was because of his Chinese dad conspiracy theory: "If we apply for the FAFSA, and the schools that you're applying to find out, you'll be less likely to get in."

I tried to explain to him that wasn't true: "Dad, these schools are need-blind. All the Ivy League colleges and competitive universities are. They don't care. The FAFSA doesn't factor in."

But my dad was firm. "I'm not willing to take that risk. I am not willing to gamble on *anything*, Vivian. You are not filling out that FAFSA form."

I low-key panicked. Coming from a home with Chinese immigrant parents, it was so ingrained in me that I was going to live that American dream and attend that top-tier caliber school and Make Something of Myself. And now that *same* mentality was expecting me to manage that *without* loans? All I could think was *How are we going to afford this?*

Even though my dad's conspiracy theory about the FAFSA affecting my admission chances is definitely *not* true (my top choice was need-blind!), I did learn something from him that day: that our parents might be teaching us the wrong lessons about money—even if they mean well.

Turns out, we all have money habits ingrained in us from a very young age—as young as seven to nine years old. We learn about money the same way we learn to speak, to communicate, to eat, to do anything: by watching, mimicking, and general osmosis. The same way you happen to hold your pencil weird like your mom, or you don't like it when your food touches like your dad, your ideas about money might stem from your parents (or the guardian adults in your life) having *interesting* habits around money themselves.

And these are not always *good* habits. In fact, sometimes they're more like tiny acts of self-sabotage.

Which is why it is crucial to unpack them on your way to thinking like a rich person.

By now, you know that being Rich AF doesn't mean being "good with numbers" or "playing the stock market" or even being born rich (remember my trash date with the credit card debt?). What it does mean is deeply understanding yourself, your goals for your money, and what's standing in the way of those two. Yes, you can do tons of research on the rules of how investing works and which banks give you the best HYSA rates, but ultimately, that Rich AF strategy you need to succeed is all within you.

By educating yourself on how money works *and* by dismantling some of those automatic, hand-me-down money habits we got from our moms and dads, you will truly set off into the world with a solid-gold mindset. So allow me to present you with one grab bag of wisdom before you go, like the gift bags they hand out at the Oscars. Here are some situations and mindsets you might have, um, inherited at some point during your life, and the true pearl of Rich AF wisdom that proves them wrong. (Sure, they might not be as tinfoil-hat-y as my dad's anti-FAFSA stance, but they're just as important to recognize and push back on.)

SOLID-GOLD TRUTH #1: Wealth Is Not Made to Be Hoarded
Whether it's that your dad "just didn't trust the banks" or your mom was firmly convinced that cash is king no matter what, your parents may have taught you that money should stay, basically, in your line of sight at all times.

This wealth-hoarding mentality can come from a genuine place of wanting to protect and provide for you. If money was tight, your parents may have been afraid to invest their money and lose (or even just lose access to) whatever small cushion of cash they had saved up. It doesn't matter how much they knew about investing and it being a "good idea" if they genuinely couldn't spare even ten bucks without the power getting turned off.

But more likely, there was a serious knowledge gap. Rich people know that just sitting on a pile of cash (literally or figuratively) is not going to get you rich, because it prevents your money from making you money—but how are regular people supposed to find that out? Your family may have been wary of investing their money or using a bank due to fear of fraud or being scammed, because they weren't aware, for example, that deposits are FDIC insured (aka backed by the government) or that there are lower-risk investment options than just buying a single company's stock. They may not have known how to get started, and therefore felt more comfortable hoarding their wealth instead of puzzling out how to set up a brokerage account. They may have assumed all investing is either "playing the stock market" or "giving twenty grand to Uncle Tony's friend to get his new restaurant off the ground" and not unreasonably been like . . . nah—I'm out.

If you grew up in that kind of environment, you probably came into the idea of investing with a lot of skepticism. You might get defensive very quickly when confronted with suggestions for how to level up your finances, or take advice personally as an insult to your abilities to "be a good saver."

What you need to remember is that good personal finance habits are skills that can be learned, not natural-born character traits that you have or you don't. You can take knowledge and facts and create strategies that work for *your* situation, *and* you can adapt as that situation changes. You won't be able to control everything—investing always has some risk— but you can control what *you* do. And you have what it takes to do this thing well.

SOLID-GOLD TRUTH #2: Spending Is Not Inherently Shameful
Look, shit costs money. Food, shelter, clothing—we have to spend our dollars on things in order to survive. But even beyond the basics, we spend money to make our lives tolerable, even *enjoyable*—and guess what? That's also okay. You may not value the exact same purchases as another person, but if it's your money, then it's your call to make, right?

Basically, the act of exchanging money for goods and/or services is inherently morally neutral. Unfortunately, *many* many people default to a mindset of "spending = shame." It's like taking "a penny saved is a penny earned" to the extreme and saying "a penny spent is a penny lost forever, you big dum-dum."

Your parents may have had good intentions to set a good example by being frugal but ended up just reinforcing the idea that spending money is bad, period. If your parents argued over one of them coming back from the grocery store with name-brand dish detergent instead of generic, or they talked smack about the neighbors buying a new car "when everyone knows those lose value as soon as you drive them off the lot," little you picked all that up.

Or maybe they actively tried to teach you to be a wise, savvy shopper who finds bargains and spends for value . . . but then they overdid it by using negative language or criticism. When you spent your allowance or after-school job dollars on candy or a new Hello Kitty notepad instead of something practical, they might chide you with "You're so wasteful with your money—candy doesn't last!" or "You should be saving your money instead of spending it, you know." That kind of language can easily make you feel guilty or ashamed for spending money.

Unfortunately, this black-and-white thinking can keep its grips on you even into adulthood thanks to the dominant cultural narratives of "stop buying Starbucks and you'll be able to buy a house." Spending shaming is truly everywhere, so if you still feel that discomfort when you pull out your credit card for a latte, you're not alone.

If this is you, think of what truly makes *you* feel good, happy, safe, healthy. Remind yourself that you earn money to be able to make those feelings a reality, and while you do have to spend to get there, you can spend efficiently by prioritizing your biggest and boldest joys.

Then remind yourself that you have so much potential. If getting what you want in your life costs more than you can afford right now? You can earn more money. It might take some time and effort, but you *can* do it.

SOLID-GOLD TRUTH #3: Money Spent to Impress Others Is Money Not Worth Spending

I like to say that the biggest money mistake I've ever made was spending money I didn't have on stuff I didn't need to impress people I didn't like.

In our keeping-up-with-the-Joneses society, this one can be huge, and even high earners can fall victim to it (remember how I went on a date with one of them?). It's like the polar opposite of spending shaming, and yet it ultimately still stems from that same ol' scarcity mindset.

As a kid, you might have seen your parents buying flashy cars or designer clothes, or going all-out on home remodels or beauty procedures just to make sure they looked as good (or better) than the people down the street.

To be clear, if this is you? It doesn't necessarily mean your parents were shallow. Again, they probably wanted to set a good example for you, to manifest outwardly that they were giving you a good life and had "made it" in the world, but somewhere along the line got their wires crossed and started overspending because they didn't know any other way to feel secure in what they had.

You might also have gotten used to compulsive spending if one of your parents may have suffered from a mental health issue that had them overbuying or hoarding possessions. Fortunately, we've come a long way in our understanding of how money problems can have a deeper underlying cause, but the lingering effects on those who grew up with them (i.e., you) still need to be unpacked.

If you now have some distance from your family, take some time to reexamine the "lessons" you learned about value from your parents. Spending money we don't have on stuff we don't need to impress people we don't like requires a *lot* of mental gymnastics, so it's likely your parents verbalized their reasoning to you as a way to make *themselves* feel justified in their approaches. Even offhand remarks like "Only poor people shop at Walmart" or "We don't want everyone at school thinking we can't *afford* a nice vacation" can lodge in your subconscious. Now that you've read about the rich-person mentalities in this book, I hope you can use them to challenge what you "know" about spending.

Also, try to reorient your sense of "payoff" from the short term to the long term. Think of what long-term gains you might be giving up by dropping cash on something right now—is it worth it to you? Maybe it is, and maybe it isn't, but only *you* (and not your parents, or your parents' friends, or the people at your parents' country club) can answer.

SOLID-GOLD TRUTH #4: Complaining but Not Doing Anything . . . Doesn't Do Anything

"My boss is such a tightwad. He's never even offered me a raise."

"The system's too screwed up. Nobody can make a real living anymore."

"We just can't get ahead no matter how hard we try."

Look, venting can be very healthy. But there's a difference between letting off steam about frustrations in a one-off bitch session and . . . whining, basically.

I'm not saying that your family didn't have very real financial issues facing them down. Debt, death, disability, divorce, disasters—there are tons of reasons that people get stuck with less money than they need to get by. Your parents may have complained about their financial situation but not done anything about it for a variety of reasons. They may not have known how to save or invest money, or they may have been afraid of taking risks with their finances. They may have felt like their current job or salary was the best they could do and that negotiating for a higher pay was not an option. They may have been too busy with other responsibilities to make any changes. Or they may have just plain felt overwhelmed by their financial situation and not known where to start.

Logically, you can see how these pile-ups can leave someone feeling defeated. But internalizing that powerlessness is *not* going to help you, especially if you're now out on your own and in your own financial situation away from your family.

If you find yourself reenacting this "nothing matters, so why bother" attitude toward money, first, you need to recognize that, as a human being, you have agency and you have value. You can do things and make choices, and you are worth something—as a worker, as a customer, as a friend and partner. And you know what you can do with agency and value? You can *negotiate*. So start there, whether it's getting a late fee knocked off a bill or asking for a big honkin' raise. Do the thing because you *can* do the thing.

You also need to practice forgiveness. If you've made what you feel are mistakes, and now feel trapped—by debt, by lack of options—hammering yourself with blame is not going to motivate you to action. Speak to yourself like you would your best friend. Use kind words, provide grace, and recognize that we all deserve second chances. Only when you accept the reality of your situation, whatever it is, *without* judgment, can you start taking steps to make it better.

No matter the money mentality you inherited from your parents, there are two more things I want you to take away here.

One: therapy is great. I highly recommend it for all to truly unpack some of this deep-down shit. But it's important to keep in mind that you break out of this scarcity mindset the same way that you break out of any bad habit. You need to actively change your thinking and behavior over time. Maybe that's saying affirmations in the mirror in the morning, maybe it's pounding the table and negotiating at your job for more money every single year, maybe it's forcing yourself to order something that *isn't* the cheapest thing on the menu. So, while yes, I *highly* recommend you talk to a therapist, you also need to be making active decisions to grow your wealth instead of just hoarding it or frittering it away.

Two: The simplest way to get out of any scarcity mindset? First and foremost, you make more money. I know, it's like, "No shit, Vivian," but don't discount how much increasing your earning can lift the burden of deep-seated money stress. It's not "mo money, mo problems" but "mo money, mo opportunities . . . and a lot less problems too."

I wanted to share these solid-gold truths with you because the not-so-solid, scarcity-and-fear-based mindsets they're taking down? Those mindsets don't arise in a vacuum. These are toxic thoughts that arise when people are stuck in toxic systems of oppression for year upon year. And these generational patterns and systemic inequalities? That's why we all need to be Rich AF.

Closing wealth gaps across communities will take more than just individual action, of course—we'll need to enact legislative change, provide public personal finance education, and support historically disadvantaged communities. But the good news is, when we overcome these kinds of financial inequality, we all win.

And that's why we all need a Rich BFF.

While there's no quick fix for all of the many problems in the world today, *upward economic mobility* is a start.

All of us deserve access to the tools that will help us be financially independent.

All of us deserve to make decisions out of a place of power and abundance instead of scarcity or desperation.

All of us deserve FU money to leave a bad ex or bad boss.

All of us deserve to build a foundation for our family and our community.

So you don't just owe it to yourself to get Rich AF. We all owe it to each other.

ACKNOWLEDGMENTS

If there's any one nonfinancial piece of wisdom you take away from this book, let it be this: there is nothing more important than who you surround yourself with. I am so incredibly lucky because my entire career, and frankly my entire existence, has been nothing but a series of serendipitous moments where the people in my life have supported me and given me opportunities to succeed. This book is a perfect example of just that.

Thank you to Alyssa Reuben, my literary agent, for being my champion and guiding me through this entire process. Your blind faith in me and uncanny ability to assuage any and all of my fears are why this book exists.

Thanks to Trish Daly, my brilliant editor at Portfolio, for your editorial insight, thoughtful comments, and MAJOR help in cutting down the word count. I'm chatty—what can I say?

I'd also like to thank the Penguin Random House team for seeing my initial vision for *Rich AF*, being an amazing squad at my back, and coming up with such a showstopping cover. A special shout-out goes out to copy editor Janine Barlow and production editor Lavina Lee for your precision and care in turning this manuscript into a real book.

Another big thank you to Blair Thornburgh and Meghan Stevenson for coaching me through the book-writing process. Our weekly meetings and your constant support made writing this book an immeasurably joyful experience. I am so grateful.

To my incredible Your Rich BFF Team, I could not do this without you. Seriously. Thank you to Alex Devlin at WME and Rana Zand and Kristen McGuinness at Range Media for managing logistics, hooking me up with incredible opportunities, and keeping me and my schedule sane through these whirlwind months. Thank you to Lauren Schwartz, my attorney extraordinaire, for not only protecting me at every turn but also being the very first member of Team Rich BFF. I'm so grateful you took a flyer on your friend's friend's random friend. Thank you to Jade Wiselogle at Persona PR for pitching, positioning, and perfecting every single piece of coverage about this book. I appreciate every news article, radio show, TV segment, magazine, and in-person interview you managed to wrangle for me.

Finally, thanks to my parents and fiancé, Greg—your never-ending support and love have charged my batteries even when I thought I was out of juice. Thank you for being my cheerleaders. I love you so much.

Tired of being told "You can't sit with us"? Join our club instead! This isn't the exclusive club where the bouncer keeps you out unless you're some kind of VIP, or the country club where you need to pay fifty grand to join. This club is for everybody. For FREE resources like budgeting templates, debt-paydown calculators, brainstorming worksheets, and other helpful stuff to get you putting your new knowledge to work, scan the QR code here, or visit us at richAF.club.

GLO$$ARY

401(k): A retirement savings plan offered by your employer that allows you to save money from your paycheck before taxes. Plus, your employer might even match your contributions (aka free money).

403(b): Similar to a 401(k), but for employees of nonprofit organizations like schools and hospitals.

APR: Stands for "annual percentage rate," which is the interest rate you pay on loans and credit cards.

APY: Stands for "annual percentage yield," which is the amount of interest you earn on savings accounts and investments.

Asset: An item of value that you own, like a house or a car. It can also refer to investments like stocks and bonds.

Balance: When we're talking bank accounts, your balance is the amount of money you have in your bank account at a given time. It's like a snapshot of your account's funds at that moment, including any deposits, withdrawals, or transactions that have been processed. When we're talking credit cards or loans, your balance is how much money you still owe to the lender.

Balance due date: The deadline for making a payment on your credit card. If you don't pay at least the minimum amount by this date, you'll be charged interest on your balance, you may be charged a late fee, and your credit score could be negatively affected.

Balance transfer: Moving debt (aka transferring a balance) from one credit card to another. You might do this to get a lower interest rate or promotional offer on the new card (although you might also pay a fee to do so).

Bank: A financial institution where you can store your money, access loans, and manage your finances.

Bond: A type of investment where you loan money to a company or government in exchange for regular interest payments.

Brokerage: A company that helps you buy and sell stocks, bonds, and other investments. You open a brokerage account online much like you would open a bank account, and use your login to transact and make investments.

Budget: A plan for how you will spend your money, including expenses like rent, food, and entertainment.

Cash back: When a credit card offers you cash back, you're essentially earning a percentage of the total dollar amount of your purchases back in the form of cash (so, like, if your card offers 1 percent cash back and you spend $200, you'll earn $2 in cash back rewards).

Checking account: A bank account where you can deposit and withdraw money, and do things like pay bills or repay friends (by linking Venmo or CashApp).

Compound interest: Interest that is earned on both the original amount of money and any interest already earned.

Consolidation: Combining multiple loans or credit card balances into one monthly payment.

Corporate bond: A bond issued by a company to raise funds. When you buy a corporate bond, you're essentially lending money to the company and earning interest in return.

CPA: Stands for "certified public accountant," someone who is trained to handle complex financial matters like taxes and audits.

Credit card: A payment card that allows you to borrow money to make purchases, with interest charged on any balances not paid in full each month.

Credit card perks: Any nice little upgrades or offers you get just for being a Valued Cardholder™. These can be stuff like free checked bags on flights, free TSA PreCheck, access to airport lounges, or discounts at certain stores or apps.

Credit card points: Another type of reward you can earn by paying with plastic: earn points by making purchases (sometimes at higher rates for different categories), and then redeem them for things like travel, merchandise, or statement credits (aka $$$ off your balance!).

Credit counseling: A service that helps you manage and pay off your debt, usually by negotiating with creditors, helping you consolidate your debts, and guiding you through making the payments.

Credit score: A number that represents your creditworthiness, based on factors like payment history and debt-to-income ratio.

Credit union: A nonprofit financial institution owned by its members, offering services like checking and savings accounts and loans.

Debt: Money you owe, like credit card balances or student loans.

Emergency fund: A savings account that you set aside specifically for unexpected expenses, such as medical bills, car repairs, etc.

ETF: Stands for "exchange-traded fund," a type of investment that tracks a basket of stocks, bonds, or other assets.

Fiduciary: Someone who is legally obligated to act in the best interest of their clients. Financial advisors who are fiduciaries can't push certain investments or products on you just because it'll make *them* more money—they are bound to serve only what's truly good for *you*.

Government bond: A bond issued by a government to raise funds. When you buy a government bond, you're essentially lending money to the government and earning interest in return.

Gross: The total amount of money you earn before taxes and deductions are taken out.

HDHP: Stands for "high-deductible health plan," a type of health insurance plan with a higher deductible and lower premiums. HDHPs are a prerequisite for opening a health savings account (see below).

High-yield bond: A bond issued by a company with a lower credit rating. They'll typically offer you higher interest rates than other bonds, but they also come with a higher risk of default (i.e., the company folds and you're left hanging).

HSA: Stands for "health savings account," a tax-advantaged account where you can sock away money to pay for medical expenses *and* invest that money while it's sitting there. To be eligible for an HSA, you'll need to have an HDHP.

HYSA: Stands for "high-yield savings account," which is a type of savings account that typically offers higher interest rates than traditional savings accounts.

Inflation: The rate at which the general price level of goods and services is increasing over time.

Interest: The cost of borrowing money or the return on an investment.

Investment account: A type of account that you use to invest your money. You can open an investment account with a brokerage firm and use it to buy stocks, bonds, mutual funds, or other assets.

IRA: Stands for "individual retirement account," a type of retirement savings account that can provide tax benefits. IRAs come in both traditional (where you don't pay taxes on contributions *now*, but *do* pay taxes when you start taking distributions in retirement) and Roth (where you *do* pay taxes up front when you contribute but don't pay taxes when you withdraw).

ISO: Short for "incentive stock option," this is one type of stock option your employer might offer you as part of compensation. It's basically a way for you to buy stock in your company at a discounted price, which can be a really good deal if the stock price goes up and you sell it later.

Leverage: The use of borrowed money to invest, with the aim of earning a higher return than the cost of borrowing.

Market correction: A sudden, medium-big drop in the value of the stock market (usually around 10 percent) over a short period of time.

Mortgage: A loan used to purchase a home or other real estate.

Municipal bond: A type of bond issued by a local government, such as a city or county. These bonds are used to fund public projects like schools, roads, and parks, and earn interest like any other bond.

Mutual fund: A type of investment that pools money from many investors to purchase a variety of stocks, bonds, and other assets.

Net: The amount of money you have left after taxes and deductions have been taken out.

Risk tolerance: The level of risk you are comfortable taking on with your investments.

RSU: A restricted stock unit, aka a type of compensation that some companies offer to their employees. Basically, you get a promise of stock in the company that you work for, but you can't sell it or trade it until a certain amount of time has passed.

Savings account: A bank account designed for storing your money and earning interest. It's a great way to save up for emergencies or long-term goals.

Sinking fund: A savings account that you set aside specifically for a future *planned* expense, such as a down payment on a house or a vacation.

Statement: A document showing all the activity in your account over a certain period of time, usually a month—things like your starting and ending balances, deposits, withdrawals, and fees, as well as any interest you've earned or charges you've incurred.

Statement closing date: The last day of your credit card billing cycle.

After this date, your credit card company will generate a statement showing all of the activity on your account during that cycle.

Stock: A type of investment that represents ownership in a company. When you buy a stock, you're buying a piece of that company's profits and assets.

Tax bracket: A range of income levels that are subject to a certain tax rate. Tax brackets in the United States are *marginal*, meaning that you owe higher rates of taxes only on income *above* a certain threshold.

Tax credit: A tax break that directly reduces the amount of taxes you owe (like getting a discount on your taxes!). Some credits are *refundable*, meaning you'll get that money back in your pocket even if you don't owe any taxes that year.

Tax deduction: An expense that you can subtract from your taxable income, reducing the amount of your money that is subject to taxes for that year.

Value-based spending: A budgeting technique that focuses on spending money on things that align with your values and goals. It's about prioritizing what's important to you and cutting back on things that *don't* bring you joy or fulfillment.

NOTES

CHAPTER 1

22 **Whatever debt that they took on:** Melanie Hanson, "Average Student Loan Debt by Year," Education Data Initiative, last modified January 22, 2022, https://educationdata.org/average-student-loan-debt-by-year.

22 **They would make enough money:** Rakesh Kochhar and Stella Sechopoulous, "How the American Middle Class Has Changed in the Past Five Decades," Pew Research Center, April 20, 2022, https://www.pewresearch.org/short-reads/2022/04/20/how-the-american-middle-class-has-changed-in-the-past-five-decades/.

22 **really only gone one way:** Emmie Martin, "Here's How Much Housing Prices Have Skyrocketed over the Last 50 Years," CNBC, June 23, 2017, https://www.cnbc.com/2017/06/23/how-much-housing-prices-have-risen-since-1940.html.

22 **redlined out of property ownership:** Candace Jackson, "What Is Redlining?," *New York Times*, August 17, 2021, https://www.nytimes.com/2021/08/17/realestate/what-is-redlining.html.

22 **without their husbands' permission:** Jessica Hill, "Fact Check: Post Detailing 9 Things Women Couldn't Do Before 1971 Is Mostly Right," *USA TODAY*, October 28, 2020, https://www.usatoday.com/story/news/factcheck/2020/10/28/fact-check-9-things-women-couldnt-do-1971-mostly-right/3677101001/.

22 **discriminated against in hiring:** András Tilcsik, "Pride and Prejudice: Employment Discrimination Against Openly Gay Men in the United States," *American Journal of Sociology* 117, no. 2 (September 2011): 586–626, https://doi.org/10.1086/661653.

24 **118 percent since 1965:** Jessica Dickler, "Home Prices Are Now Rising Much Faster Than Incomes, Studies Show," CNBC, November 10, 2021, https://www

.cnbc.com/2021/11/10/home-prices-are-now-rising-much-faster-than-incomes -studies-show.html.

26 **about one in ten young people:** "Living Arrangements of 25-34-Year Old Individuals in the United States in 2021, by Gender," Statista, February 11, 2022, https://www.statista.com/statistics/1074730/living-arrangements-30-year-olds -usa/.

26 **one in three adults:** Jenn Hatfield, "Young Adults in the U.S. Are Less Likely Than Those in Most of Europe to Live in Their Parents' Home," Pew Research Center, May 3, 2023, https://www.pewresearch.org/short-reads/2023/05/03/in -the-u-s-and-abroad-more-young-adults-are-living-with-their-parents/.

26 **Median price of a home:** Robin Rothstein, "Housing Market Predictions for 2023: When Will Home Prices Be Affordable Again?," *Forbes,* May 4, 2022, https://www.forbes.com/advisor/mortgages/real-estate/housing-market -predictions/.

26 **Average amount of student loan debt:** Alicia Hahn, "2023 Student Loan Debt Statistics: Average Student Loan Debt," *Forbes,* last modified May 9, 2023, https:// www.forbes.com/advisor/student-loans/average-student-loan-statistics/.

26 **Average price of a used vehicle:** Michael Wayland, "Used Vehicle Prices Rising at an Unseasonably Strong Rate," CNBC, March 7, 2023, https://www.cnbc.com /2023/03/07/used-vehicle-prices-rising-at-an-unseasonably-strong-rate.html.

28 **around 2 percent per year:** "The Importance of Inflation and GDP," Investopedia, last modified June 29, 2021, https://www.investopedia.com/articles/06/gdpin flation.asp.

28 **its own kind of bad news:** Kate Ashford, "What Is Deflation? Why Is It Bad for the Economy?," *Forbes,* last modified February 14, 2023, https://www.forbes.com /advisor/investing/what-is-deflation/.

28 **the inflation we see now:** Danilo Cascaldi-Garcia, Musa Orak, and Zina Saijid, "Drivers of Post-Pandemic Inflation in Selected Advanced Economies and Implications for the Outlook," FEDS Notes, Board of Governors of the Federal Reserve System, January 13, 2023, https://www.federalreserve.gov/econres/notes /feds-notes/drivers-of-post-pandemic-inflation-in-selected-advanced -economies-and-implications-for-the-outlook-20230113.html.

28 **a pretty famous study:** Daniel Kahneman and Angus Deaton, "High Income Improves Evaluation of Life but Not Emotional Well-Being," *Proceedings of the National Academy of Sciences* 107, no. 38 (September 21, 2020): 16,489–93, https://doi .org/10.1073/pnas.1011492107.

28 **A 2021 study:** Matthew A. Killingsworth, "Experienced Well-Being Rises with Income, Even above $75,000 per Year," Proceedings of the National Academy of Sciences 114, no. 4 (January 18, 2021): e2016976118, https://doi.org/10.1073/pnas .2016976118.

29 **through a bull market:** Hannah Miao and Amina Niasse, "Boomers Got Hooked on Stocks. Now They Can't Let Go," *Wall Street Journal,* June 18, 2023, https://

www.wsj.com/articles/boomers-got-hooked-on-stocks-now-they-cant-let -go-8589ff74.

30 *more* **expensive to be poor:** "It's Expensive to Be Poor," *The Economist*, September 3, 2015, https://www.economist.com/united-states/2015/09/03/its-expensive-to-be -poor.

32 **only thirteen cents:** "Fact Sheet: Biden-Harris Administration Announces New Actions to Build Black Wealth and Narrow the Racial Wealth Gap," The White House, June 1, 2021, https://www.whitehouse.gov/briefing-room/statements-releases /2021/06/01/fact-sheet-biden-harris-administration-announces-new-actions-to -build-black-wealth-and-narrow-the-racial-wealth-gap/.

32 **Black women in the United States:** "Data About the Gender Pay Gap for Black Women," Lean In, https://leanin.org/data-about-the-gender-pay-gap-for-black -women, accessed May 9, 2023.

32 **an active part of the workforce:** "Labor Force Characteristics by Race and Eth- nicity, 2021," U.S. Bureau of Labor Statistics, last modified January 2023, https:// www.bls.gov/opub/reports/race-and-ethnicity/2021/home.htm.

32 **the** *same. Exact. House*: Vanessa Romo, "Black Couple Settles Lawsuit Claiming Their Home Appraisal Was Lowballed Due to Bias," NPR, last modified March 9, 2023, https://www.npr.org/2023/03/09/1162103286/home-appraisal-racial-bias-black -homeowners-lawsuit.

33 **the bottom tenth percentile:** Rakesh Kochhar and Anthony Cilluffo, "Income Inequality in the U.S. Is Rising Most Rapidly Among Asians," Pew Research Cen- ter, July 12, 2018, https://www.pewresearch.org/social-trends/2018/07/12/income -inequality-in-the-u-s-is-rising-most-rapidly-among-asians/.

33 **the H-1B visa:** M. Hanna and J. Batalova. "Immigrants from Asia in the United States," Migration Policy Institute, Migration Policy Institute, January 29, 2020, https://www.migrationpolicy.org/article/immigrants-asia-united-states-2020.

33 **crucial to the organized labor movement:** "Latino Civil Rights Timeline: 1903 to 2006," Learning for Justice, accessed May 9, 2023, https://www.learningforjus tice.org/classroom-resources/lessons/latino-civil-rights-timeline-1903-to-2006.

33 **10 percent "savings":** Rosina Todaro. "Braceros: History, Compensation" UC Davis Migration Research Cluster, UC Davis Migration Research Cluster, Octo- ber 29, 2019, https://migration.ucdavis.edu/rmn/more.php?id=1112.

33–34 **seventy-three cents to the dollar ... as white entrepreneurs:** Lucy Pérez et al., "The Economic State of Latinos in America: The American Dream Deferred," McKinsey & Company, December 9, 2021, https://www.mckinsey.com/featured -insights/sustainable-inclusive-growth/the-economic-state-of-latinos-in -america-the-american-dream-deferred#/.

34 **like religious exceptions:** Regina Stuart, "What the Supreme Court Giveth Can Religious Schools Taketh Away: The Title VII Religious Exemption After Bostock," American Bar Association, July 5, 2022, https://www.americanbar.org/groups /crsj/publications/human_rights_magazine_home/intersection-of-lgbtq-rights

-and-religious-freedom/what-the-supreme-court-giveth-can-religious
-schools-taketh-away/.

34 **been illegal to reject:** "Housing Discrimination and Persons Identifying as Lesbian, Gay, Bisexual, Transgender, and/or Queer/Questioning (LGBTQ)," U.S. Department of Housing and Urban Development, accessed May 9, 2023, https://www.hud.gov/program_offices/fair_housing_equal_opp/housing_discrimination_and_persons_identifying_lgbtq.

34 **The "pink tax":** Kelley R. Taylor, "Pink Tax: What Does Price Discrimination Cost Women?," Kiplinger, March 8, 2023, https://www.kiplinger.com/taxes/pink-tax-womens-products-price-discrimination.

34 **less competent if we don't:** Catherine Saint Louis, "Up the Career Ladder, Lipstick in Hand," *New York Times,* October 12, 2011, https://www.nytimes.com/2011/10/13/fashion/makeup-makes-women-appear-more-competent-study.html.

34 **woman's lifelong earning potential:** Linda Gorman, "How Childbearing Affects Women's Wages," *National Bureau of Economic Research Digest* 4, April 2011, https://www.nber.org/digest/apr11/how-childbearing-affects-womens-wages.

CHAPTER 2

52 **people who stayed with a company:** Cameron Keng, "Employees Who Stay in Companies Longer Than Two Years Get Paid 50% Less," *Forbes,* June 22, 2014, https://www.forbes.com/sites/cameronkeng/2014/06/22/employees-that-stay-in-companies-longer-than-2-years-get-paid-50-less/?sh=5ccf466e07fa.

78 **at least 99 percent of people:** Jon M. Taylor, MBA, PhD, Consumer Awareness Institute, "Chapter 7: MLM's Abysmal Numbers," *The Case (for and)* Against Multi-level Marketing, 1999, https://www.ftc.gov/sites/default/files/documents/public_comments/trade-regulation-rule-disclosure-requirements-and-prohibitions-concerning-business-opportunities-ftc.r511993-00008%C2%A0/00008-57281.pdf.

CHAPTER 3

91 **around 0.42 percent interest annually:** Liz Knueven and Sophia Acevedo, "What Is the Average Interest Rate for Savings Accounts?" Bankrate, June 7, 2023, https://www.businessinsider.com/personal-finance/average-savings-account-interest-rate.

CHAPTER 4

134 **the Great Depression:** Richard H. Pells and Christina D. Romer, "Great Depression," Britannica, last modified April 28, 2023, https://www.britannica.com/event/Great-Depression.

135 **about 0.07 percent in interest:** Alisa Wolfson, "The Average Savings Account Now Pays Just 0.06%, So Is It Even Worth It to Put Money in a Savings Account?," MarketWatch, last modified February 23, 2022, https://www.marketwatch.com/picks/the-average-savings-account-now-pays-just-0-06-so-is-it-even-worth-it-to-put-money-in-a-savings-account-01645560701.

135 **five hundred bucks per customer:** "Statistics," FI Works, https://www.fiworks.com/resources/statistics.

138 **don't themselves have a bank charter:** Ivana Pino, "What Is a Neobank? Here's What to Know About These Online-Only Banks," *Fortune*, October 26, 2022, https://fortune.com/recommends/banking/what-is-a-neobank/.

143 **anywhere from 4 to 5 percent interest:** Ann Carrns, "Many Banks Pay High Rates on Savings. So Why Aren't You Moving Your Money?," *New York Times*, February 3, 2023, https://www.nytimes.com/2023/02/03/your-money/savings-account-rates-banks.html.

143 **brick-and-mortar consumer banks:** Hugh Son, "Rarely-Humbled Goldman Sachs Concedes Missteps in Plan to Take on Megabanks in Retail Finance," CNBC, October 18, 2022, https://www.cnbc.com/2022/10/18/goldman-sachs-pivot-from-marcus-shows-that-disrupting-retail-banking-is-hard.html.

152 **average sale price of home:** Robin Rothstein, "Housing Market Predictions For 2023: When Will Home Prices Be Affordable Again?," *Forbes*, last modified June 8, 2023, https://www.forbes.com/advisor/mortgages/real-estate/housing-market-predictions/.

CHAPTER 5

170 **and not come out of it:** Isabella Simonetti and Niraj Chokshi, "What Is a Recession, and When Is the Next One Going to Begin?," *New York Times*, June 24, 2022, https://www.nytimes.com/2022/06/24/business/what-is-a-recession.html.

170 **85 percent of day traders:** Bob Pisani, "Attention Robinhood Power Users: Most Day Traders Lose Money," CNBC, November 20, 2020, https://www.businessinsider.com/personal-finance/average-savings-account-interest-rate.

172 **over the past thirty years:** Vartika Gupta et al., "Markets Will Be Markets: An Analysis of Long-Term Returns from the S&P 500," McKinsey & Company, August 4, 2022, https://www.mckinsey.com/capabilities/strategy-and-corporate-finance/our-insights/prime-numbers/markets-will-be-markets-an-analysis-of-long-term-returns-from-the-s-and-p-500.

187 **to the performance of a particular index:** "ETFs vs. Mutual Funds," Charles Schwab, accessed May 9, 2023, https://www.schwab.com/etfs/mutual-funds-vs-etfs.

187 **a minimum dollar amount:** "Mutual Funds and ETFs: A Guide for Investors," U.S. Securities and Exchange Commission, accessed May 9, 2023, https://www.sec.gov/investor/pubs/sec-guide-to-mutual-funds.pdf.

189 **is largely unregulated:** Kevin Roose, "The Latecomer's Guide to Crypto," *New York Times*, March 18, 2022, https://www.nytimes.com/interactive/2022/03/18/technology/cryptocurrency-crypto-guide.html.

189 **much more volatile:** Nicole Lapin, "Explaining Crypto's Volatility," *Forbes,* December 23, 2021, https://www.forbes.com/sites/nicolelapin/2021/12/23/explaining-cryptos-volatility/?sh=4f5c3f377b54.

190 **those legacy firms got ~disrupted~:** Maggie Fitzgerald, "The End of Commissions for Stock Trading Is Near as TD Ameritrade Cuts to Zero, Matching Schwab," CNBC, October 2, 2019, https://www.cnbc.com/2019/10/02/the-end-of-commissions-for-stock-trading-is-near-as-td-ameritrade-cuts-to-zero-matching-schwab.html.

195 **up to a total of $66,000 (for 2023):** "One-Participant 401(k) Plans," Internal Revenue Service, accessed May 9, 2023, https://www.irs.gov/retirement-plans/one-participant-401k-plans.

210 **Robo-advisors are online platforms:** "Investor Bulletin: Robo-Advisers," U.S. Securities and Exchange Commission, February 23, 2017, https://www.investor.gov/introduction-investing/general-resources/news-alerts/alerts-bulletins/investor-bulletins-45.

214 **study by NerdWallet:** Tanza Loudenback, "There's Almost No Chance Young Investors Will Lose Money over 40 Years," *Business Insider*, August 1, 2017, https://www.businessinsider.com/chance-lose-money-investing-long-term-stock-market-2017-7.

214 **a decline of 10 percent or more:** "What Is a Stock Market Correction?," *New York Times*, February 27, 2020, https://www.nytimes.com/2020/02/27/business/what-is-a-stock-market-correction.html.

CHAPTER 6

224 **a 1.5 to 3.5 percent fee:** "What Is a Processing Fee?," National Merchants Association, accessed May 9, 2023, https://www.nationalmerchants.com/what-is-a-processing-fee/.

230 **came about in 1956 . . . since 1989:** Kimberly Adams and Daniel Shin, "History of Credit Score Algorithms and How They Became the Lender Standard," Marketplace Tech, July 5, 2022, https://www.marketplace.org/shows/marketplace-tech/the-history-of-credit-score-algorithms-and-how-they-became-the-lender-standard/.

231 **five major factors:** "What's in My FICO® Score?," myFICO, accessed May 9, 2023, https://www.myfico.com/credit-education/whats-in-your-credit-score.

234 **more than 30 percent of your available credit:** "How Do I Get and Keep a Good Credit Score?," Consumer Financial Protection Bureau, last modified September 1, 2020, https://www.consumerfinance.gov/ask-cfpb/how-do-i-get-and-keep-a-good-credit-score-en-318/.

239 **over 1.2 billion:** "Kim Kardashian," *Forbes,* last modified June 12, 2023, https://www.forbes.com/profile/kim-kardashian/?sh=3437aa305230.

239 **she got a mortgage:** Keith Griffith and Alesia Stanford, "Kim Kardashian Took Out a Staggering $4.8 MILLION Mortgage to Buy . . . ," *Daily Mail*, last modified February 25, 2023, https://www.dailymail.co.uk/news/article-11791453/Kim-Kardashian-took-staggering-48M-mortgage-buy-Malibu-mansion.html.

251 **not as severe:** "Accuracy-Related Penalty," Internal Revenue Service, https://www.irs.gov/payments/accuracy-related-penalty.

255 **lobbyists to work:** Justin Elliott and Paul Kiel, "Inside TurboTax's 20-Year Fight to Stop Americans from Filing Their Taxes for Free," *ProPublica,* October 17, 2019, https://www.propublica.org/article/inside-turbotax-20-year-fight-to-stop-americans-from-filing-their-taxes-for-free.

255 **using targeted ads:** Justin Elliott and Lucas Waldron, "TurboTax Just Tricked You into Paying to File Your Taxes," *ProPublica,* April 22, 2019, https://www.propublica.org/article/turbotax-just-tricked-you-into-paying-to-file-your-taxes.

257 **$13,850 for single filers . . . in 2023:** "How Much Is My Standard Deduction?," Internal Revenue Service, February 1, 2023, https://www.irs.gov/help/ita/how-much-is-my-standard-deduction.

263 **interests of their clients:** "What Is a Fiduciary?," Consumer Financial Protection Bureau, last modified August 5, 2016, https://www.consumerfinance.gov/ask-cfpb/what-is-a-fiduciary-en-1769/.

265 **get paid jack shit:** "Social Worker Salaries in New York City, NY Area," Glassdoor, accessed May 9, 2023, https://www.glassdoor.com/Salaries/new-york-city-social-worker-salary-SRCH_IL.0,13_IM615_KO14,27.htm.

CONCLUSION

276 **seven to nine years old:** David Whitebread and Sue Bingham, "Habit Formation and Learning in Young Children," Money Advice Service, May 2013, https://mascdn.azureedge.net/cms/the-money-advice-service-habit-formation-and-learning-in-young-children-may2013.pdf.

INDEX

Note: Italicized page numbers indicate material in tables or illustrations.